A Practical Guide
to Neural Nets

Technical
Publishing
Advisory Board

A Practical Guide to Neural Nets

Marilyn McCord Nelson
and W. T. Illingworth

**Addison-Wesley Publishing
Company, Inc.**
Reading, Massachusetts • Menlo
Park, California • New York •
Don Mills, Ontario •
Wokingham, England •
Amsterdam • Bonn • Paris •
Milan • Madrid • Sydney •
Singapore • Tokyo • Seoul •
Taipei • Mexico City • San Juan

Many of the designations used by manufacturers and sellers to distinguish their products are claimed as trademarks. Where those designations appear in this book and Addison-Wesley was aware of a trademark claim, the designations have been printed in initial caps or all caps.

The programs and applications presented in this book have been included for their instructional value. They have been tested with care, but are not guaranteed for any particular purpose. The publisher does not offer any warranties or representations, nor does it accept any liabilities with respect to the programs or applications.

Library of Congress Cataloging-in-Publication Data

Nelson, Marilyn McCord.
    A practical guide to neural nets / Marilyn McCord Nelson and W. T. Illingworth.
    p.   cm.
    Includes bibliographical references.
    ISBN 0-201-52376-0
    1. Neural networks (Computer science)   I. Illingworth, W. T.   II. Title.
QA76.87.N44   1990
006.3—dc20
                                                                        90-34627
                                                                        CIP

The Publisher offers discounts on this book when ordered in quantity for special sales. For more information please contact:
    Corporate & Professional Publishing Group
    Addison-Wesley Publishing Company
    Route 128
    Reading, Massachusetts 01867

Sponsoring Editor, Ted Buswick
Cover design by Hannus Design Associates
Text design by Joyce C. Weston
Set in 10½ point Palatino by DEKR Corporation, Woburn, MA

Book/disk package ISBN 0-201-52376-0
Book only ISBN 0-201-56309-6
3 4 5 6 7 8 9–MA–9594939291
Third printing, March 1991

Contents

11. What Is the Current Research?   221

12. Where Do We Go from Here?   247

List of
Illustrations

Figures

Tables

Acknowledgments

We are grateful for the encouragement and support from many of our colleagues at Texas Instruments.

Stanton William (Bill) Davis receives our special thanks; without his talent and effort there would not be a diskette to accompany this book. Bill created the dynamic graphics display contained in the interactive diskette with the aid of three software packages that we wish to mention: the neural networks graphics screens themselves were created using NeuralWorks Professional II (compliments of NeuralWare), the timing and sequencing of these graphics screens used the Presents program portion of Dr. Halo (thanks to Media Cybernetics), and the packaging and control was provided by the Personal Consultant Plus expert system runtime disk (courtesy of Texas Instruments). In addition, Bill contributed significantly to the neural network simulation research and background for chapter 9.

Sandra Richey was also indispensable; she produced all of our graphics (using her gifted proficiency with GEM® Draw), created the copy for appendix C, and designed a number of the figures. We appreciate her attention to detail and her willingness to accommodate "yet one more small modification."

The assistance given by the Texas Instruments Technical Library staff was outstanding: Cecilia Tung and Sue Jennings (at the Spring Creek site) and Phyl Barrus and Steve Searl (at the North Building site) performed literature searches, located articles, and furnished source information. Richard O'Bryant and Tom May (co-workers in the AI Group of Technology Systems Education) loaned materials and provided direction on initial drafts, and Eric Dillinger (of HTX International in Manhattan, KS) also supplied timely articles, assistance on quotes, and other helpful suggestions.

We appreciate the contributions of researchers in various companies and academia who took the time to talk with us, share their ideas and their work, and correct our summaries of conversations.

Preface

The responsibility for change . . . lies within us. We must begin with ourselves, teaching ourselves not to close our minds prematurely to the novel, the surprising, the seemingly radical.

—Alvin Toeffler

This book originally existed as a half-day seminar, developed during the spring and summer of 1988. The target audience was and still is technical managers and people in other technical fields who want to find out something about neural networks.

We expanded our seminar materials, dropping some things and adding several new sections. The presentation still somewhat parallels our previous work. Many of the graphics used as overhead transparencies in the seminar have been reproduced here. It is difficult in book form, however, to "break" and show software examples. We have tried to overcome this by including numerous examples in the text. Chapter 9 is our own "show-and-tell" chapter. In addition, the diskette gives you some opportunity to see for yourself how a neural network works and to participate in the development of a small project.

The style is one in which we let ideas grow. First we mention topics, then we build on them. If you find yourself wanting to know more, you may well find that we pick up on your particular interests again later. The bibliography/reading list in appendix B provides further references for study. Many of our ideas came from these references as well as from conversations with our seminar students and various people in the field. Other ideas came from our own work with some of the software packages. In general, people working in neural networks are very willing to share their writings, their work, and their ideas.

When we did our initial seminar study in 1988 we kept track of what our own questions were and what organization of topics made sense to us. These questions formed the outline for our twelve chapters. Some of our notes became part of the chapters as well as the appendixes. Many articles were initially too technical for us; some still are. By having started at the beginning ourselves, we feel we are in a good position to piece things together for novices and for the casual reader.

Chapter 1 explores the utility questions: What can you do with neural networks? Why would anyone want to use them? What kinds of things are being done currently? What are some of the issues and problems this technology seeks to address?

Chapter 2 is also brief: What are neural networks? Why have they hit the media so hard in the past couple of years? What is going on in the current technological climate that supports this particular new technology?

Our questions in chapter 2 lead us to **chapter 3,** a review of the developments of the past few decades. Both of us have spent the majority of our efforts over the past few years in pursuing projects related to AI (artificial intelligence). We knew there were similarities and differences in the historical developments of these related technologies. We wanted to provide a context.

The biological underpinnings of neural networks were of interest to us for a variety of reasons. We have some rough ideas of how we, as humans, process information and learn. Because this new style of computing is so different from conventional computing, it helps to have a few familiar analogies. **Chapter 4** begins with a look at the biological metaphor and some of the terminology. We want to point out here, and again throughout the book, that this metaphor is responsible for a great deal of confusion. Many people consider the name *neural network* itself to be an unfortunate choice (just as many consider that the name *artificial intelligence* has *not* been in the best interests of the field), yet it is the name most widely recognized today in popular writing. There is a definite effort by many people in the field to use nonbiological terms, emphasizing the differences between this new style of computing and the functions of the human brain. Yet, we wonder if some of the original biological terminology won't stick. Even though we begin by talking about the metaphor, the heart of chapter 4 is a discussion of the components of a typical artificial neural network and how they work together.

Chapter 5 explores some of the characteristics and limitations of these artificial neural networks. What are they like? What are their strengths and weaknesses? Where have they encountered problems?

From our own background in AI, we have been extremely interested in the relationship of these two technologies, as well as how neural networks relate to statistical methods. Some early neural network aficionados came down rather hard on traditional AI—probably an overreaction to being the "step-child" for so many years. We are not a part of that camp. Both AI and neural networks have their strengths and uniqueness. We see the blending of these two as being extremely useful, each contributing their best to the overall effort in many projects. **Chapter 6** compares technologies, relates some of the claims of each side, then settles into promoting the amalgam that will surely result from combining the strengths of the various approaches.

Chapter 7 grew out of a single overhead transparency in the original course which asked the question, "How many different ways can you organize a neural network?" This chapter takes the components outlined in the last part of chapter 4 and develops variations and possibilities. This diversity is responsible for the assortment of neural network paradigms that have already surfaced and those that are being developed. We end chapter 7 by noting some of the earliest and best-known models.

Perhaps the key feature of a neural network is its ability to adapt, or learn. **Chapter 8** examines the question "How do neural networks learn?" The word *learning*, as popularly used, is often synonymous with *training*, though some people make a distinction between the terms. Looking at learning/training aspects of a neural network necessitates drawing again on the components presented in chapters 4 and 7. Several common learning laws are listed, along with some tables that compare various neural network models with respect to their learning features.

Chapter 9 gets to the question most asked by participants in our early seminars: "How do you move from theory to applications?" We use some of the current software simulations and our own work experience at Texas Instruments to walk you through five detailed case study examples of how to get started. Some things worked well for us, others did not. We learned a lot and often found ourselves excited by our discoveries. Companion information and graphics are also on the diskette, so you can see some of the variable components of a network in time-lapse sequences. If a picture is worth a thousand words, the diskette should be invaluable.

In **chapter 10** we look at the question, "How are neural networks being implemented?" A few general categories are commonly used for comparing implementations, and we look first at those. Although many current neural networks are software simulations, many researchers are putting significant effort into hardware implementations. Both approaches have their niche. We look at commercially available implementations and some of the research categories. Hardware includes special-purpose hardware for conventional computers, new types of computers, chips, optical and holographic implementations. Wetware is a new category. Some researchers are building neural networks using biological materials. There are biochips, for example, with actual cells on an electrode grid.

"What has been happening in neural net research?" **Chapter 11** looks at some of the recent research in terms of issues, problems, and directions. Some companies have shared with us stories of specific research questions and projects. Here we have an opportunity to expand on some of the ideas mentioned only briefly earlier.

Chapter 12 wraps it up. We found ourselves asking more questions even in our summarizing. What is intelligence? Are neural networks truly intelligent? How do we separate the hype from the facts? There are plenty of wild-sounding claims. Where do people say this technology is going? And how do we feel about it ourselves?

Appendix A provides the material that accompanies the diskette. It not only illumines our rationale but also gives tips on how to best use the diskette. **Appendix B** contains our bibliography and reading list. Some of this list is annotated. At the end of appendix B you can find information on some of the currently available journals and newsletters. **Appendix C** elaborates on some of the mathematics involved in designing neural networks. **Appendix D** uses Lotus® 1-2-3® to demonstrate the training process for a single artificial neuron.

Obviously we have been interested enough to spend a considerable amount of time on artificial neural networks. Not only are we interested in them, we are excited about them. Enough so that we want to take as much as we can of what we have learned and share it with you. While you are looking for facts and using the keen analytical logic for which our era is well-known, keep an open mind, and maybe even dare to dream a little about a possible new future.

What Can You Do with a Neural Network?

Any time we're tempted to think that our technology has gone about as far as it can go, we should stop and remember a certain Commissioner of the U.S. Patent Office. In 1895 he proposed to Congress that the Patent Office be closed because all the great inventions had already been discovered.

—Bits & Pieces

Introduction

Biologically inspired computing is different from conventional computing. It has a different feel; often the terminology doesn't sound like it's talking about machines. The activities of this new computing sound more human than mechanistic as people speak of machines that learn, forget, and remember.

Biology is and has been the inspiration, but we don't want to mislead you. Although the resulting computational units, often referred to as *neural networks*, work in ways similar to how we think the neurons in the human brain work, the mainstream of the technology is not trying to produce biological clones. Much of the technology is trying to mimic nature's approach in order to mimic some of nature's capabilities. Assumptions that are not biologically accurate are used in building artificial, as opposed to biological, neural systems.

Alongside these efforts are others that *do* have goals of replicating biology. Some researchers are trying to understand more about how the brain works. Others simply believe it is important to pay attention to and learn from nature's designs. Although this book deals predominately with the former, we by no means wish to dismiss the latter. Just as the space program brought us technological breakthroughs in medicine, materials, and miniaturization, the pursuit of neural network computers holds similar promise. The benefit to us will come not just in the development of better computers. Each approach has its own appeal, and threads of both approaches appear throughout this book.

This biologically inspired research has its rewards. Exciting things are being accomplished. Neural networks are performing tasks that have posed stumbling blocks for previous technologies. They are doing some things in real time that, with other methods, have taken too long to be of practical value. Of interest to researchers for several decades, neural networks are now beginning to interest corporations and governments. Products are beginning to appear; people are talking about money-saving possibilities.

There are many questions you might ask about neural networks. We hope to address most of them in the chapters that follow. We'll explain the components, how the systems work, how they learn, how this technology compares to other ones you may know about, what advantages neural networks might buy you, issues and directions. As we said in the preface, our style is to mention ideas and then build on them as we go.

What we want to do first, though, is to pique your interest by sharing some of the accomplishments. The success stories are impressive. People don't tend to share their failures so readily, however, and a fair assessment needs to point out limitations as well as achievements. That will be done later.

Existing Applications

Most of the applications currently on the neural network scene are prototypes or research projects. Although only a few commercially available products exist at the time of this writing, we are convinced that more are awaiting their debut. Too many good minds are delving into this area for it not to produce fruit.

Most current commercially fielded applications run on personal computers. Few, if any, use any special-purpose neural network hardware, but you can bet that's coming. Every month technical publications reveal new products and new breakthroughs.

The next few paragraphs talk about telephones, mortgages, airplane security, fluorescent bulbs, manufacturing plant inspections, and heaters for Fords. Mundane stuff. Mundane, except when there is static on *your* important long distance call or when it's *your* mortgage application that is being evaluated. When it's your flight, airport security may be frustrating, but you sure want it to be thorough. These next applications deal with everyday occurrences, and neural networks are playing a part in each of them.

Adaptive Noise Canceling

An application we can all appreciate, and one that received the Institute of Electrical and Electronic Engineers' Alexander Graham Bell award, is that of adaptive noise canceling in telecommunications. This contribution cleans up echoes on telephone lines and reduces transmission errors on modems. Every time you make a long distance telephone call, your voice is processed through an adaptive filter. If you use a modem, you are using a small neural network. The adaptive filtering process was developed in the 1950s by Bernard Widrow, a pioneer in the field, and it represents the longest-running successful application. Widrow recently delighted the audience at a Neural Networks for Computation Conference by demonstrating one of his original machines, called an ADALINE. It has worked perfectly for more than twenty-five years.[1]

Mortgage Risk Evaluator

Nestor, one of the earliest neural network companies, has a product that appraises mortgage applications, the Mortgage Risk Evaluator. It helps loan officers identify people who may be likely to default on their payments. The system was trained on several thousand actual applications, about half of which were accepted and the other half of which were rejected by the human underwriters. Learning from the successes and failures of this body of experience, the system looks for patterns in the data to determine what constitutes a bad risk. Additionally, you could configure the product to be conservative or optimistic in its assessments.

There are three levels of problems: mortgage origination underwriting, mortgage insurance underwriting, and delinquency risk assessment. The difficulty of the task increases at each level, along with the level of risk.

Two goals were uppermost in creating this product: to automate the underwriting process, thereby reducing processing costs, and to improve on current practice. Many statistics have been kept to compare the performance of this tool with the performance of human underwriters. Results are promising. In a comparison with human underwriters, the neural network was more consistent in its classification of files, produced a higher quality of certified files, and significantly reduced delinquencies.[2]

AVCO Financial Services, in Irvine, California, uses this neural network system for credit risk analysis. The system was trained on more than 10,000 credit case histories. A *New York Times* article reported that one test indicated there would have been a 27-percent increase in profits if the neural network system had been used instead of the computerized evaluation system previously used by AVCO.[3]

Bomb Sniffer

In August of 1989, the Federal Aviation Administration installed a new bomb detector system at New York's JFK International Airport. Traditional methods of determining such risks have limitations: human operators can become tired and can be distracted. Science Applications International Corporation. (SAIC), working under an FAA program, developed a neural network approach called Thermal Neutron Analysis (TNA), or more commonly, SNOOPE.

The bomb-sniffing system runs automatically and does not get distracted or tired. SNOOPE has been trained on the characteristics of explosive materials by learning to identify their characteristic pattern of gamma-ray emissions. It can tell the nitrogen in a bomb from the nitrogen in cheese, for example. About 2.5 pounds of explosives will trigger the machine.

Around ten pieces of luggage can be examined every minute. If SNOOPE is unsure about any bag, that piece can be rerouted to a human inspector. Currently the data sets on suspect baggage are saved and used for future improvements on the system.

Future enhancements may include the immediate incorporation of the new data into the knowledge and behavior of the system. People are continuously adaptable. Why not systems, too, even systems of neural networks? That's what learning is all about. As neural network learning techniques become more sophisticated, applications will be able to refine their knowledge and understanding during and even after training. Without such

A Practical Guide to Neural Nets

learning there would be little difference between neural networks and standard statistical modeling.

SNOOPE has been certified as safer than X-rays for humans, and safe for film and electromagnetic media, food, and drugs. The low-energy neutrons are not radioactive. But SNOOPE is an expensive system, costing around $1.1 million. And it would not have caught the small amount of explosives believed to have blown up Pan American World Airways Flight 103 over Lockerbie, Scotland, in December of 1988. The FAA's initial plans are to install only six of them at high-risk international airports, such as the one at JFK. More are in the works for domestic airports as well.[4]

GTE Process Monitor

GTE Laboratories is using a neural network in its fluorescent bulb manufacturing plant. The intent of the project is to identify those parameters which most affect the production process. The system monitors the production line, tracking such things as variations in heat, pressure, and the chemicals used to make the bulbs. Inputs from these sensor measurements are compared to factory yield and performance. This information will be used to help determine optimum manufacturing conditions, to indicate what controls need to be adjusted, and potentially to even shut down the line when something is wrong.[5]

GTE's John Doleac talked to us about the project: "Researchers may develop a process 'to a T' in the lab, but in the real world you can't control everything. You can't have the same viscosity at all temperatures, for example. Things are related. If you knew what counted, you could map out a 'flight envelope'; you could watch the normal, everyday changes in parameters which cause the process to vary." He shared a conceptual diagram, shown in figure 1.1. We'll repeat this diagram and supply more details in chapter 11, but you can readily see what types of input factors are being considered.

Although the system is still young and "inexperienced," Doleac expects a "huge payback." Tests are usually expensive. They involve design, materials, coordination, downtime on equipment, and evaluation. In this case, sensors had been placed on the line for another project anyway, so there was little cultural upheaval and very little cost. Although the use of artificial neural networks

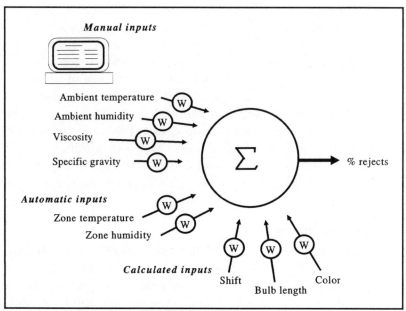

FIGURE 1.1   PROCESS CONTROL INPUT PARAMETERS

was considered a cutting edge project, it was also seen by many as one of the least likely to succeed. Now, six months later, the system has been embedded and is running. Doleac is justifiably proud of the progress: "If the system tells us about the 'flight envelope,' which I really expect, the benefits will be undeniable."

Conventional statistical analyses could perform the same comparisons, but with a few significant differences. The neural network collects its data incrementally, every five minutes. Linear regression, for example, requires all the data to be collected ahead of time and then processed all at once. This means the neural network system requires less memory, provides relatively current statistics, and is more responsive to changes in the data. Future steps could include moving from process monitoring to process control.

Word Recognizer

A project does not have to be large to be useful. Intel built a small application that capitalizes on the expressiveness of human speech. By limiting the system to a single speaker at a time and limiting the vocabulary to around a hundred isolated words or phrases, the speech recognition system provides better than 99-percent accuracy for the speaker who trains the system. This voice-controlled data entry system has been used in various manufacturing applications since 1983.[6]

Here's the way it works. An inspector in a manufacturing plant could wear a headset microphone with a two-way radio link. The speech recognition system could prompt the inspector, and in turn, the system could receive information back concerning the manufacturing process or product. There would be no need to carry a clipboard; hands would be free for other tasks. The machine's prompts could insure correct sequence or completeness in the inspection. Resulting information could be routed to company computers immediately without manual entry of the inspection data. Simple and efficient.

Blower Motor Checker

Siemens, an electrical equipment maker in West Germany, had a problem. Some of the blower motors they were making for Ford car heaters were noisy. If they tried to detect them by having people listen to all the motors, the people got tired and became bored. Conventional approaches didn't have much more success than the human approach. So they tried a neural network. This succeeded with greater than 90-percent accuracy, and now a neural network checks all the blower motors.[7] (See similar story on diagnosing engine faults at Ford Motor Company in a report by Tom J. Schwartz, "IJCNN '89."[8])

Prototype and Research Activity

Many of today's neural network examples fall into the prototype or research category. They are interesting, show potential, and work well in a limited setting. Such results are not the same as having a fielded, commercially successful application, but the winners have to start somewhere, and there appear to be plenty of candidates.

Physicians at Brown University have used a simulated network of medical knowledge to relate information on cases, symptoms, and treatments. Researchers at Los Alamos National Laboratory are using a neural network to predict whether particular DNA sequences represent genetic codes for the manufacture of proteins. U.S. Postal Service officials are investigating neural networks for use in reading handwritten addresses.[9] A law enforcement agency is using a neural network to try to determine whether the psychological profile of people who commit a particular type of crime is changing.

Other research applications include text-to-speech, target recognition, broom balancing, and fast pattern searching. The following sections expand on a few stories that seem like more fun than just a sentence or two would show. Additional stories will come in subsequent chapters.

Airline Marketing Tactician (AMT)

Here is a proof-of-concept prototype from a company called BehavHeuristics, Inc. (Silver Spring, Maryland). This system advises users on airline seat yield management. It is comprised of two different neural networks, a rule set, and a graphics interface. One neural network is in a perpetual training mode to learn the patterns of seat bookings, pricing, no-show rates, and so on. This information allows the system to predict things like demand and no-show rates. Although the prototype currently simulates these activities, actual airline operations will be used in production models.

The second network works at maximizing profit and minimizing overbookings. It advises a user to raise or lower the number of seats at each fare. Rules incorporate more traditional expertise in handling situations like bumping and alternate carrier vouchers. One of the enticing possibilities is that AMT can monitor all flights, not just a sampling, and it can do it quickly enough to allow changes in strategy.[10]

Sonar Classifier

The ability to detect undersea mines remotely in shallow water is essential for harbor and coastline security. Having a reliable, automatic means of doing this would be of great benefit.

Paul Gorman of Bendix Aerospace has captured naval interests with his neural network that can recognize underwater targets by sonar.[11] It can tell the difference between a mine and a rock shaped like a mine. Sonar signals were taken by a diver with a sonar gun, taking about a hundred "shots" at each target from various angles. These sonar returns provided the inputs to the system.

A Practical Guide to Neural Nets

Distinguishing between active sonar returns from mines and returns from rocks and debris on the sea floor is difficult. In experiments, the network classifier performed better than either the trained human listeners or a traditional technique called a nearest neighbor classifier. The network system was almost perfect in classifying a training set of data (99.8 percent), and correctly classified 90 percent of the returns in a test set of new data.[12]

Bellcore Chip

Bellcore is a research group owned by seven regional Bell Telephone Companies. They developed an experimental neural network chip that can perform 100,000 times faster than a computer simulation running the same functions.[13] Parallel processes can be done simultaneously rather than one step at a time as on a digital computer. Instead of needing to be programmed with every rule and exception, the chip learns by example. It is well suited to speech and pattern recognition applications, and makes neural networks an add-on technology to existing processing. Optimization of switching and routing circuits are likely application possibilities.

List of Possible Applications

What can you do with neural networks? A lot of things in a lot of different categories. There are so many fascinating research activities going on that we devote an entire chapter to them (chapter 11). The intervening chapters provide a primer for understanding, but the real excitement is in examining the probabilities and the possibilities for our future.

Applications and potential applications are popping up like wildflowers after a spring rain. Here is an assortment of possibilities, which has been sort of a "wish list" for research and which has prompted the first few commercial applications:

Biological
  Learning more about the brain and other systems
  Modeling retina, cochlea

Business
  Evaluating probability of oil in geological formations
  Identifying corporate candidates for specific positions

Mining corporate databases
Optimizing airline seating and fee schedules
Recognizing handwritten characters, such as Kanji

Environmental
Analyzing trends and patterns
Forecasting weather

Financial
Assessing credit risk
Identifying forgeries
Interpreting handwritten forms
Rating investments and analyzing portfolios

Manufacturing
Automating robots and control systems (with machine vision
and sensors for pressure, temperature, gas, etc.)
Controlling production line processes
Inspecting for quality
Selecting parts on an assembly line

Medical
Analyzing speech in hearing aids for the profoundly deaf
Diagnosing/prescribing treatments from symptoms
Monitoring surgery
Predicting adverse drug reactions
Reading X-rays
Understanding cause of epileptic seizures

Military
Classifying radar signals
Creating smart weapons
Doing reconnaissance
Optimizing use of scarce resources
Recognizing and tracking targets

What are common features in this list of applications? Most
of them have to do with pattern recognition. They find the patterns in a series of examples, classify patterns, find the complete
pattern from a partial set, or reconstruct the correct pattern from
a distortion. Many of the examples have to do with perception

and sensory data—visual, auditory, and other signals. Some involve filtering or mapping a set of inputs to a set of outputs. In general, the examples exhibit behaviors that are more characteristic of people than of conventional computers.

Summary

So far we've tried to emphasize what you can do with a neural network without getting into too many other details. It's sort of like looking at the tip of the iceberg, though. The neural network picture is still building. There are predictions of a billion dollar market by the end of the 1990s.[14] By no means have we been complete; even with examples sprinkled throughout the remainder of this book, there will still be applications and research we should have mentioned and didn't.

Now, or soon, we will see neural networks used for many of the same kinds of capabilities exhibited in the preceding examples. There will be automated parts inspection in industry. Cameras, sonar, and radar will be used for recognizing people or equipment. Speaker/signature verification systems will be developed. Complex diagnostics and controls will be possible in industries such as nuclear power. Parts will be allowed to age normally without aging dangerously. Pattern recognition applications will proliferate.

Perhaps it will take three to five years to achieve commercial neural network products for things like voice-operated word processors and machines that read to the blind. It may take another ten to fifteen years to make practical household robots that can act as partners. We can be sure that one success will trigger another, and there will be a cascade of new ideas about how to use this technology.

The tasks that neural networks are already doing, and those that seem possible if given a research nudge, form an impressive list. We find it interesting that the government-funded DARPA Neural Network Study interviewed a number of researchers about their applications and commented that each one "expressed an inspirational fascination in one way or another."[15] (DARPA stands for Defense Advanced Research Projects Agency.)

Researchers are excited by what they are finding. Executives are, too. Ford Executive Vice President John A. Betti calls the neural network computers "probably the most exciting team effort presently under way."[16]

We didn't start out to write a book; we were simply caught up in the fascination. Here is a technology with promise. We feel it offers significant opportunities for the betterment of our future. We want to understand it better and to encourage openness and experimentation in these early stages. This book gives us a chance to share our excitement.

1. James A. Anderson and Edward Rosenfeld, eds., *Neurocomputing: Foundations of Research* (Boston: MIT Press, 1988) p. 125.

2. *DARPA Neural Network Study*, (Fairfax, VA: AFCEA International Press, November 1988), appendix G, pp. 429–43.

3. Andrew Pollack, "More Human Than Ever, Computer Is Learning to Learn," *New York Times*, September 15, 1987, section C, p. 2.

4. See R. Colin Johnson, "Neural Nose to Sniff Out Explosives at JFK Airport," *Electronic Engineering Times*, issue 536 (May 1, 1989): 1, 86. See also Tom J. Schwartz, "IJCNN '89," *IEEE Expert*, vol. 4, no. 3 (Fall 1989): 77–78 and Richard Doherty, "FAA Adds 40 Sniffers," *Electronic Engineering Times*, issue 554 (September 4, 1989): 16.

5. *DARPA Neural Network Study*, (Fairfax, VA: AFCEA International Press, November 1988), appendix D, pp. 411–13.

6. *DARPA Neural Network Study*, (Fairfax, VA: AFCEA International Press, November 1988), appendix E, pp. 417–20.

7. Brian O'Reilly, "Computers That Think Like People," *Fortune*, vol. 119, no. 5 (February 27, 1989): 90–93.

8. Tom J. Schwartz, "IJCNN '89," *IEEE Expert* (Fall 1989): 77.

9. Fred Reed, "USPS Investigates Neural Nets" (p. 10) and "Neural Networks Fall Short of Miraculous But Still Work" (p. 28), *Federal Computer Week*, vol. 3, no. 4 (January 23, 1989).

10. EDventures Holdings, *Release 1.0 Newsletter* (New York: July 9, 1989), pp. 8–9. See also Lee Green, "Neural Networks Still Waiting on the Brink," *Information Week*, issue 186 (September 12, 1988): 52.

11. R. P. Gorman and T. J. Sejnowski, "Analysis of Hidden Units in a Layered Network Trained to Classify Sonar Targets," *Neural Networks*, vol. 1, no. 1 (1988): 75–89.

12. June Kinoshita and Nicholas G. Palevsky, "Computing With Neural Networks," *High Technology* (May 1987): 24–31. See also *DARPA Neural Network Study*, (Fairfax, VA: AFCEA International Press, November 1988), appendix F, pp. 421–25.

13. Reuters U.S., Dialog File 649, September 9, 1988. See also Amy Cortese, "Bellcore Puts Neural Nets on a Chip," *Computerworld*, vol. 22, issue 38 (September 19, 1988): 23.

14. "Neural Networks to Stimulate Investment and Development," *EDP Weekly* (March 20, 1989), p. 6–7.

15. *DARPA Neural Network Study,* (Fairfax, VA: AFCEA International Press, November 1988), p. 249.

16. News feature, *Ford Aerospace,* April 25, 1989.

Next Questions: What and Why?

The important thing is not to stop questioning. Curiosity has its own reason for existing.

—*Albert Einstein*

What Is a Neural Network?

Many definitions of neural networks assume that you already know the basics of such networks, or that you are at least math-literate and comfortable with calculus and differential equations. Although mathematical models of computation are valuable, it's easy for nontechnical persons to be intimidated by them. Other definitions tend to be jargony, and still others end up being esoteric or vague. Often they talk about a new computing architecture inspired by biological models.

As is indicated in figure 2.1, neural networks are a new information processing technique. They are computer-based simulations of living nervous systems, which work quite differently than conventional computing. For those who care about such things, they do have a rigorous, mathematical basis. Having a statistically valid set on which to train a network is important. Although at points we show some of the mathematics involved, our goal is to provide a hands-on guide without making too many assumptions about your skill level and without being tedious.

If you gain enough background to read some of the professional journals and understand some of the complexities of neural networks, that would make a fine beginning to a study of the subject. Managers could "get a leg up" on the "techies" and be

> A new form of computing, inspired by biological models.
>
> A mathematical model composed of a large number of processing elements organized into layers.
>
> " . . . a computing system made up of a number of simple, highly interconnected processing elements, which processes information by its dynamic state response to external inputs."
>
> —— (Maureen Caudill's paraphrase of Robert Hecht-Nielsen)

FIGURE 2.1   WHAT IS A NEURAL NETWORK?

```
                                              D_N'T   THR_W   _W_Y

                                              TH_   _LD   B_CK_T
     _ ST_TCH _N        _ P_NNY   S_V_D
                                              _NT_L   Y__   KN_W
     T_M_  S_V_S        _S _ P_NNY
                                              WH_TH_R   TH_   N_W
     N_N_               __RN_D
                                              _N_   H_LDS   W_T_R.
```

FIGURE 2.2   SEQUENTIAL VERSUS GESTALT EXPERIMENT

able to better evaluate briefings and proposals. See chapter 9, "How To Get Started," for other ideas.

A couple of experiments may suggest the flavor of neural networks and help you begin developing a more intuitive understanding of what they are.

Experiment 1

Imagine what it would be like to try to understand figure 2.2 if you could read it only serially, one character at a time, in order, across the page. (You could take a sheet of paper, make a little hole in it just big enough for one character, and move it across the page in a simulation of a serial procedure.) That's how a conventional computer processes its input—one thing at a time. Working sequentially, it's much harder to detect patterns that become obvious when you can see the whole picture at once.

Our eyes look at the whole. We see that the vowels are missing. We can identify three different groupings, and know that simply reading across an entire line would mix words from the different groups. The first grouping is easy. Once we see that it's a proverb, the second grouping falls into place. Knowing the pattern, we can fill in the missing spaces to complete the third grouping. We may not have known this Swedish proverb, but that doesn't matter now—we're feeling like old hands at this game.

Neural networks have more in common with the second approach (parallel processing) than they do with the first (sequential processing). They process many inputs at once, reinforcing some, diminishing others, working toward a stable picture. Of course, this is a simplification, but it's a reasonable place to start.

Experiment 2

Suppose one of us tossed an eraser to you. Most likely you would catch it, even if you might be a bit startled. Tracking the state of dynamic systems, such as the path of an eraser thrown at you, is a nontrivial task for a computer. Yet, you can probably do this quite easily. You estimate the speed, the trajectory, the weight (whether to catch it or duck), and so on. And you do it in real time, immediately.

Compare your task to what a serial computer would have to do to track a satellite or the position of a ship. There are quite a few navigation components: coordinates in a three-dimensional space (x, y, z); velocities in each direction; and variations in the attitude of the vessel, such as roll, pitch, and yaw. Algorithms taking these components into account are quite complicated. Tracking is computable, but sometimes just barely. It depends on how sophisticated your computing resource is.

The speed of the computation affects the sampling size and speed of updates. When a weather service needs to update each hour, there's plenty of time to compute the new data. When you use updates to influence the course of a vessel (such as a spacecraft), the calculations must be done in real time. Even very powerful computers reach the limits of reasonable computation when the number of components gets large (say around 25 different variables).

Our processor, the brain, is significantly slower than today's computers, yet we can evaluate all the components quickly enough to react and catch the eraser. Why? Parallel processing. The massive parallelism of our brains gives us a lot of processing capability in real time. Neurocomputers (computers based on the parallelism of neural networks) offer good possibilities for increasing the size of the system we can observe and keep up with.

We've looked at a couple of examples of what *we* can do with our biological neural networks. Now let's look at some of the accomplishments of current artificial neural systems.

Pattern-Recognition Examples

Neural networks have proved adept at pattern-recognition tasks (see figure 2.3). One system can recognize handwritten numbers on checks. Another network was built to analyze customer signatures for banks. The latter claims a success rate between 96 and 98 percent in detecting authentic examples (even when the forger has a copy of the signature available)[1] and has done better than most humans can do in catching forgeries.

An experimental neural network at Stanford University in the

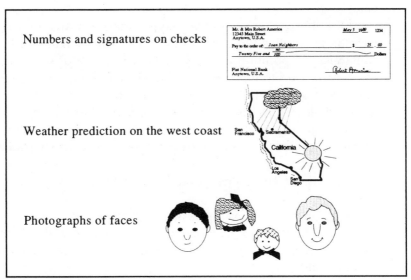

FIGURE 2.3 PATTERN-RECOGNITION EXAMPLES

1960s predicted weather patterns.[2] Data were collected for 33 days—things like barometric pressure and precipitation. The goal of the network was to predict precipitation based on the input patterns. This simple network performed as well or better than the weatherman during a two-week test. You could create an ongoing system by continually updating the network and removing old data.

A Finnish experiment illustrates the pattern-recognition capabilities of neural networks by using photographs of ten people.[3] Each face was photographed at five different angles to produce a data set of fifty photos. Each photograph was subsequently associated with a bar in a bar graph by correlating with light intensities at specified points on the photographs. A different bar was used for each person; the five views of each person were all associated with the same bar. All fifty name-face pairs were stored in a mathematical model. Next, a picture of one of the original ten people was taken from a new angle (though still vertical and the same size as the reference figures) and its intensity pattern was combined with the previous model. The output was a bar graph to show how much the new input resembled each of the ten people. The neural network had no trouble correctly matching the new picture. The height of the bar corresponding to the actual person photographed was many times higher than the other nine bars.

One innovative nonmilitary application to prove neural net technology studies the communication of killer whales.[4] General Dynamics Corporation and scientists at Sea World in San Diego have teamed up to tape whale calls, which curiously change over time. Do Alaskan whale sounds show up in the calls of Norwegian killer whales? (Or, can neural nets prove valuable in military applications such as analyzing radar and sonar?) Yet another novel example applied a neural network based on a Soviet statistical model. Using the answers to twelve yes/no questions, the net predicted that George Bush would win the 1988 U.S. presidential election.[5]

We'll share more examples as we go along. That's how we've learned—by examples. They give a more holistic understanding than resources such as reference manuals, which emphasize syntax and rules.

Other Names for Artificial Neural Networks

Some researchers make a point of saying "artificial neural networks," just as you might say that airplanes are "artificial birds."

Nature's successes provide a basis for our understanding, but there is still so much we don't know. Researchers differ in their opinions about whether we should continue trying to learn more about nature in order to copy it (after all, nature has spent a lot of time trying to get things right) or whether we should depart from nature and move in new directions. Airplanes, for example, are designed to carry heavier loads and fly faster than nature's models. Where the goal is the solution of a specific problem, it makes sense to move in whatever directions seem most promising. Where the goal is learning more about the brain and how it works, then obviously you have to pay attention to biology. Both approaches have their place, and both will likely end up contributing to the other's store of knowledge.

Neural networks go by many aliases. Although by no means synonyms, the names listed in figure 2.4 all refer to this new form of information processing. You'll see some of these terms again when we talk about implementations and models. In general, though, we will continue to use the words *neural networks* to mean the broad class of artificial neural systems. This term appears to be the one most commonly used.

- Parallel distributed processing models

- Connectivist/connectionism models

- Adaptive systems

- Self-organizing systems

- Neurocomputing

- Neuromorphic systems

FIGURE 2.4   OTHER NAMES FOR ARTIFICIAL NEURAL NETWORKS

Why Neural Networks Now?

Neural networks aren't new. Why the emphasis now? (See figure 2.5).

Current technology has run into a lot of bottlenecks—sequential processing, for one. When a computer can handle information only one small piece at a time, there are limits to how fast you can push a lot of information through. Even with many processors working in parallel, much time is wasted waiting for sequential operations to complete. It's also difficult to write programs that can use parallel operations effectively.

Even though today's supercomputers may amaze us with their speed and number-crunching abilities, they cannot do other tasks that a child can do easily . . . recognizing faces, learning to speak and walk, knowing when cookies are in the oven. Sequential architectures may be good at the highly procedural task of walking trees (such as decision trees and binary trees used in programming), but neural networks are better at picking which branch to walk.

Artificial intelligence (AI), touted as all sorts of wonderful things, has not been able to deliver on many of its anticipated promises. Although some things that were thought to be difficult

---

Current problems and potentials:

    Bottlenecks in sequential processing

    Limitations of current AI approaches

    Potential for solving today's technological problems

    . . . such as: pattern recognition
                     speech/image understanding
                     sensor processing
                     robotic controls
                     expert systems
                     learning

FIGURE 2.5 WHY NEURAL NETWORKS NOW?

A Practical Guide to Neural Nets

have proved to be easy, some things that researchers thought would be easy to do have proved to be difficult. AI representations must be formal, and you can't do common sense or intuitive thinking that way. Logic machines have turned out to be poor at dealing with images and making analogies. Rule-based computers are limited in their ability to accommodate inaccuracies or fuzzy information.

A number of today's technological problems are in areas where neural network technology has demonstrated potential: things like pattern recognition and classification, speech and image understanding, sensor processing, robotic controls, optimization, learning . . . and without the need for application-specific software.

Figure 2.6 lists some additional reasons for the current interest in neural networks. Improvements in hardware and software have created a climate that has encouraged experimentation and simulation. You don't have to have the power of an IBM mainframe or a VAX to do neural nets. Many excellent simulation examples and learning aids run on desktop computers;[6] some cost less than $100. This means that just about anybody can get into the game.

The past couple of years have witnessed an explosion in the number of neural network articles appearing in computer maga-

---

Current improvements and impacts:

    Hardware and software improvements

    Impact of neural networks on technology

    Impact of "Everybody's doing it"

        Articles, conferences, companies

        Neural networks in Europe and Japan

        DARPA study

FIGURE 2.6 WHY NEURAL NETWORKS NOW? (CONTINUED)

zines. Entire issues have been devoted to the topic. (*IEEE Computer*, March 1988; *MD Computing*, May/June 1988; *AI Expert*, August 1988 and June 1990; *PC AI* November/December 1988 and May/June 1990.) Articles are also showing up in nonindustry publications such as *Time* magazine and the *New York Times*. Neural nets have even made the Dick Tracy comic strip (January 1989)!

With all the attention given to neural networks in the media, people and businesses are beginning to take notice. They don't want to get left too far behind the leading edge of new technological advances. Potential advantages are worth knowing about and evaluating.

Annual conventions and conferences that didn't even exist a few years ago now offer you many opportunities to listen, learn, and share ideas. Again, the interdisciplinary nature of this field is refreshing. Meetings are sponsored by such diverse groups as IEEE, Wright-Patterson Air Force Base, European Physical Society, USSR Academy of Sciences, Johns Hopkins University, Institute for International Research, University of Miami, UCLA, Society for Computers in Psychology, Center for Neurobiology of Learning, Society of Photo-optical Instrumentation Engineers, and many others. The agendas can be as varied as the sponsorship. The 5th Interdisciplinary Workshop held in Paris in June 1988, for example, included topics from hydrodynamics, quantum statistical mechanics, biophysics, chaos, convection patterns, electric lines, magnetic chains, materials science, optical lines, nonlinear phenomena, lattice dynamics, and neural networks.

More than 40 start-up companies in neural network technology showed up in the short space of 18 months in 1987–88, pushing their software, hardware, applications, consulting services, education, and whatever else they deem marketable. Along with computer giants like AT&T, Texas Instruments, Motorola and Fujitsu, smaller companies are moving full-steam ahead with research. Battelle-Columbus Labs has established a neural network clearinghouse to track for their clients the developments of researchers and companies working on neural network computers.[7]

Money is being spent on neural network research in continents besides North America. Japan is turning its post-fifth generation computer attention to neural network research in a government-sponsored program called "The Human Frontiers."

Although most of the effort has been conducted at universities, corporations are getting into the game. Fujitsu is working on mobile robots controlled by neural networks, Asahi Chemical is marketing a speech recognition network, and NEC Corporation has come out with a personal neurocomputer.[8] Some 200 machines, equipped with "neuro-engine" boards and neural network software, were shipped by the summer of 1989.[9] These systems can be used for applications such as sound recognition, fault diagnosis, robot control, and character recognition.

Europe's neural network effort, ESPRIT II, is a five-year project involving eight countries and several hundred worker-years of effort.[10] The designers propose to build the first neural computers complete with architectures and algorithms for neural processors and a high-level programming language. Potential applications include image and speech understanding, robot control, route planning, and medicine. Real financial returns are expected in a few years as a result of their research. In early 1989, ESPRIT announced a new program, the Application of Neural Networks for the Industry in Europe (ANNIE).[11] Six million dollars has been budgeted to create a strong European presence in neural nets.

In addition to the ESPRIT projects, neural network projects are being developed in individual European countries. The West Germans have appropriated about $250 million for neural-network research over the next five years.[12] France has perhaps the most active development; six neural-based microchip projects are underway in Paris alone.[13] In the Netherlands, the previously independent neural network research of biophysicists and computer scientists is now being coordinated and funded by a government committee. The U.K. has a project funded at $470 million. The Scandinavian countries have a four-year, $12-million program. Rumors are already suggesting an ESPRIT coordination of the neural net efforts of all Common Market countries.

The U.S. government funds much technological research. One significant government agency is the Defense Advanced Research Projects Agency, DARPA. When DARPA speaks, budget makers generally listen.

Jasper Lupo, the deputy director of the Tactical Technology Office of DARPA, called the neural network technology "more important than the atom bomb."[14] The results of the DARPA-funded neural network study, published in November of 1988, are the first major assessment of the state of neural network technology. This six-part report includes an executive summary followed by an analysis of prospects and limitations of the technology. When DARPA embarked on an eight-year neural network program, many people wanted a slice of the $390 million pie. Even when the original funding was reduced to $33 million over 17 months as a seed program, there were still a lot of applicants for the grants.

Summary

Neural networks are rough models of the mental processes their name implies. Because of their massive parallelism, they can process information and carry out solutions almost simultaneously. They learn by being shown examples and the expected results. Or, they form their own associations without being prompted and rewarded. They are good at pattern-matching types of problems.

Because the kinds of things neural nets can do address many of today's problems, a new industry is emerging. This is happening on several continents and involves a wide variety of disciplines. Researchers are forming alliances, holding conferences, publishing. Neural networks have progressed from conception to actual products. This is a time of optimism and promise, but also of caution and reserve. The next chapter attempts to clarify the interplay of optimism/pessimism by looking at some events in the history of neural networks.

1. Mickey Williamson, "Neural Networks," *Digital News* (January 9, 1989): 33.

2. Bailey, Thompson, and Feinstein, "The Practical Side of Neural Networks," *PC AI*, vol. 2, no. 4, (November/December 1988): 34.

3. Dreyfus and Dreyfus, *Mind Over Machine* (New York: The Free Press, 1986), p. 93.

4. Mimi Bluestone, "Why Computer Scientists Are Eavesdropping on Whales," Developments to Watch, *Business Week* (August 8, 1986): 53.

5. R. Colin Johnson, "Soviet Model Picks Bush," *Electronic Engineering Times*, issue 508 (October 17, 1988): 51. (A copy of the program is available by sending a blank disk and mailer—or $6—to Source Translation and Optimization, P.O. Box 404, Belmont, MA 02178.)

6. Di Schwartz and Mark Jurik, "Neural Nets on a Personal Computer," *PC AI*, vol. 2, no. 4 (November/December 1988): 37. See also Tom J. Schwartz,

"12-Product Wrap-Up: Neural Networks," *AI Expert,* vol. 3, no. 8 (August 1988): 73–85.

7. News Release, April 15, 1988, Columbus, OH. Contact Dr. Klaus Obermeier, Battelle-Columbus Labs, 505 King Avenue, Columbus, OH 43201–2693, phone 614–424–5570.

8. Miyoko Sakurai, "Personal 'Neurocomputer' Ready to Go, NEC's 'Neuro'," *Electronic Engineering Times,* issue 494 (July 11, 1988): 19. See also "NEC Develops PC Neuro-Computer System," *Comline Computers* (December 1, 1988): 2.

9. Shohei Kurita, "Expanding Neural Marketplace Challenges Japanese Engineers," *Electronic Business* (Asia/Pacific Business section) (September 18, 1989): 80.

10. Angeli Mehta, "Nations Unite for Electronic Brain," *Computer Weekly,* issue 1148 (January 11, 1988): 1.

11. Harvey P. Newquist III, "Parlez-Vous Intelligence Artificielle?," *AI Expert,* vol. 4, no. 9 (September 1989): 60.

12. R. Colin Johnson, "DARPA Neural Awards Stress Practical Use," *Electronic Engineering Times,* issue 558 (October 2, 1989): 22.

13. R. Colin Johnson, "French Research: Vive le Neuron" and "nEuro '88 Abuzz With nEuropean Activity," *Electronic Engineering Times,* issue 492 (June 27, 1988): 57.

14. R. Colin Johnson and Tom J. Schwartz, "DARPA Backs Neural Nets," *Electronic Engineering Times,* issue 498 (August 8, 1988): 1, 96.

 # A Brief History of Neural Networks

Erwin Schrodinger, the great physicist, once said that it takes at least fifty years before a major scientific discovery penetrates the public consciousness—half a century before people realize what truly surprising beliefs are held by leading scientists. The human species can no longer afford the luxury of such long double-takes or the leisurely changes of heart of entrenched scientists. The cost is too great. . . . We are duty-bound to search, question, open our minds.

—Marilyn Ferguson

This chapter discusses the history of neural networks, from their conception to their current state. Figure 3.1 summarizes this history.

Conception (1890–1949)

Attempts to understand the human brain go back a long way, even centuries. In *Intelligence: The Eye, the Brain, and the Computer*, Fischler and Firschein mention the work of Hippocrates as well as the less familiar *Edward Smith Papyrus*.[1] The latter is a surgical treatise which describes the location of certain sensory and motor control areas in the brain. It was written around 3000 B.C.

A more recent text by William James, *Psychology (Briefer Course)*, 1890, contains insights into brain activity and foreshadows current theories. Take this quote as an example: "Let us assume as the basis of all our subsequent reasoning this law: When two elementary brain-processes have been active together or in immediate succession, one of them, on reoccurring, tends to propagate its excitement into the other."[2]

Alan Turing was the first to use the brain as a computing paradigm, a way of looking at the world of computing. That was in 1936. In 1943, Warren McCulloch, a neurophysiologist, and

A Practical Guide to Neural Nets

Present	late 80s to now	Interest explodes with conferences, articles, simulations, new companies, government funded research.
Late Infancy	1982 ——	Hopfield at National Academy of Sciences
		Some research continues
Stunted Growth	1969 ——	Minsky & Papert's critique, *Perceptrons*
		Excessive hype
Early Infancy	late 50s, 60s ——	Research efforts expand
		AI & Neural Computing Fields launched
Birth	1956 ——	Dartmouth Summer Research Project
Gestation	1950s ——	Age of computer simulation
	1949 ——	Hebb, *The Organization of Behavior*
	1943 ——	McCulloch & Pitts paper on neurons
	1936 ——	Turing uses brain as computing paradigm
Conception	1890 ——	James, *Psychology (Briefer Course)*

FIGURE 3.1 A BRIEF HISTORY OF NEURAL NETWORKS

Walter Pitts, an eighteen-year-old mathematician, wrote a paper about how neurons might work.[3] They modeled a simple neural network with electrical circuits. Though oversimplified by today's standards, this paper was saved from possible obscurity when John von Neumann used it in teaching the theory of computing machines. Researchers began to look to anatomy and physiology for clues about creating intelligent machines.

Another important book was Donald Hebb's *The Organization of Behavior* (1949), which highlights the connection between psychology and physiology, pointing out that a neural pathway is reinforced each time it is used. Hebb's Learning Rule, as it is sometimes known, is still used and quoted today.

Gestation (1950s)

Improvements in hardware and software in the 1950s ushered in the age of computer simulation. It became possible to test theories about nervous system functions. Research expanded; neural network terminology came into its own.

Nathaniel Rochester and others from the IBM research laboratories conducted a software simulation of a neural network model based on Hebb's work. The first attempts failed, but with collaboration from Hebb and others, successful adaptations were made. Theories began to be modified as details that could be overlooked on paper became essential in the laboratory of the computer.

Birth (1956)

The Dartmouth Summer Research Project on Artificial Intelligence (AI) in the summer of 1956 provided momentum for both the fields of AI and neural computing. Putting together some of the best minds of the times unleashed a whole raft of new work. Some efforts took the "high-level" (AI) approach in trying to create computer programs that could be described as "intelligent" machine behavior; other directions used mechanisms modeled after "low-level" (neural network) processes of the brain to achieve "intelligence."

Early Infancy (Late 1950s, 1960s)

The year following the Dartmouth Project, John von Neumann wrote material for his book *The Computer and the Brain* (Yale University Press, 1958). Here he makes such suggestions as imitating simple neuron functions by using telegraph relays or vacuum tubes. Also in 1957, Frank Rosenblatt (Cornell) began work on the Perceptron, a neural network model about which we will hear more later. Built in hardware, it is the oldest neural network and still has use today in various forms for applications such as character recognition.

In 1959, Bernard Widrow and Marcian Hoff (Stanford) developed models for ADALINE, then MADALINE (Multiple ADAptive LINear Elements). This was the first neural network applied to a real-world problem—adaptive filters to eliminate echoes on phone lines. As we mentioned before, this application has been in commercial use for several decades.

One of the major players in neural net research from the 1960s to current times is Stephen Grossberg (Boston University). He has done considerable writing (much of it tedious) on his extensive physiological research to develop neural network models. His 1967 network, Avalanche, uses a class of networks to perform activities such as continuous-speech recognition and teaching motor commands to robotic arms. More on the models later. . . .

Excessive Hype

Affected by the predominantly rosy outlook of the time, some people exaggerated the potential of neural networks. Biological comparisons were blown out of proportion. In the October 1987 issue of the *Neural Network Review,* newsletter editor Craig Will quotes Frank Rosenblatt from a 1958 issue of *The New Yorker:*[4]

> "Our success in developing the perceptron means that for the first time a nonbiological object will achieve an organization of its external environment in a meaningful way," Dr. Rosenblatt said. "That's a safe definition of what the perceptron can do. My colleague [Marshall Yovits, from the Office of Naval Research] disapproves of all the loose talk one hears nowadays about mechanical brains. He prefers to call our machine a self-organizing system, but, between you and me, that's precisely what any brain is."
>
> Of what practical use, we asked, would the perceptron be? "At the moment, none whatever," Dr. Rosenblatt said cheerfully.
>
> What, we asked, *wasn't* the perceptron capable of? Dr. Rosenblatt threw up his hands. "Love," he said. "Hope. Despair. Human nature, in short. If we don't understand the human sex drive, how can we expect a machine to?"
>
> Reprinted by permission; © 1958, 1986 *The New Yorker* Magazine, Inc.

Some observers were disappointed as promises were left unfulfilled. Others felt threatened by the thought of "intelligent machines." Could we be out-manipulated by contemporary equivalents of Hal, as in the movie 2001? An Oklahoma newspaper headline typifies the impending hype/over-reaction climate: "Frankenstein Monster Designed by Navy Robot That Thinks."

AI had made some of the same mistakes. Enthusiastic proponents had dreamed big dreams and made sweeping predictions. "Intuition, insight, and learning are no longer exclusive possessions of human beings: any large high-speed computer can be programmed to exhibit them also," Herbert Simon wrote about AI in 1958.[5] *Deja vu.*

Needless to say, our expectations have changed significantly, though overly optimistic predictions are still with us. Healthy skepticism may guard against repetitions of such excess.

Stunted Growth (1969–1981)

In 1969, in the midst of such outrageous claims, respected voices of critique were raised that brought a halt to much of the funding for neural network research. Marvin Minsky and Seymour Papert published *Perceptrons,*[6] an influential book condemning Rosenblatt's "baby," the Perceptron. The limitations of the Perceptron were significant; the charge was that it could not solve any "interesting" problems. Many researchers turned their attention to AI, which looked more promising at the time.

The undaunted continued working. These researchers included James Anderson, a neurophysiologist at Brown University, who developed a network model with the catchy name of Brain-State-in-a-Box (BSB—again, we will return to the models later). In Japan and Europe, research also continued. Current government-sponsored projects are targeting both research and commerce. Kunihiko Fukushima developed the Neocognitron, a neural network model for visual pattern recognition. Teuvo Kohonen, an electrical engineer at Helsinki University, developed a similar model to Anderson's, but independently. And there were others, plugging away quietly in their labs: Grossberg, Rumelhart and McClelland, Marr and Poggio, Amari, Cooper, and many more.

Late Infancy (1982–Present)

In 1982, the time was ripe for renewed interest in neural networks. Several events converged to make this a pivotal year.

John Hopfield (Caltech) presented his neural network paper to the National Academy of Sciences. Abstract ideas became focused as he pulled together previous work on neural nets. Where previous models had been brain models first and useful devices second, Hopfield reversed the priorities. Practicality was key.

With clarity and with mathematical analysis, he showed how such networks could work and what they could do. A distinguished physicist, he brought a new respectability to the struggling science. His images of retrieval of complete data or images from fragments intrigued military minds. One of the big failures of artificial intelligence—automatic guided vehicles—again looked possible with this new tool. That Hopfield has also been described as being very charismatic didn't hurt the cause. In fact, some accounts of the times attribute about 80 percent of the revived interest in neural networks directly to Hopfield. Other writers simply point out that many people were doing work that was converging in similar directions.[7]

But there were other threads pulling at the neural network picture as well. Also in 1982, the U.S.-Japan Joint Conference on Cooperative/ Competitive Neural Networks was held in Kyoto, Japan. Japan subsequently announced their "Human Frontiers" program, or Sixth Generation effort, as it is sometimes called. Fujitsu began development on "thinking computers" for robotics applications. Interest was building.

In 1985, the American Institute of Physics began what has become an annual Neural Networks for Computing meeting. This was the first of many more conferences to come. In 1987, the Institute of Electrical and Electronics Engineers' (IEEE) First International Conference on Neural Networks drew more than 1,800 attendees and 19 vendors (although there were few products to show yet). Later the same year, the International Neural Network Society (INNS) was formed under the leadership of Grossberg in the U.S., Kohonen in Finland, and Amari in Japan. Within two years' time the INNS has achieved a membership of more than 3,000.

Six different IEEE societies were cosponsors of the INNS conference, with funding from DARPA (more about this agency elsewhere), the National Science Foundation, and others. Although there were two competing conferences in 1988, the spirit of cooperation in this new technology has resulted in joint sponsorship (INNS and IEEE) for semiannual meetings. The International Joint Conference on Neural Networks (IJCNN), held in June 1989, produced 430 papers, 63 of which focused on application development. The January 1990 IJCNN in Washington, D.C. included an hour's concert of music generated by neural networks.

The Neural Networks for Defense meeting, held in conjunction with the June 1989 IJCNN above, gathered more than 160 representatives of government defense agencies and defense contractors giving presentations on neural network efforts. Bernard Widrow, in his after-lunch talk, told his audience that they were engaged in World War IV, a war of commerce, ("World War III never happened") where the battlefields were manufacturing and world trade.[8] Widrow suggested that governmental agencies should redirect 50 percent of their budgets to commerce and R&D for commerce.

When the U.S. Department of Defense announced its 1990 Small Business Innovation Research Program, 16 topics specifically targeted neural networks.[9] An additional 13 topics mentioned the possibility of using neural network approaches.

When simulations are abundant, applications are starting to come out of the closet, and high-level redirection of resources is being urged, can tools be far behind? Of course not. Many new products are emerging to help the neural network developer. A number of them run on PCs. Dave Trowbridge, a spokesman for Hecht-Nielsen Corporation, claims, "What spreadsheets did for financial analysis, Netset [their neural network product] will do for pattern recognition."[10]

1989 was a year of unfolding application possibilities, some of which were featured in chapter 1. On September 27, 1989, the IEEE and The Learning Channel sponsored a 3-hour satellite videoconference entitled Neural Networks: Capabilities and Applications—For Today and The Future. Although networks on a chip soon followed the events of 1982, the continuing development in implementations (see chapter 10) promises to be one of the next hot spots. Over half a dozen neural network newsletters are now being published (see appendix B).

Who Are the Key Players?

The multidisciplinary approach to neural networks is exciting. When some of the best minds from so many areas are converging on a common interest (see figure 3.2), there must be some powerful brew in the pot.

The ICNN in 1987 included attendees from computer science, electrical engineering, physiology, cognitive psychology, medicine, and even a philosopher or two. There were financial types as well as people from the defense establishment, buyers, sellers,

- Medical and theoretical neurobiologists
  Neurophysiology, drug chemistry, molecular biology
- Computer and information scientists
  Information theory
- Adaptive control theorists/psychologists
  Merging learning and control theory
- Adaptive systems researchers/biologists
  Self-organization of living species
- AI researchers
  Machine learning mechanisms

FIGURE 3.2 WHO ARE THE KEY PLAYERS?

and interested observers. That's been a fairly typical representation for most conferences.

Nobel laureates such as Francis Crick (DNA structure) and Leon Cooper (superconductivity theory) have joined the ranks of those interested. In fact, Cooper is one of the founders of Nestor Corporation, one of the first new companies in the neural network game today.

New coalitions combining educational and commercial concerns around this new field are beginning to emerge. In May of 1988, the North Texas Commission Regional Technology Program convened a study group for the purpose of reviewing the opportunities for developing a metroplex-based center of excellence in the emerging field of computational neuroscience. Their report of October 1988 concludes that the present is a critical time to establish such a center.

A quote from John von Neumann sets the tone for the North Texas Commission report: "I suspect that a deeper mathematical study of the nervous system . . . will affect our understanding. . . . in fact it may alter the way in which we look at mathematics and logic proper."[11] Believing that a better scientific understanding of the brain and the subsequent application to computing technology could have significant impact, they assess their regional strengths in electronics and biomedical science. Their goals are both academic and economic. You can sense excitement and commitment in their plans.

There are a number of key individuals in this field. It would be risky to list them, because no doubt we'd leave out someone important. We've already mentioned a number of notable people in the preceding history and more are scattered throughout this book. See the bibliography for other names. Claims to fame include research in theory, application and implementation, writing of books and articles, and helping to build a new industry.

Summary

The history of neural network development has been eventful, exciting, and somewhat rocky. Pamela McCorduck said, "To know intelligence well enough to be able to build a working model of it is surely one of the most intellectually exciting and spiritually challenging problems of the human race."[12] She applied this to artificial intelligence, but it also applies to neural networks. The imagination and perspiration of many have gone into this pursuit. Hopefully, the rich blend of intellects and backgrounds and divergent objectives will continue the quest. We may well come to understand ourselves in new ways as a result.

1. Fischler and Firschein, *Intelligence: The Eye, the Brain, and the Computer* (Reading, MA: Addison-Wesley, April, 1987), p. 23.

2. Anderson and Rosenfeld, eds., *Neurocomputing: Foundations of Research*, (Cambridge, MA: MIT Press, 1988), p. 5. Quoting from James, *Psychology (Briefer Course)*, (New York: Holt, 1890), p. 256.

3. Warren S. McCulloch and Walter Pitts, "A Logical Calculus of the Ideas Immanent in Nervous Activity," *Bulletin of Mathematical Biophysics* (1943), 5:115–33.

4. "Rival: Perceptron," *The New Yorker*, "Talk of the Town," (December 6, 1958): 44–45.

5. Herbert A. Simon and Allen Newell, "Heuristic Problem Solving: The Next Advance in Operations Research," *Operations Research* 6 (January-February 1958):6.

6. Minsky and Papert, *Perceptrons* (Cambridge, MA: MIT Press, 1969).

7. Craig A. Will, "Neural Networks Go Public," *Neural Network Review* (October 1987): 11.

8. Edward Rosenfeld, "Neural Networks for Defense Highlights Applications, Chips," *INTELLIGENCE Newsletter,* June 1989, P.O. Box 20006, NY, NY 10025–1510.

9. *Neural Network Review* (newsletter), Craig Will, editor, vol. 3, supp. 1 (October 1989) published by Lawrence Erlbaum Associates.

10. Ann Sussman, "Neural Networking Conference Shows Commercial Uses," *PC Week,* vol. 5, no. 31 (August 1, 1988): 8.

11. "Computational Neuroscience: An Opportunity for Technological Leadership for the Metroplex." A report of the North Texas Commission Panel on Computational Neuroscience, October 1988, p. 1.

12. Pamela McCorduck, *Machines Who Think,* (New York: W. H. Freeman and Company, 1979), p. 113.

How Do Neural Networks Work?

It does not seem that there is anything in the construction, constituents, or behavior of the human beings which is essentially impossible for science to duplicate and synthesize. On the other hand. . . .
                                                                    —*Loren Eiseley*

Anthropomorphism: The Biological Metaphor

A discussion of anthropomorphism may seem like a digression, but it may be a worthwhile one if it helps explain the terminology of artificial neural networks. Ascribing human characteristics to nonliving things sometimes helps promote understanding (see figure 4.1). After all, we can all relate to ourselves as rather typical (translated, "above average") humans. We more or less know about ourselves.

Along with the gift of understanding there is also a danger. Anthropomorphism can lead to misunderstanding when the metaphor is carried too far. In fact, some researchers doing a lot of substantive work in this new technology are deliberately calling their efforts "connectionism" rather than neural networks. This is an attempt to distance themselves from comparisons with those doing research in brain modeling. Nevertheless, we believe that much of the current neural network language will survive, and that knowledge of the biological origins is beneficial in developing an understanding of the work of both the connectionists and the brain modelers.

FIGURE 4.1 ANTHROPOMORPHISM

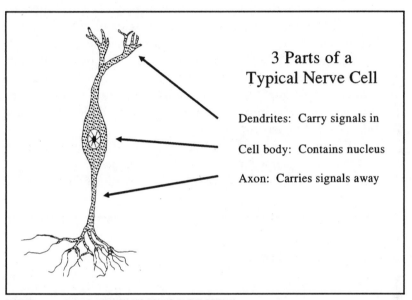

3 Parts of a
Typical Nerve Cell

Dendrites: Carry signals in

Cell body: Contains nucleus

Axon: Carries signals away

FIGURE 4.2 A SIMPLE NEURON (AS FOUND IN THE RETINA)

A Simple Neuron

A neuron is a nerve cell with all of its processes. Neurons are one of the main distinguishing features of animals. (Plants do not have nerve cells.) Between seven and a hundred different classes of neurons have been identified in humans. The wide variation is related to how restrictively a class is defined. We tend to think of them as being microscopic, but some neurons in your legs are as long as three meters.

The type of neuron found in the retina is shown in figure 4.2 as an example. It is a bipolar neuron, which means it has two processes. The cell body contains the *nucleus*. Leading into the nucleus are one or more *dendrites*. These branching, tapering processes of the nerve cell, as a rule, conduct impulses toward the cell body. The *axon* is the nerve cell process that conducts impulses away from the cell body. Although we could look at many other types of neurons, this one gives us the functionality and vocabulary we need to make analogies.

Nerve Structures and Synapses: Bundles of neurons, or nerve fibers, form *nerve structures* (see figure 4.3). In a simplified scenario, nerves conduct impulses from receptor organs (such as eyes or ears) to effector organs (such as muscles or glands). The point between two neurons in a neural pathway, where the termination of the axon of one neuron comes into close proximity with the cell body or dendrites of another, is called a *synapse*. At this point, a microscopic gap, the relationship of the two neurons is one of contact only. The impulse traveling in the first neuron initiates an impulse in the second neuron.

Impulses pass in one direction only, at rates varying from 10 to 120 meters per second. Here's the sequence. The end of a nerve fiber is stimulated to or above its sensitivity threshold level.

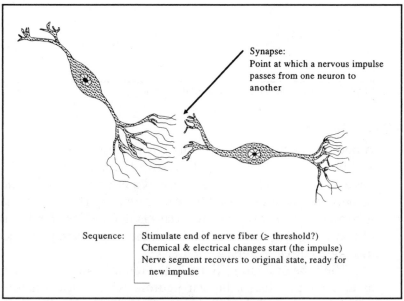

Synapse:
Point at which a nervous impulse passes from one neuron to another

Sequence:
Stimulate end of nerve fiber (≥ threshold?)
Chemical & electrical changes start (the impulse)
Nerve segment recovers to original state, ready for new impulse

FIGURE 4.3   BUNDLES OF NEURONS FORM NERVE STRUCTURES

A Practical Guide to Neural Nets

Chemical and electrical changes start—that's the impulse. When the impulse reaches the termination of the fiber, it may induce an impulse in another nerve cell, eventually resulting in physiological activity or inhibition.

Once the impulse is transmitted, the nerve segment recovers to its original state, ready for a new impulse.

Synapse Activity: In breaking the synaptic activity down, the points shown in figure 4.4 are important for our neural network analogy.

Signals come into the synapses. These are the inputs. They are "weighted." That is, some signals are stronger than others. Some signals excite (are positive), and others inhibit (are negative). The effects of all weighted inputs are summed.

If the sum is equal to or greater than the threshold for the neuron, then the neuron fires (gives output). This is an "all-or-nothing" situation. Either a neuron fires or it doesn't fire.

The ease of transmission of signals is altered by activity in the nervous system. Synapses are susceptible to fatigue, oxygen deficiency, and agents such as anesthetics. These events create a resistance to the passage of impulses. Other events may increase the rate of firing. This ability to adjust signals is a mechanism for learning. Threshold functions integrate the energy of incoming signals over space and time.

- Signals come into synapses,
  are "weighted,"
  and resulting quantities are summed

- If sum $\geq$ threshold for neuron
  Then neuron fires

- Activity in nervous systems can adjust signals

- Threshold functions integrate energy of
  incoming signals over space and time

FIGURE 4.4 SYNAPSE ACTIVITY

Computers and the Brain

A conventional computer is typically a single processor acting on explicitly programmed instructions. Programmers break tasks into tiny components, to be performed in sequence rapidly. The tasks are usually logical and precise.

On the other hand, the brain is comprised of ten billion or so neurons. Each nerve cell can interact directly with up to 200,000 other neurons (though 1,000 to 10,000 is typical). The power comes from the sheer numbers and multiple connections of so many units operating in concert.

Because a neuron either fires or doesn't fire, the rate of firing, not the amplitude, conveys the magnitude of information. The brain accepts inputs and generates responses to them. The responses are a combination of genetic programming and *learning*—how the self organizes in response to the inputs (see figure 4.5).

So . . . what if a computer were built to operate in a similar fashion? That is the issue. Can such a machine be built? How? How closely should you try to model the biology? Should you model the entire structure as closely as possible, or model only the end results or capacities? Opinions differ widely.

● Contains around 10 billion neurons

● Maximum firing rate is around 1,000 pulses/second

● Accepts inputs and generates responses to them

   Combination of genetic programming

   and

   Learning — organizing self in response to inputs

What if . . . a computer were built to operate in a similar fashion?

FIGURE 4.5   THE HUMAN BRAIN

A Practical Guide to Neural Nets

Machines, Not Brains: Artificial neural networks are based only loosely on biology (see figure 4.6). We don't understand how the brain works or what intelligence really is. Researchers are working on that, and it promises to be a lengthy project.

Kunihiko Fukushima, a senior research scientist at NHK (Japan Broadcasting Corporation) and inventor of the Neocognitron neural network model, describes his technique as a synthetic modeling approach. " . . . We try to follow physiological evidence as faithfully as possible. For parts not yet clear, however, we construct a hypothesis and synthesize a model that follows the hypothesis. We then analyze or simulate the behavior of the model and compare with that of the brain. If we find any discrepancy in the behavior between the model and the brain, we change the initial hypothesis and modify the model. . . . We repeat this procedure until the model behaves in the same way as the brain."[1]

Neural computing is about machines, not brains (see figure 4.7). We are trying to build machines that draw upon the highly successful designs used in biology. As we keep saying, there are two camps: one group is interested in the machines purely for what functionality they can provide us (an engineering problem), and the other group is interested in the machines for the biological

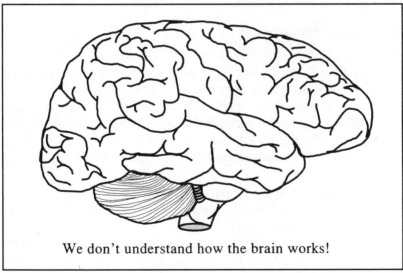

We don't understand how the brain works!

FIGURE 4.6 ARTIFICIAL NEURAL NETWORKS ARE ONLY LOOSELY BASED ON BIOLOGY

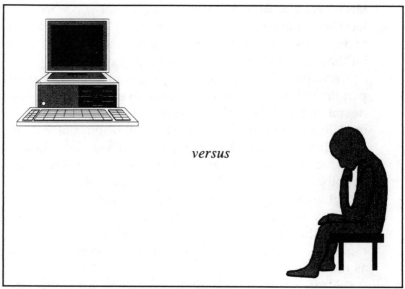

FIGURE 4.7 CONVENTIONAL COMPUTERS VERSUS BRAINS

information they illuminate (a scientific problem). One approach to models is synthetic. The other is analytical. Neither group has delusions about building an artificial brain.

Neural Network Activities

Although neural networks are not really considered to be artificial brains, the metaphor is strong enough that when we describe the activities of a neural network, it is fairly common to talk about how the network "behaves" or "reacts" to various inputs (see figure 4.8). Some networks are called "self-organizing"; others are said to "generalize." Networks that "learn" are so important that we have an entire chapter just to explore that feature. Sometimes networks have to learn to "forget" old learnings when situations change. These are all part of the accepted neural network vocabulary, whereas "executing programs" belongs to the arena of conventional computing.

That's probably enough said about the biology which serves as the inspiration. On to describing the nature of the artificial systems.

A Practical Guide to Neural Nets

Neural networks . . .

behave

react

self-organize

learn

generalize

forget

. . . rather than execute programs

FIGURE 4.8   NEURAL NETWORK ACTIVITIES

The Basic Components

Attempts to implement neural networks started with paper and pencil models. We'll start there as well. Subsequent hardware improvements made computer simulations possible. Although it may seem strange to simulate a parallel process on a sequential machine, there have been many benefits. It has bought time for the real objective of implementing neural networks in hardware, and it has illuminated problems in earlier models. Simulations have allowed us to better understand and improve the technology, and to tell in advance how well a particular neural network will perform in a given application. In addition to simulations, analog neural network circuits have been built and tested. We'll provide more implementation details in chapter 10.

The basic components we will describe are fairly typical. Keep in mind that there are many different types of neural network architectures. Chapter 7 will consider some of the interesting variations among several of the common models.

A Single Processing Element

Our paper and pencil model starts by copying the simplest element, the neuron. Call our artificial neuron a *processing element,* or *PE* for short. The word *node* is also used for this simple building block, which is represented by a circle in figure 4.9A.

These artificial neurons bear only a modest resemblance to the real things. It is easier to observe and measure electrical activity than it is to understand the chemical properties. Tom Schwartz (president of the Schwartz Associates, a consulting firm in Mountain View, CA), notes that "processing elements are barely a first order approximation of biological neurons. Processing elements model approximately three of the processes we know neurons perform. We know that there are at least 150 processes performed by neurons in the human brain."[2]

The PE handles several basic functions. It must evaluate the input signals, determining the strength of each one. Next, it must calculate a total for the combined input signals and compare that total to some threshold level. Finally, it must determine what the output should be.

Inputs and Outputs: Just as there are many inputs (stimulation levels) to a neuron, there should be many input signals to our PE. All of them should come into our PE simultaneously. In response, a neuron either "fires" or "doesn't fire," depending on some *threshold* level. Our PE will be allowed a single output signal, just as is present in a biological neuron. Many inputs, one output.

In addition, just as real neurons are affected by things other than inputs, some networks provide a mechanism for other influences. Sometimes this extra input is called a *bias term*, or a *forcing*

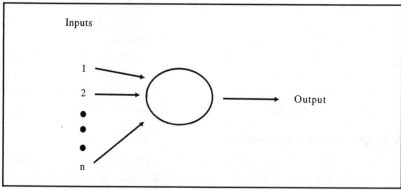

FIGURE 4.9A   A SINGLE NODE (OR PROCESSING ELEMENT, PE, OR ARTIFICIAL NEURON)

A Practical Guide to Neural Nets

term. It could also be a forgetting term, when a system needs to unlearn something.

Weighting Factors: Each input will be given a relative *weighting*, which will affect the impact of that input (see figure 4.9B). This is something like the varying synaptic strengths of the biological neurons—some inputs are more important than others in the way they combine to produce an impulse. Weights are adaptive coefficients within the network that determine the intensity of the input signal. Think of them as a measure of the connection strength. The initial weight for a PE could be modified in response to various inputs and according to the network's own rules for modification.

Mathematically, we could look at the inputs and the weights on the inputs as vectors, such as $(i_1, i_2 \ldots i_n)$ and $(w_1, w_2 \ldots w_n)$. The total input signal is the dot, or inner, product of the two vectors. You multiply each component of the i vector by the corresponding component of the w vector, and add up all the products. $Input_1 = i_1 * w_1$; $input_2 = i_2 * w_2$, etc. Then add $input_1 + input_2 + \ldots + input_n$. The result is a scalar, not a vector. Geometrically, the inner product of two vectors can be considered a measure of their similarity. If the vectors point in the same direction, the inner product is maximum; if the vectors point in opposite directions (180 degrees), their inner product is minimum. (If you want visual images of dot products, dust off your analytic geometry. It works well here.)

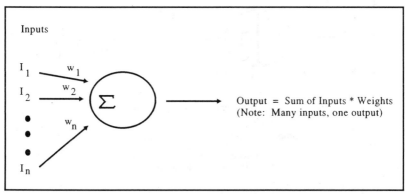

FIGURE 4.9B   A SINGLE NODE (OR PROCESSING ELEMENT, PE, OR ARTIFICIAL NEURON) WITH WEIGHTED INPUTS

Neuron Functions: Several important activities take place within the design of the processing element, or neuron. We will look at the highlights of these mathematical functions next; they will be examined in more detail later (and in appendix C).

First, let's examine the *summation function* (represented in figures 4.9B and 4.9C). All of the products will be summed (which could be more complex than simple summation) and compared to some *threshold* to determine the output. If the sum of the inputs is greater than the threshold value, the processing element generates a signal. If the sum of the inputs is less than the threshold, no signal (or some inhibitory signal) is generated. Both types of response are significant.

Activation Functions: The result of the summation function could be input to an activation function before being passed on to the transfer function (represented by T in figure 4.9C). The purpose of introducing another function here would be to allow the outputs to vary with respect to time. This is pretty much a research area, and most current implementations use the identity function as an activation function (which is equivalent to not having one). Additionally, such a function might likely be a component of the network as a whole rather than a PE component.

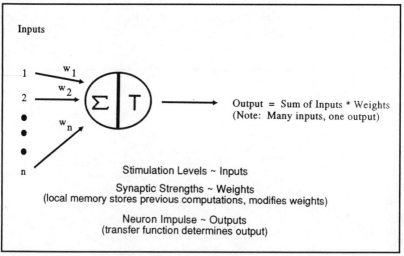

FIGURE 4.9C   A SINGLE NODE (OR PROCESSING ELEMENT, PE, OR ARTIFICIAL NEURON)—SUMMATION FUNCTION

A Practical Guide to Neural Nets

Transfer Functions: The threshold, or *transfer function*, is generally nonlinear. Linear (straight-line) functions are limited—boring, even, because the output is simply proportional to the input. But more than that, linear functions are not very useful. That was the problem noted in *Perceptrons*.[3] Only a few problems can be separated neatly into two categories with a straight line. The "eXclusive OR," XOR, is a classic example (see figure 4.10).

The transfer function could be something as simple as 0. Then the output depends upon whether the result of the summation is positive or negative. The network could output 1 and -1, or 1 and 0, etc., and the transfer function would then be a "hard limiter" or "step" function (figure 4.11a). It has only binary output.

Another type of transfer function, the threshold or ramping function (figure 4.11b), could mirror the input within a given range (say 0–1), but could function as a hard limiter outside that range. It is a linear function that has been clipped to minimum and maximum values, which then makes it nonlinear.

Yet another option would be a sigmoid or S-shaped curve (such as is shown in figures 4.11c and 4.11d). The curve approaches a minimum and maximum value at the asymptotes.

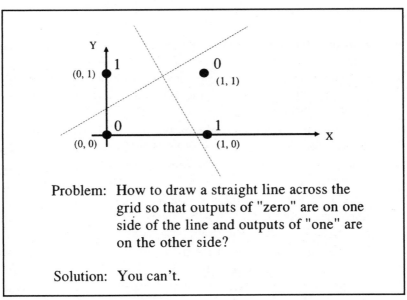

Problem: How to draw a straight line across the grid so that outputs of "zero" are on one side of the line and outputs of "one" are on the other side?

Solution: You can't.

FIGURE 4.10 EXCLUSIVE-OR PROBLEM

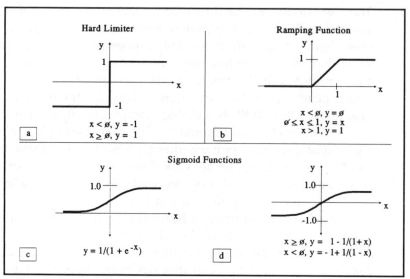

FIGURE 4.11   SAMPLE TRANSFER FUNCTIONS

Mathematically, the exciting feature of these curves is that both the function and its derivatives are continuous. This option works fairly well and is often the transfer function of choice. Any of these options, and others, would introduce nonlinearities into the network.

Learning Functions: What we said before about signals coming into biological neuronal synapses applies here as well: signals can be positive (excitatory) or negative (inhibitory). A positive input promotes the firing of the PE, whereas a negative input tends to keep the PE from firing.

If we attach some local memory to our PE, we can store results of previous computations and modify the weights used as we go along. This ability to change the weights allows the PE to modify its behavior in response to its inputs, or *learn*. For example, suppose a network identifies a dog as "a cat." On successive iterations, connection weights that respond correctly to dog images are strengthened; those that respond to other images, such as cat images, are weakened until they fall below the threshold level. It's more complicated than just changing the weights for dog recognition; the weights have to be adjusted so that all images are correctly identified.

A Practical Guide to Neural Nets

When weight adjustments are made in preceding layers of feedforward networks by "backing up" from outputs, the term *back propagation* is used. This is an important concept, because a high percentage of all networks today employ back propagation algorithms. Chapter 8 will emphasize the difference between training and learning and will expand on how neural networks "learn."

Combining Elements

Now, suppose we take our processing element and combine it with other PEs to make a *layer* of these nodes. Inputs could be connected to many nodes with various weights, resulting in a series of outputs, one per node. (See figure 4.12.) The connections correspond roughly to the axons and synapses in a biological system, and they provide a signal transmission pathway between the nodes.

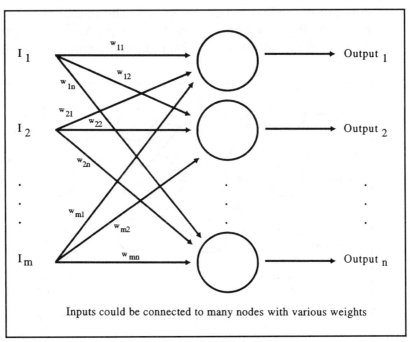

Inputs could be connected to many nodes with various weights

FIGURE 4.12 COMBINED WITH OTHER NODES . . . TO MAKE A LAYER

Combining Layers

Carrying the design yet another step, we can interconnect several layers. The layer that receives the inputs is called the *input layer.* It typically performs no function other than the buffering of the input signal. The network outputs are generated from the *output layer.* Any other layers are called *hidden layers* because they are internal to the network and have no direct contact with the external environment. Sometimes they are likened to a "black box" within the network system. But just because they are not immediately visible doesn't mean you can't examine what goes on in those layers. There may be from zero to several hidden layers.

The connections are multiplied by the weights associated with that particular interconnect. They convey analog values. Note that there are many more connections than nodes. The network is said to be *fully connected* if every output from one layer is passed along to every node in the next layer. Our example in figure 4.13 is *not* fully connected, nor does it make use of feedback, described next.

Connectivity Options: Connectivity has to do with how the outputs are channeled to become inputs. The output signal from a node may be passed on as input to other processing elements, or even possibly sent back as an input to itself. When no processing

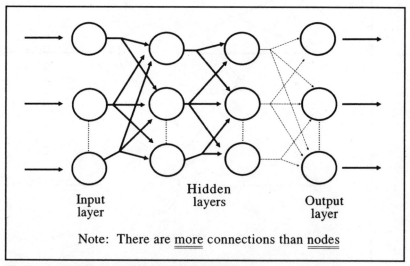

Note: There are more connections than nodes

FIGURE 4.13 AND SEVERAL LAYERS ARE INTERCONNECTED . . .

element output can be an input for a node on the same layer or a preceding layer, the network is described as a *feedforward network*. When outputs can be directed back as inputs to previous or same-level nodes, the network is a *feedback network* (figures 4.14A and 4.14B). Feedback networks that have closed loops are *recurrent systems*.

The classic traveling-salesman problem is a good illustration of nodes and connections issues. Given an itinerary of cities, the objective is for the salesman to travel to each city once and yet

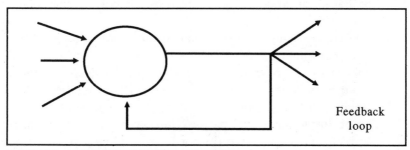

FIGURE 4.14A   A SINGLE NODE WITH FEEDBACK TO ITSELF

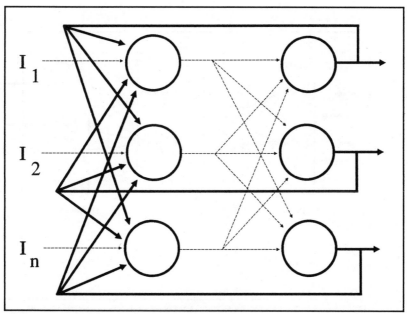

FIGURE 4.14B   NETWORK WITH FEEDBACK TO PREVIOUS MODES

How Do Neural Networks Work?   51

keep the total travel distance to a minimum. This example has important applications to situations involving routing, use of scarce resources, placing components on a board, and so on.

Filters: The layers in a neural network can act as *filters* (see figure 4.15). For example, the input signals could be the pixel pattern for the letter "A," as shown in the 5-by-7 matrix. The network could then generate an output pattern of the ASCII code for the input letter, or "0100 0001" for the letter A. Even an imperfect or partial letter could be recognized as the correct exemplar by the network.

This example represents a mapping, or feedforward network. The mappings, or associations of objects in the input set with objects in the output set, are also called transformations. Each input is matched to some output but is not restricted to simple single-input and single-output applications. That is, we could input any letter's pixel pattern and have the network output the correct ASCII code. We do not have to have a separate network for each element in the set.

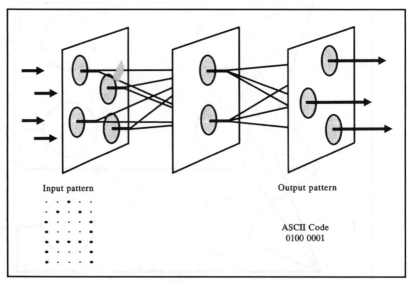

Input pattern

Output pattern

ASCII Code
0100 0001

FIGURE 4.15   LAYERS CAN ACT AS FILTERS (ADAPTED AND REPRINTED BY PERMISSION OF *AI EXPERT*.)

The internal layers form an intermediate representation of the input data. If too many nodes are available in the hidden layers, it becomes hard for the network to make generalizations. Too few nodes available leads to an inability to form adequate midway representations and to encode what the network thinks are the significant features of the input data. The network "forgets" too easily. Hidden layers hold the key to more complex computations.

An Illustration: NETtalk

NETtalk[4] is a program that teaches itself to read out loud. It was developed in the summer of 1986 by Terrence Sejnowski of Johns Hopkins University and Charles Rosenberg, a graduate research assistant at Princeton. Input is text. Codes are converted to sounds for the outputs by using DECtalk, a complex rule-based expert system voice synthesizer. In one well-publicized example, the input text was a first grader's conversation.

The implementation was a serial simulation on a VAX computer. Although the numbers varied from simulation to simulation, for continuous speech examples there were 309 "neurons" with 18,629 connections in 3 layers, fully connected, in a feedforward network.

The input layer had 7 neural groups, each with 29 "neurons" (one for each letter of the alphabet, space, comma, and period). The middle (hidden) layer was comprised of 80 units and attempted to improve the feature detection needed for the I/O transformation. The output layer had 26 units that encoded phonemes and stresses and drove the sound synthesizer.

There were no rules. NETtalk examined a window of seven characters at a time, keying from the middle character and the context of the surrounding triples. Errors were corrected, and corrections were back-propagated from the output to the input layer. After training (a transcription of a person reading the text), the system inferred rules about vowels, spaces, etc., and adjusted weights. At first the talk was gibberish, then babylike, and after a night, it achieved a 95-percent performance level, reading with few mistakes.

English spelling and pronunciation are full of exceptions. People handle these inconsistencies fairly well, but a rigid rule-based system might encounter significant problems. According to the creators, "this model can be trained on any dialect of any language and the resulting network can be implemented directly in hardware." NETtalk is a good example of applying neural networks to problems handled well by this technology.

Yet, NETtalk's goal is not to synthesize speech. Although it does translate English text into appropriate speech sounds with a reasonable degree of accuracy, the real goals are aimed at fundamental research.[5] How do neural networks learn to solve problems? And what internal representations do they create to accomplish their tasks? Can the model help explain how human cognitive processes work? Can damaged networks, for example, help us understand reading errors experienced by humans suffering from dyslexia?

A Simple Hardware Illustration

If you don't speak analog, you may want to skip this section. Doug Conner, regional editor for *EDN* magazine, describes in an article his experiences[6] in building two simulations and then an analog circuit to perform the transform of x to $\sin(x)$.

The simple circuit used as a building block (see figure 4.16) was "almost an exact analog representation of the desired processing element." Resistors were used for the weights. A weighted summing amplifier served as the summer. A simple diode clamping circuit provided the activation function, limiting the voltage to +/- Vclamp. Because the weights could have positive and negative values, the circuit provided complementary outputs, either of which could be used as input to other processing elements.

The article shows a schematic of the complete circuit and graphs of the outputs (which were quite accurate); it also discusses approach and results. Conner points out that the learning algorithm is not related to the particular task and could also be used in a training period to set weights for other transforms, such as mapping x to the square root of x.

As processing elements such as this are packed into integrated circuits, large numbers of processing elements and real-time processing speed will allow neural networks to become practical.

(For additional ideas on hardware components for network implementation, and an experimental software implementation

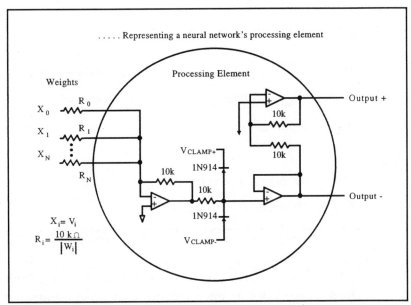

Representing a neural network's processing element

Processing Element

Weights

X_0 R_0

X_1 R_1

X_N

R_N

V_{CLAMP+}

1N914

10k

10k

1N914

V_{CLAMP-}

10k

10k

10k

Output +

Output −

$X_i = V_i$

$R_i = \dfrac{10\,k\Omega}{|W_i|}$

FIGURE 4.16   A SIMPLE ANALOG CIRCUIT (REPRINTED FROM *EDN*, MAY 12, 1988, © 1990 CAHNERS PUBLISHING COMPANY, A DIVISION OF REED PUBLISHING USA.)

description with source code listings, see the article "An Artificial Neural Network Experiment."[7] The source code is available on disk.)

Programmer Tasks

A neural net programmer would not write algorithms but would need to specify transfer functions (equations to determine thresholds), training laws (rules that set initial weights and equations that modify weights), and the structure of the network (number of nodes, layers, and interconnections). In addition to all of this, some sort of scheduling function would be needed to determine if and how often the processing elements would update (continuously or periodically). This new breed of programmer would need to understand statistics in order to select training sets and evaluate output results adequately. Neural networks require a different set of skills from that required by conventional programming (see figure 4.17).

Information is not stored in a single memory location, as in conventional computing, but is distributed throughout the sys-

The programming task is to specify:

- Transfer functions (equations to determine thresholds)
- Training laws (equations that modify weights)
- Interconnections

The power is in collective computational abilities;

The result is a new information-processing paradigm.

FIGURE 4.17   A NEURAL NET PROGRAMMER DOES NOT WRITE ALGORITHMS . . .

tem. This feature makes for the robustness of neural networks—you could lose a percentage of the processing elements and still not lose the information stored there. The power is in the collective computational abilities. The result is a new information-processing paradigm.

Summary

Neural nets are computer models inspired by the brain's own hardware. They consist of processing elements, or units, that attempt to model some of the properties of neurons. The brain has sensory receptors for input and motor neurons for output. Similarly, the artificial units that form the input layer act as "sensors," receiving their inputs from outside the network. Units not in the input layer receive their inputs from other units. These collective inputs are processed. If the total strength of the input signals exceeds a certain threshold, the unit sends a signal on to other units. The units in the outer layer produce the "activity," the external output of the system.

Various rules are used to adjust the internal processing. The way in which the weights are adjusted, for example, affects the self-adaptation (learning) of the system. The power, as in the brain, is in the interconnections among these units. No single unit

A Practical Guide to Neural Networks

gives much of a clue to the overall picture—it is the overall pattern of interactions among units which determines the properties of the network.

Learning more about how the brain works is one goal of this field. Perhaps in the future we may come to better understand more complex processes, such as memory and learning. The other goal is more immediately commercial: to use these nets as tools to solve some of our current problems, carry out complex analytical tasks, and study complex systems such as economics, or weather.

Francis Crick, of the Salk Institute, works at maintaining a healthy perspective regarding biological analogies. "No one actually claims this is how the brain works, but there is a tacit assumption that it might be. There is a tendency to believe."[8] Crick points out that much of the current artificial net implementation techniques are very "unbrainlike," and encourages more attention to neuroscience.

The understanding of the brain is, in Sejnowski's words, "one of the biggest challenges left in science." Neural nets are powerful tools, just as calculus is a tool, applicable to many areas. Models that do not necessarily follow biological structure may still help us understand fields such as psychology. Even simple models can provide new insights. As long as researchers in both neuroscience and connectionism pay attention to one another, benefits will accrue to all.

1. Kunihiko Fukushima, "A Neural Network for Visual Pattern Recognition," *IEEE Computer,* vol. 21, no. 3 (March 1988): 65–76.

2. Tom J. Schwartz, "Neural Networks: Capabilities and Applications," IEEE 31st Videoconference, Sept. 27, 1989.

3. Marvin Minsky and Seymour Papert, *Perceptrons* (Cambridge, MA: MIT Press, 1969; expanded edition, 1988).

4. Terrence J. Sejnowski and Charles R. Rosenberg, "NETtalk: a Parallel Network that Learns to Read Aloud," *Johns Hopkins University Electrical Engineering and Computer Science Technical Report,* JHU/EECS–86/01, 1986. (See *Neurocomputing: Foundations of Research,* edited by Anderson and Rosenfeld, pp. 661–71.)

5. Craig A. Will, "NETtalk: Learning to Pronounce English Text," *Neural Network Review,* vol. 2, no. 2 (1988): 61–64.

6. Doug Conner, "Data Transformation Explains the Basics of Neural Networks," *EDN*, vol. 33 (May 12, 1988): 138–44.

7. Robert Jay Brown, "An Artificial Neural Network Experiment," *Dr. Dobb's Journal*, vol. 12, no. 4 (April 1987): 16.

8. Leslie Roberts, "Are Neural Nets Like the Human Brain?," *Science*, vol. 243 (January 27, 1989): 481.

What Are Neural Networks Like?

It was SIX MEN of Indostan
　　To learning much inclined,
Who went to see the elephant
　　(Though all of them were blind),
That each by observation
　　Might satisfy his mind.
　　　　　　　—John Godfrey Saxe

Several characteristics of neural network technology set it apart from conventional computing and artificial intelligence approaches. This chapter looks at qualities such as the strong mathematical basis, inherent parallelism, storing of knowledge, fault tolerance, adaptability, and pattern-recognition skills (see figure 5.1). We also consider some of the limitations of neural networks. Comparisons to other technologies, such as statistical methods and expert systems, comprise the bulk of chapter 6.

Mathematical Basis

Neural networks are one of the few AI-related technologies that have a rigorous, mathematical foundation. This provides a measure of comfort for the general scientific community and allows mathematicians some great sport. In fact, it was partly the clear mathematical and statistical underpinnings of this technology that attracted the attention of the National Academy of Sciences when Hopfield presented his work on neural networks in 1982. In contrast, expert systems rely heavily on heuristics, or rules of thumb, which are much less formal.

Some of the math is quite sophisticated, using differential equations, linear algebra, and covariance matrices. Weights, sum-

---

- Mathematical basis

- Parallelism

- Distributed associative memory

- Fault tolerance

- Adaptability

- Pattern recognition

- Intuition and statistical pattern recognition

FIGURE 5.1 NEURAL NETS ARE NOTED FOR . . .

ming and transfer functions, and learning algorithms all rely heavily on mathematics. These equations affect inputs, memory, recall, determination of energy levels, convergence, and stability. Although the mathematics are integrally related to the design, functioning, and tuning of neural networks, it is not necessary to be a mathematician to understand the basic principles of operation. Aspects of the mathematics will be referred to in various examples throughout the book, but for a more concise presentation, see appendix C.

Inherent Parallelism

Not only are neural networks structurally parallel, but the processing sequence is parallel and simultaneous. The total scheme of the system as well as the individual elements combine theory and practice in parallel performance. The processing elements in one layer are all operating in concert. Computation is distributed over more than one processing element and is done simultaneously.

Although digital computers have to simulate this parallelism, true neural network hardware will really perform the operations in parallel. Very fast decisions will be possible and will be able to be made in real time.

A Practical Guide to Neural Nets

Storing Knowledge

Knowledge within a neural network is not stored in specific memory locations, as it is in conventional computing. Knowledge is distributed throughout the system; it is the dynamic response to the inputs and the network architecture. Because knowledge is distributed, the system uses many connections to retrieve solutions to particular problems.

Not only is the memory in a neural network distributed, it is also *associative*. "An associative memory is a mapping from data to data, a mathematical abstraction from the familiar associative structure of human and animal learning."[1] A neural network system looks for closest matches, much as our brains locate memory contents by matching an input stimulus rather than by any addressing scheme. For example, if you hum a few bars of a tune and it is one we have heard before, we may be able to "name that tune." Another, more personal illustration: junior high school teachers can become very good at reading the virtually illegible handwriting of some of their students. In spite of variations, distortions, and omissions, humans are good at retrieving the correct pattern. So are neural networks.

Compare this approach with that of conventional digital computers using RAM (random access memory) and ROM (read-only memory). Each fact is stored in a unique location. A fact is retrieved by providing the address, even though there is no particular relationship between the fact and the address. Neural networks don't work this way at all (see figure 5.2). Computers that retrieve data in an associative manner, rather than by address, are now becoming commercially feasible.[2]

- Is not stored in specific memory locations

- Is related to network structure

- Consists of the overall state of the network at some equilibrium condition

---

FIGURE 5.2 KNOWLEDGE WITHIN A NEURAL NETWORK

Associative memories have two major benefits: the ability to store a large number of complex patterns (such as speech templates, visual scenes, robot movements, spatiotemporal behavior, social behavior, and so on), and the ability to classify new patterns to stored patterns quickly. Although conventional computers, by comparison, excel at high-speed serial computation, they do poorly at such real-time pattern recognition.[3]

The special category of neural network pattern recognition that combines automatic associative recall is sometimes called content-addressable memory (CAM). Here, memory is really a representation of the information it contains. Fixed tag and data words can be matched exactly according to the contents of the word, so multiple responses are possible for each search key. The more general "associative memories" can access or modify cells based on their contents, but do not rely on an exact match with a data key.

Knowledge is also related to network structure—how the output signal of a node is connected to the input signals of many other nodes—and the relative weighting of each input to a node. Knowledge consists of the overall state of the network at some equilibrium condition after it has responded to the input patterns. In his 1982 presentation to the National Academy of Sciences, Hopfield talked about energy minima. Other researchers started with a learning rule, and then looked at interesting results. Hopfield began at the opposite end, describing the function of the system as that of developing stability. Processing elements respond to inputs, and network modifications continue until a stable state (an energy minimum) is reached. Networks do not compute answers like conventional computers do; sometimes it's more a matter of memorizing the answers for given inputs.

Example: Pac-Man

A number of good visual examples serve to illustrate a network going through a learning period and finally settling into a steady pattern. One such network was created by Harry Klopf at Wright-Patterson Air Force Base. The graphics show a "Pac-Man-like" symbol who "eats" red and green disks. Half of the nodes process input in Pac-Man's visual field and half generate motion. The learning rules of the system reinforce the eating of green disks, and the red disks are deemed "not good."

When the simulation begins the little symbol devours any disk in sight. Soon, however, there is a marked decrease in the appetite for the red disks until, finally, they are avoided altogether. At the same time, green disks appear to have more and more appeal. The association is not just one of contact but also of seeing the object. The Pac-Man-like symbol has "learned" which disks are "good to eat" and which ones "taste bad." The behavior of the system stabilizes.

As an aside, if the bad-tasting red disks are strongly reinforced, avoiding pain can become more important than seeking pleasure. After a number of iterations, the symbol finally turns and "hides in the corner" at the beginning of the simulation (see figure 5.3). Just seeing one of the red disks stimulates him to make sure these hateful things are avoided altogether!

Klopf's work concentrates more on learning paradigms than on some of the other aspects of neural networks. Reward and punishment activities here are not unlike the classical conditioning behavior in animals (remember Pavlov's dogs). In truth, much of the ongoing research in neural networks today is involved with

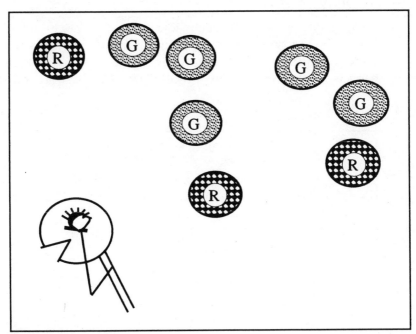

FIGURE 5.3 PAC-MAN EXAMPLE

learning. There are so many questions related to training and learning functions. What happens if training is incomplete? Or wrong? Or based on conflicting data? How valid is the network output under such circumstances? It's important to know answers to questions like these before assigning significant tasks to neural networks.

Fault Tolerance

Neural networks are extremely fault tolerant and degrade gracefully. They can learn from and make decisions based on incomplete data. Because knowledge is distributed throughout the system rather than residing in a single memory location, a percentage of the nodes can be inoperative without significantly changing the overall system behavior. Resistance to hardware failure is therefore much greater in a neural network than in conventional computers, where hardware failure is usually catastrophic.

Adaptability

Adaptability is the ability of a whole neural network to self-adjust. This is one of two features of neural networks particularly highlighted by the DARPA study. As figure 5.4 shows, there are four aspects to the adaptability process: learning, self-organization,

● Learning (a single PE)

● Self-organization (many PEs)

● Generalization

● Training

    - Supervised

    - Unsupervised

FIGURE 5.4 ADAPTABILITY INCLUDES . . .

generalization, and training. We'll look at each of these separately, though they are related and the categories tend to spill over.

Learning

Learning is at the level of a single PE. Learning "occurs" when the weighted connections are adjusted. Specific algorithms for each problem the network needs to solve would pose a major problem and make the network so specific that its use would be severely limited. As an example, suppose you were using a network to adjust the angle of a robot arm in response to feedback from camera images. If accuracy to within one degree was required, an algorithm would need to allow for 360 different variations within a given plane. That could pose a problem of considerable proportions, especially in three-dimensional space. A neural network, however, could generate its own algorithm by adjusting the weighted connections between the processing elements.

Example: Forklift Robot: Martin Marietta has trained a robot arm to recognize and pick up pallets even when they are at cockeyed angles.[4] The industrial robot has a forklift as its end-effector. It uses a variety of infrared sensors to determine the location and position of objects that are to be lifted and moved. A neural network guides the movements in six dimensions to determine the x, y, z point in space and the pitch-roll-yaw attitude adjustments required to insert the forklift into a pallet.

These control functions are learned rather than programmed. A human teacher shows the robot how to do it. During training, the robot matches the information from its proximity sensors to the trajectory command given by the human operator via a joystick or keyboard. Once the network has made the internal adjustments to mimic the patterns, it can perform on its own.

Results have been encouraging. In some cases, with as few as seven teaching points, the network learned to pick up the pallet from any arbitrary starting position. A teaching point is simply a point on the path, not the entire trajectory. The network's ability to generalize the trajectory from a small number of points is one of its most impressive features. To allow a similar flexibility using algorithms would be an overwhelming task.

Self-Organizing

Self-organizing is the modification of many processing elements at once. Training sessions exercise the rules for learning as modifications take place throughout an entire network system. It is as if neural networks are developing their own heuristics as they go through the iterations. The network converges, or settles down to a stable response.

Example: Nakano's Robots: Kaoru Nakano, an associate professor at the University of Tokyo, has used neural networks in building a number of different self-organizing robots over the past 20 years.[5] His robots have "learned" to do a variety of things: repair themselves, walk, talk, play ball. The self-organizing behavior becomes apparent when the actions randomly tried are successful and yet are totally unlike anything a human might have programmed. Take the act of throwing a ball. The robot, with a number of servos controlling its flexible arm, was rewarded or punished on the basis of how far the ball went. As it learned, some of the throws looked like conventional human overhand throws. In addition, however, some bizarre, albeit successful, movements were used.

Generalization

Generalization is the ability of the network to respond to input that it has not seen before. The input may be partial or incomplete, as discussed later in the paragraph on intuition, prediction, and statistical pattern-matching. Generalization takes the ability to learn and self-adjust a step further. The system can "hypothesize" a response.

Two other self-organizing robots of Nakano's learned to make "words." Observing the world around them, they attached labels to concepts. When two robots recognized they were having the same experience, they interchanged "words." The internal words of each could be modified to achieve a closer match. Thus, they invented their own language and communicated with other robots.

The ability to learn complicated control functions, and the ability to respond to changing or unexpected environments, expands the usefulness of robots. This technology could be useful for unmanned land and underwater craft, in automated machinery, on assembly lines, and for hazardous tasks such as disposal of radioactive materials.

Training

Training is the way a neural network learns. Training may be supervised (Hopfield models and Perceptrons are examples using supervised training) or unsupervised (Kohonen networks). The former provides the network with examples of the desired response; the latter provides no output examples but the network may create clusters of like features (such as robots creating "words"). Reinforcement, grading the network on its performance, is somewhere in between. Nakano's robots were given no advance training. They had to learn on their own, but they were given reinforcement related to their actions.

Training may include such activities as providing exposure to databases, placing objects in front of sensors, or presenting other examples. One example of supervised training would be teaching a network to recognize images of numbers. You could present inputs of numeral images *with* the expected outputs. It's like telling the network, "When you see this pattern (a 7, for example), give me a '7'." All of this is done to achieve a particular self-organization of the system.

After training, the system is ready for use. Depending on the task to be done, the network may have its currently learned weights "frozen," thus disabling its learning laws. This would be appropriate for an application doing text-to-speech. It would not be appropriate, however, for a system that must continue to adjust to changing conditions, such as a network to do real-time process control.

Pattern Recognition

Many different types of networks are under consideration for various research and application projects. Differences in models are mostly due to the number of processing elements, how they are connected, and what the learning laws are. These structural differences create different learning paradigms by which neural networks are classified. You can find more information on various paradigms in chapter 7.

The structure of a neural network allows it to be good at particular kinds of learning. Many networks are good at recognizing patterns. Others might be called classification builders. Some systems extract features, such as edges of solids, and are regularity detectors. Still other networks are automatic associators. Quite a variety of tasks can be undertaken, but most of them relate somehow to an ability to discern patterns.

Overall, pattern recognition is what neural networks are best noted for. Networks have the ability to pick out a set of features previously learned, or they may select and generate their own pattern features in response to inputs. This isn't limited to static patterns, either. The potential for processing complex, dynamic patterns that vary in time and space provides promise for exciting new solutions in real time.

Example: NestorWriter

One commercial example of pattern matching is NestorWriter, a handwriting recognizer (Nestor's first product, which runs on an IBM PC AT and is partially based on a neural network pattern recognizer). Input is in the form of handwriting on a digitized pad. After being trained on a set of typical handwriting samples, NestorWriter can interpret handwriting it has not seen previously. And this can be accomplished in spite of changes in scale, shifts in position, distortions, and idiosyncrasies in style.

The flexibility of the system extends to accepting other symbols such as Kanji, Japanese characters. Difficult computer entry is eliminated. Not only can networks detect patterns, they can do it both in time (as in auditory signals) and in space (using visual data).

Incomplete Patterns

Suppose part of the input pattern is missing or contains misleading, or noisy, information? (See figure 5.5.) What then?

Just as you can recognize people when you see only a part of their face, neural networks are good at looking at partial patterns and guessing the whole. Call it intuition. This capability is combined with an ability for statistical pattern reconstruction, where the computed pattern is the one closest to the partial pattern. (In a least-mean-squares sense, this means that the computed pattern is the one that best fits the data. If you take a point

A Practical Guide to Neural Nets

FIGURE 5.5   WHAT ABOUT PARTIAL PATTERNS, SUCH AS THIS PARTLY OBSCURED OBJECT?

on the partial pattern, and find the corresponding point on the computed pattern, the sum of the squares—squaring eliminates problems in summing positive and negative errors—of the distances between all these corresponding sets of points is as small as possible.) The characteristics of *intuition, prediction,* and *statistical pattern reconstruction* allow neural networks to deal with situations in which the input may be fuzzy, incomplete, or ambiguous, or may even have some corrupted data.

Because most of the data in this world is inexact, this characteristic becomes highly significant. It also ties back to adaptability—the ability of a net to learn, self-organize, and generalize—and provides the key to this feature.

Appropriate Tasks

Sometimes, tasks appropriate for neural networks are ones humans know how to do. Recognizing faces (remember the Finnish example in chapter 2) is a relatively easy accomplishment, even for a small child, but has been one of the traditional AI monster problems. Continuous speech recognition and synthesis are additional examples of tasks neural networks are undertaking with reasonable success.

There are plenty of good counterexamples, though. Some tasks at which neural networks excel have been difficult for humans to do well. Quality control of solder joints is currently done by blowing up a digitized image of the joint and having humans inspect it. They make a qualitative judgment on whether the solder joint is acceptable or unacceptable. Quality control is a priority for the manufacturing industry, but it is not easily accomplished. Neural networks can take the digitized image as input and come up with quantitative data as well as a more accurate qualitative assessment. (See chapter 9 for more details about this example.) Statistical methods are at work with neural network enhancements.

Initially, many tasks for neural networks had large sets of examples available, or could generate suitable examples. In some applications it is difficult to formalize rules, but lots of data and examples are available. This is true for some classification problems. Remember the story in chapter 1 about AVCO Financial Services, in Irvine, California. They used more than ten thousand examples of past loans to train their neural network, which evaluates loan applications. Weather predictor systems based on neural networks also key off a large volume of past data to forecast future conditions. Note, however, that changing trends in the input examples will be picked up by the network, so a moving window of historical data would allow a network to continue to learn and adapt.

Current work in neural networks is examining ways to reduce the size of the training set required. Texas Instruments, for example, is finding good success with applying data compression techniques to the training sets. Here's one possibility: If the input is a matrix of 100 by 100 pixels, sum the rows across and simply input a 1-by-100 matrix instead.

Tasks often involve mappings of objects in one set with objects in another set. Many significant commercial issues are really mapping problems. For example, to accomplish text-to-speech (as in NETtalk), a network must be able to associate the inputs of letters, spaces, and punctuation with the outputs of sounds, pauses, and intonations. Visual images may need to be digitized, coded, rotated, transformed, and matched with an appropriate category for a corresponding output image. Data-compression techniques may need to map inputs to some smaller data set (for transmission), which can later be mapped back to the original set. Neural networks can be viewed as a statistically based mapping technology. "After people understand that neural networks are just a highly parallel, very rapid computing technology that works statistically on a trial-and-error basis to solve problems you don't know how to solve any other way, then they will start a revolution in the computer industry," says Robert Smithson, director of Lockheed's neural network program.[6]

Some current network systems require that all necessary input data be available at one time. Such a system would have no possibility for interaction. Contrast this with the use of an expert system, which prompts the user for inputs as the consultation proceeds. Also, with neural networks, the input must be numeric and is generally binary or continuous-valued (analog). This requirement may necessitate preprocessing of input data. Other systems, such as the weather predictor mentioned above, can continuously integrate new data as they become available. Adaptable systems must have this capability.

Types of Problems Addressed

The kinds of problems addressed by this technology comprise another sort of characteristic. Although a few of the main areas of research have been mentioned, we'd like to emphasize here some of the current directions and potential applications (while reserving other research examples for chapter 11). Figure 5.6 shows some of the major research and application areas.

Neural network projects are working on the problems of natural language processing, such as continuous speech recognition [7] and synthesis and text-to-speech transformations. Products are available that do character recognition and handwriting analysis, including analysis of complex characters.

Additional complex pattern-recognition problems being worked on include image-recognition problems of several types. This area is of particular interest to the military for applications such as "friend-or-foe" determination.

- Speech recognition and synthesis
  - Natural language processing
  - Text-to-speech

- Character recognition
  - Handwriting, complex characters

- Image recognition
  - Auto-associative / Hetero-associative

- Image (data) compression

- NP-Complete problems (combinatorial explosion)

FIGURE 5.6 RESEARCH AND APPLICATION AREAS

If a partial image leads to the complete version, the term auto-associative is used to describe the network. On the other hand, if the object is identified from input that is distorted or disoriented, the term hetero-associative applies. Although an auto-associative network would give you an improved or completed version of the input, the hetero-associative network usually gives you the missing information only.

Examples of auto-associative networks would be ones identifying an object from seeing only part of it, such as identifying an obscured object in a picture or retrieving a bibliography given only some key words. Another example would be one involving an association with some characteristic: If an animal climbs trees, then maybe it's a cat.

Hetero-associative examples (see figure 5.7) would include seeing a target at different angles but still identifying it as the same object, or recognizing someone "in disguise," or signature verification. Banks have so many checks pass through on a daily basis that it's impossible for humans to examine each one for correctness. BancTec (in Dallas) is one company making use of neural nets to read checks.

Neural networks used for robotics and control applications have been around for a relatively long time. They offer several

FIGURE 5.7   HOW DO NEURAL NETWORKS HANDLE NOISY OR "DISGUISED" DATA?

advantages over conventional approaches. Transformations can be learned from examples rather than having to be derived and explicitly programmed. Real-time adaptive and learning controllers based on neural networks become possible because of such net capabilities as on-line learning with minimal intervention, ability to use delayed feedback, and an ability to learn internal models of the external world. With the networks, robotic systems can be more flexible, respond to variations within their own system, and move in less precisely defined environments.

Michael Kuperstein, president of Neurogen, Inc., has prototyped this flexibility in developing a neural robot called Infant (Interacting Networks Forming Adaptive Neural Topographies).[8] Infant uses two cameras positioned as eyes and has a jointed arm with a clipper hand. As a baby can explore the world and learn through its movements, so Infant explores its world and expands its capabilities. It walks on uneven terrain, grasps new objects, and learns coordinated movement by associating what it experiences.

Image (data) compression is another task undertaken by some neural networks. One experiment demonstrated reducing an 8-bit gray-scale image into 1 bit per pixel. Such techniques show promise also for compressing complex sensor data during conventional processing.

Tasks called *np-complete problems* (combinatorial explosion toughies such as the traveling salesman problem—*np* means non-polynomial), once thought to be intractable, are being tamed. Neural systems are doing the job of routing telephone network traffic, locating chips on a board for good wiring layout, and other similar resource allocation problems. Not only do routing solutions attempt to minimize delays, sometimes they must also have the potential to respond rapidly to radically changing environmental conditions. This would often be true for military communications systems. The neural network may not find the best solution (which could take an enormous amount of time even on a supercomputer), but finds a "good enough" answer (such as within 1 percent of the optimal solution).

Limitations and Concerns

Along with the good news there is bad news. There are a number of problems that neural networks do *not* handle well (see figure 5.8).

The networks are not good if precise answers are required. You would not want to use an artificial neural network, for example, to keep your finances. We mentioned before that networks

---

- Learning is hard —
  You have to build on what you know

- Cannot justify answers

- Not good if precise answers are required

- Can't count (sees forest, not trees)

- Can't (yet) do things conventional computers can do

- Designing a network is still a somewhat mysterious process

FIGURE 5.8 LIMITATIONS

are generally good at tasks people do well. Extending the analogy, we could say that there are many people who don't handle finances particularly well, either.

Neural networks can't count; they see the forest, not the trees. Counting, after all, is hard to do in parallel. Even we have to go into sequential mode and concentrate when it's time for serious counting. This is the nature of systems which generalize.

Learning is hard; you have to build on what you know. There are no standards for learning algorithms or for training networks. Off-line training is difficult and sometimes tedious. The number of trials required can be significantly large. Designing a network is still a somewhat mysterious process. When you are building one, you try one learning rule here, a different transfer function there. Then you have to tweak, evaluate, and see what works. Designing the architecture is a painstaking trial-and-error effort.

A difficult problem that neural networks must overcome is in evolving serially in the time domain. To solve speech recognition, natural language understanding, and varying aspects of visual perception, it will be necessary to design neural networks that adapt continuously in time. Present investigation has involved mostly spatial representations with some very interesting temporal properties, but additional studies are needed (and are in progress) with regard to time.

In general, a neural network cannot justify its answers. There is no facility to match the *"how"* or *"why"* found in expert systems. There is no way to stop the system and say, "What are you doing now?" It's as if the network were instead saying, "Trust me, trust me."

In response to this problem, Stephen Gallant of Northeastern University has come up with an explanation facility.[9] His patented, two-program package constructs connectionist expert systems from training examples. Hecht-Nielsen Neurocomputer Corporation has licensed Gallant's method, and other corporations, such as NeuralWare and Nestor, are also working on justification systems. "The ability of a neural network to produce rule sets could potentially provide explanations for network credit-scoring models, and identification of problems in diagnostic systems."[10]

Scaling is another issue. Toy problems may converge in a reasonable amount of time; real problems may magnify the task beyond reasonable limits. A small prototype may work just fine in the lab, but it may be quite another story to build a full-blown, commercially viable model.

When networks generalize, or guess, they may be wrong. Mistakes may be hard to undo, or forget. Errors are spread out over the connections in the same way the correct answers are, so it's hard to know which PEs to blame. (Back propagation algorithms address this issue, but have limitations such as requiring extensive off-line training.)

Neural networks can't yet do things that conventional computers do effortlessly (such as number-crunching). "When they do something that can't be done any other way, that will be revolutionary," says Marvin Minsky, AI researcher at MIT.[11] Attempts to make neural networks more like traditional computers (i.e., do logic, store and retrieve large amounts of information with high accuracy) are not employing the true virtues of neural networks. At the same time, exploring the limits of neural nets with regard to their computing power may reveal they have more potential in this arena than is currently being realized.

Inescapably, there are the hardware limitations. Although it may be useful to study a parallel process by simulating it on a sequential machine, simulation is not the goal. Parallel machines are needed for parallel processes to achieve speed and cost-effectiveness in mass implementation. But the hardware barrier is beginning to crumble.

Other Concerns

Even after a neural network system is built, there's still a lot to do (see figure 5.9). Appropriate training materials need to be developed. The quality of information and training provided for the network is ultimately related to the quality of the decisions the network makes. Unfortunately, no current standards exist for training methodology or training data. Good teachers may be more important here than good programmers.

There is also the issue of I/O. Inputs and outputs must all be configured properly. This could include things like file conversion, voice synthesis, codification of forms, collection of light waves from objects on assembly lines, digitization of handwriting, and so on. Moreover, the representational techniques used when pres-

A Practical Guide to Neural Nets

FIGURE 5.9   EVEN AFTER A NEURAL NETWORK SYSTEM IS BUILT, THERE'S STILL A LOT TO DO

enting the input data or training set are more important than the selection of learning algorithms.

Like any other system, a network must be integrated with other components for seamless operation. It may need to talk to other computers, input devices, PC screens. End users will need to know how and when to use the network. People concerns and technology transfer issues will need to be addressed.

Summary

Neural nets are a complete change from the von Neumann approach to computing. "According to one group of researchers, neural nets carry out tasks that are not only beyond the scope of conventional processing but also cannot be understood in the same terms."[12] They do not compute the same things. The characteristics of neural nets come from its structure—many interconnected elements operating in parallel.

Useful commercial neural net applications are beginning to appear. The technology is showing a great deal of promise in areas that have posed problems for conventional systems. Pattern recognition, real-time control, classification problems, optimization problems (such as airline fares or military resource allocation), and others.

Along with the positive features of neural nets, some limitations need to be noted. Such networks are not the answer to every problem. There is no question of making conventional computers obsolete. The neural net technology is only one of several and it needs to be applied to appropriate problems. How it relates to other technologies and how these various technologies might work together is the subject of the next chapter.

1. Bart Kosko. "Constructing an Associative Memory." *Byte,* vol. 12, no. 10 (September 1987): 137.

2. Lawrence Chisvin and R. James Duckworth, "Content-Addressable and Associative Memory: Alternatives to the Ubiquitous RAM," *IEEE Computer,* vol. 22, no. 7 (July 1989): 51.

3. Bart Kosko. "Constructing an Associative Memory." *Byte,* vol. 12, no. 10 (September 1987): 137.

4. *DARPA Neural Network Study,* (Fairfax, VA: AFCEA International Press, November 1988), appendix H.

5. R. Colin Johnson, "Nakano's Positive Perceptron Perception," *Electronic Engineering Times,* Issue 534 (April 17, 1989): 35.

6. R. Colin Johnson, "DARPA Neural Awards Stress Practical Use," *Electronic Engineering Times,* issue 558 (October 2, 1989): 22.

7. Alex Waibel and John Hampshire, "Building Blocks for Speech," *Byte,* vol. 14, no. 8 (August 1989): 235–42. See also D. J. Burr, "Experiments of Neural Net Recognition of Spoken and Written Text," *IEEE Transactions of Acoustics, Speech, and Signal Processing* vol. 36, no. 3 (July 1988): 1162–68; and Teuvo Kohonen, "The 'Neural' Phonetic Typewriter," *Computer,* vol. 21, no. 3 (March 1988): 11–22.

8. "New Robot Has Neural Net," *Newsletter Digest* (June 1989): 36.

9. Stephen I. Gallant, "Connectionist Expert Systems," *Communications of the ACM,* vol. 31, no. 2 (February 1988): 152–69.

10. "Next for Neural Nets," Product Showcase, *AI Expert,* vol. 4, no. 9 (September 1989): 65.

11. June Kinoshita and Nicholas G. Palevsky, "Computing with Neural Networks," *High Technology* (May 1987): 28.

12. Peter Judge, "Neurocomputers Are News," *New Electronics,* vol. 21, no. 5 (May 1988): 36.

How Do Neural Networks Relate to Other Technologies?

Beware of the solution that requires one side to be totally the loser and the other side to be totally the winner. The reason there are two sides to begin with usually is because neither side has all the facts. Therefore, when the wise mediator effects a compromise, he is not acting from political motivation. Rather, he is acting from a deep sense of respect for the whole truth.

—*Stephen R. Schwanbach*

You might ask, "What will using this technology buy me over, say, using statistical techniques and standard expert systems?" It's a fair question, and makes for some interesting comparisons. We've been making comparisons between conventional computers and artificial neural networks, so here we'll focus particularly on statistics and artificial intelligence (AI) comparisons.

Statistical Methods

Neural networks have more than once been described as a biologically motivated, statistical-mapping technology. "Neural-network learning procedures are inherently statistical techniques,"[1] says Halbert White, professor of economics and an expert in neural networks and econometrics. To get a better handle on the comparisons, we chose this definition of statistics:

> The science of the collection and classification of facts on the basis of relative number of occurrence as a ground for induction; systematic compilation of instances for the inference of general truths.[2]

Scientists needed to make sense of what they observed. They measured everything. They looked at relationships among different measurements. This "collection, analysis, interpretation, and presentation of masses of numerical data"[3] has come to be recognized as "statistics."

The ability to model, and perhaps eventually control, incompletely known and understood systems provides great incentive for the application of neural networks to statistical process control. The neural network approach requires fewer resources than conventional statistical methods, and further, can process data in real time.

Statistical process control is a technology that uses statistics to monitor the steps in a process, often a manufacturing process. Massive amounts of production process statistical data must be collected and scrutinized in an attempt to determine whether the process is properly meeting product specifications. Goals include both the improvement of product quality and the reduction of product cost through elimination of rejected parts and the need for rework. Methods used can help discover problems such as poor product design and worn out machines and tools.

Process control has reams of output data that need organizing and interpreting. Neural networks could be called, in simplistic terms, information processing systems that are literally looking for reams of input data that require organizing and interpreting. "One might easily be convinced that neural networks were designed specifically for the sole use of statistical process control in a closed-loop, real-time manufacturing environment."[4] Neural networks can organize the data, analyze statistics, spot trends, adapt and learn from the data, take corrective control action, and predict future product specifications. And do it in real time.

GTE Laboratories is working on neural networks for process control. Controllers that learn are a major focus of their efforts. According to GTE researchers, "Connectionist networks are a promising technique for real-time adaptive and learning controllers because of their capabilities for on-line learning with minimal external intervention, for real-time response, for utilizing delayed feedback, for learning internal models of the external world, for robustness and noise-tolerance, and for learning nonlinear mappings."[5]

One of GTE's applications (mentioned in chapter 1) involves using neural networks to analyze quality control on a fluorescent lamp manufacturing line. The company wants to know how quality is affected by variations in raw materials, environmental factors such as weather, wearing and aging of the machinery, and changes in operators. Using past experience, the networks find correlations between approximately 100 sensory measurements. Currently the data are turned over to engineers responsible for making all actual changes in the running of the plant. This responsibility may fall to controller networks in the future.

Researchers at GTE are comparing conventional (batch) and connectionist-learning (incremental) techniques. Simulations have shown that "connectionist learning networks can monitor manufacturing processes to determine causal relationships with an accuracy competitive with that of conventional statistical techniques."[6] Add to that the advantages of on-line operation in real time and they predict substantial savings as compared to conventional computer-integrated manufacturing (CIM) techniques. Further, if the time per step for a network is $O(n)$, where n is the number of sensors, then the total processing time required by a conventional method such as linear regression is estimated to be approximately $O(n^3)$. This means that the network can be implemented on a much smaller computer, or can be used with significantly larger numbers of sensors, or the sensors can be sampled much more frequently. A reduction in computational complexity will provide greater flexibility in choice of models used to predict outcomes and correlations.

At Los Alamos National Laboratory investigators are applying neural networks, machine learning algorithms, statistical analysis, and information theory to DNA sequence analysis.[7] The major goal is to determine the biological function of certain DNA sequence segments.

An additional goal is the evaluation of the various information-processing procedures. This is important because of the large amounts of data available from the Human Genome Project.[8] Automated, accurate, and verified symbolic information-processing techniques (without recourse to biological laboratory work) will be essential for use in sifting and preprocessing raw data. Such methods can help discern biochemically important features and reduce the amount of subsequent laboratory work required to answer questions of biological interest. Some methods work better for certain problems, so surveying a number of methods is useful. The value of any method, however, depends on its accuracy.

In comparing the various methods used, the Los Alamos researchers noted that simple statistical weighting schemes commonly used in DNA analysis were a subset of general neural network approaches, "and therefore neural nets may be more general and more useful." Further, in comparisons with various classic statistical and discriminant analysis techniques, the more powerful neural network formalisms had an advantage in automatically being able to form appropriate internal representations of the data. Their conclusions showed that "neural set methods provided the highest accuracies. These accuracies significantly exceeded those previously reported in the literature."

While the scientists at Los Alamos express caution that much more work needs to be done (and is in progress) to properly assess the relevance of the techniques used, they are optimistic. "Simple statistical weighting schemes commonly used in previous methods are related to the simplest neural net approaches. More powerful neural net approaches, therefore, yield additional algorithms that can be used for various problems, and increased accuracies can result."

In another comparison study, researchers at Peat Marwick developed two models to predict commercial bank failures.[9] A conventional statistical approach (logistic regression) was used in one model and the other used neural networks (two back propagation models with slightly differing architectures). Using a large sample of failed and solvent banks classified by asset size, and using the same predictor variables for both approaches, the two were compared. Each technique generated predictions for a holdout sample of banks that failed/nonfailed in 1987.

In the study, the simple neural network did slightly better on the holdout data, essentially misclassifying less of the time, and "performed well in comparison to the logistic regression model." The authors of the article caution that the study is only tentative and continuing research is being done, but that the neural network project "may eventually end up on the auditor's desk as part of the decision-aiding tool package being created." (For more information, contact the study authors: Timothy Bell, Gary Ribar,

Jennifer Verchio, KPMG Peat Marwick, Audit Research Group, Montvale, NJ.)

Halbert White, quoted in the first paragraph of this section, has also done some comparisons on neural networks and statistical methods.[10] To make the task manageable, he limited the networks to hidden-layer feedforward and back propagation models (which he claims provides a good generalization). He points out that neural network output functions correspond precisely to specific families of regression curves; the network inputs are the explanatory variables and the weights are the regression curve parameters. "Back propagation and nonlinear statistical regression can be viewed as alternative statistical approaches to solving the least squares problem."

White emphasizes the gains to be made from interaction between each approach. Statistics have much to offer in analyzing neural networks and associated learning methods. Neural-network models have much to offer statistics. "Applications of such neural-network models [those with multiple hidden layers and recurrency] to new and existing data sets could advance empirical understanding of disciplines as diverse as genetics, linguistics, and economics."

Artificial Intelligence

Science fiction abounds with examples of our dreams of creating machines that can pilot our space ships, fight our battles, perform menial chores, or otherwise assist us. Artificial intelligence (AI) is a field of computer science concerned with building machines that do things we would call intelligent.

Since Alan Turing proposed his famous test in 1950, researchers have been after a machine that could pass it. Roughly the test goes like this (see figure 6.1): Put a human and a computer behind a curtain and then stand on the other side of the curtain. Ask questions on any subject and receive written answers. If you can't tell whether the answers come from the machine or the person, the computer passes the test and is called "intelligent." (*Note:* the computer couldn't be too quick with numbers here, or the difference would be obvious!)

FIGURE 6.1   CLASSICAL TURING TEST

Similarities and Differences

Neural networks have some of the same objectives as AI and are
very much a part of the effort to build more useful and intelligent
machines. Both AI and neural network approaches claim to model
human reasoning, artificially. Both technologies have researchers
who are attempting to better understand the nature of human
intelligence. Both have common events in their history, such as
the Dartmouth Conference of 1956.

However, the two areas approach the task of remaking intelligence from different directions. Neural network efforts pay more
attention to how the brain functions. Again, we want to point out
that some researchers are simply trying to achieve similar results
while others are working on a more literal interpretation, attempting to model the brain's circuitry. That task is much harder than
trying to duplicate the function of isolated components. An enormous number of simplifications and guesses have to be made in
the process. When the problem is so big, you settle for the pieces
you can solve.

As figure 6.2 illustrates, the neural network approach is from

A Practical Guide to Neural Nets

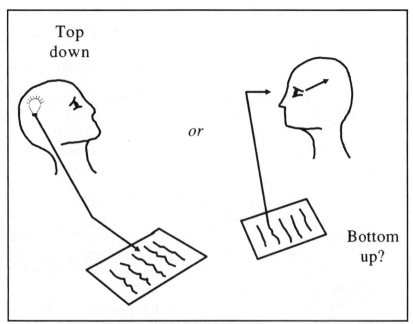

FIGURE 6.2   SHOULD INTELLIGENCE BE TOP DOWN OR BOTTOM UP?

the "bottom up" and attempts to model the biology. Beginning with the simplest units, artificial neurons, functionality is then added by combining these nodes into layers with multiple inter-connections. The learning, or intelligence, comes from generaliz-ing experience. What is unknown is likely unnecessary.

Traditional AI approaches have been "top down" and have attempted to model theories rooted more in psychology. They work more on "what" the brain does than on "how" it does it. This seems reasonable because "how" was even less well under-stood in the 50s than it is now. Intelligence is programmed in, such as in the form of explicit "if-then" rules. AI systems are more deductive than inductive, and the organization of intelligence must take place "up front."

AI is sometimes called fifth-generation computing, and neural networks are sometimes called sixth-generation computing, or neurocomputing. First-generation computing used switches and wires; the development of the transistor led to second-generation computing; solid state technology, leading to the use of integrated circuits in computers, produced the third-generation computers and third-generation programming languages; end-user tools became known as fourth-generation languages and produced fourth-generation computing.

Table 6.1 compares numerous aspects of AI and neural networks.

One of the big differences in the two technologies is self learning. This is an important goal, and neural networks do it fairly well. Generally, the more data they get, the more accurate and complete their learning. Another item, software effort, relates to this. Software has been an increasingly significant portion (and cost) of major projects. If a network is trained rather than programmed, a different set of skills will be required.

Another big difference has to do with speed and the ability to perform in real time. The parallel architecture of neural networks provides a huge advantage in this department. Decisions can be made quickly, and the system is highly resistant to hardware failure.

The AI effort to create general problem solvers ran into serious difficulty. As the complexity of a problem increased, so did the possible number of solution paths. Systems required too much

Table 6.1: Comparisons of Computers

Characteristic	Von Neumann Used for AI	Neural Networks Used for Pattern Recognition
1. Processing elements	VLSI	Artificial neural networks; variety of technologies
2. Memory and processing	Separate	The same
3. Hypotheses pursued	One at a time	Multiple, simultaneously
4. Connections	Externally programmable	Dynamically self-programming
5. Self learning	Only algorithmic parameters modified	Continuously adaptable
6. Fault tolerance	None	Significant
7. Use of neurobiology in design	None	Moderate

A Practical Guide to Neural Nets

resource and became too slow. The AI approach became feasible only within narrowly defined domains. In addition, heuristics, or rules of thumb, were used to "prune the tree" and thereby limit the search space. Programmers applied their own experience (their own internal neural networks) to improve the efficiency of systems. These approaches produced successes, and the subfield of expert systems became commercially viable.

Aside from this success in expert systems, AI has encountered significant problems (see figure 6.3). Areas such as vision, continuous speech recognition and synthesis, and machine learning have been hard. Theoretical speed limits for a single processor are being approached. Rules are often hard to specify, and experts rarely "speak in rules." Some algorithms are too complex and too slow to be implemented practically. An algorithm specifying robot control for all possible positions of an assembly piece would be a good example.

Although many of the goals of AI research remain unchanged, neural networks are seen by many as a help for AI projects that have bogged down. Real-time processing problems like automatic target recognition, autonomous vehicles, and voice

---

AI has experienced some problems . . .

   In vision

   In continuous speech recognition and synthesis

   In machine learning

   In theoretical speed limits for a single processor

   And sometimes rules are hard to specify

   For many tasks, algorithms are too complex to
   implement practically.

FIGURE 6.3 AI PROBLEMS

identification have been persistently hard to solve with alternate technologies. The ability of neural nets to handle novelty means that you wouldn't have to tell the net in advance what it is supposed to do for all possible situations.

Competitors or Complements?

The July 1987 issue of the newsletter *NeuroComputers* reported that the first International Neural Network Conference (held in San Diego in June, 1987) repeated the theme "AI is dead — long live Neural Networks." After neural network research had been conducted as an underground movement for a couple of decades, the feelings expressed were no doubt born of the vindication that has come with the recent and explosive new growth of this field. But forecasting the demise of AI was premature at the least, and we believe that it was just plain inaccurate. IBM announced recently that it now has more people working on AI than on data base.[11] R. F. Stoisits of ARCO says that ". . . expert systems and neuronets, implementations of symbolic processing, will be a routine part of our tool kit in the future. In fact, they may be more widespread than numerical analysis tools, because people apply information and logic more often than they solve numerical analysis problems."[12]

Learning and parallelism will augment conventional AI. For one example, consider knowledge acquisition, which has been a stickler for AI. We have heard Avron Barr (one of the editors of the *Handbook of Artificial Intelligence*) talk about "extracting" knowledge from an expert. He points out that the process is about as pleasant as going to the dentist. Beyond that, the knowledge obtained often contains assumptions and biases of programmers as well as of experts. Neural networks, along with other AI efforts in automating knowledge acquisition, can help by inducing the rules from the examples (see figure 6.4).

Neural Networks as Expert Systems

Expert systems (or knowledge-based systems) are a particular application of artificial intelligence techniques. Before we talk about neural networks as expert systems, we should say another word or two about what an expert system is.

Typically an expert system consists of a piece of software called an *inference engine* and another piece called a *knowledge base*.

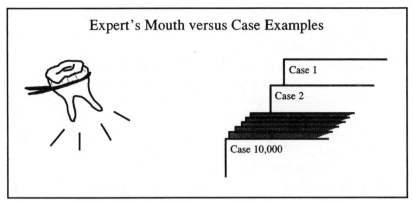

FIGURE 6.4   KNOWLEDGE ACQUISITION FOR RULES

The inference engine is generic, and it handles the logistics of a consultation. Scheduling decisions, user interface menu systems, external file or program access, etc., would be tasks of the inference engine. The knowledge base, on the other hand, contains all of the information that is specific to a particular application. This could include things like parameters and their possible values, rules that specify the relationships among various parameters, and the particular graphics or other relevant external files and programs.

Many see these systems as advisors to humans in areas such as planning and design, scheduling, diagnosis and trouble-shooting, training, and other knowledge-intensive decision-making situations. Others, such as Aion Corporation with its mainframe shell, see expert systems technology as a set of tools for productivity, whether or not they are used for traditional AI applications. This is partly because the inference engine can be predefined and pretested, leaving only the task of specifying the specific application aspects. "Taking expert systems into DP/MIS is the biggest factor in the realization of AI," says John Popolizio, director of custom consulting at New Science Technology Research and Consulting.[13]

Additional productivity gains are realized in the iterative refinement style, which makes it relatively easy to modify and update expert systems. This has been a significant factor in the success of systems in which the knowledge base changes rapidly (such as a 30-percent turnover in parts monthly).

Neural networks are both a rival and a companion to expert systems. Neural networks are good at recognizing patterns and can do this rather quickly. Like the brain, they are self-organizing and essentially self-programming. In an expert system for medical diagnosis, for example, the input nodes could describe the symptoms and the output nodes could suggest possible diagnoses, perhaps including suggested treatments and possible side effects. The network would be trained to associate symptoms and diagnoses from a database of case histories.

Sophisticated monitoring equipment and sensing devices for medical diagnosis have been available for some time. They have, unfortunately, some limitations. Often the output of this equipment is ambiguous, and the accuracy of interpretation depends on the education and experience of the physician as well as the conditions under which the diagnosis has been made. For example, an emergency or operating room is not the best environment for monitoring subtle variations in heartbeats. In addition, analysis of data by either a cardiologist or a computer is expensive and time-consuming; the availability of heartbeat analysis is limited to only a portion of the patient population. An expanded and automated heartbeat-recognition system could provide doctors with an important diagnostic tool at a lower cost than was previously possible.

In James Anderson's example of a medical system on drugs and diseases,[14] vectors of 25 characters are used to interrogate a knowledge base that has been coded as 31 character strings arranged in fields. Known portions of information in the vector are filled in to provide the input. The neural network cycles through the data and attempts to find the appropriate matching vector. If the input, for example, is "SiEf _____ Amphote," that could be interpreted as a request to the system to find out the side effects of the drug Amphotericin. The output after 27 iterations through the database shows the matching vector, "SiEfKidneys++K ____ e Amphote." The possible side effects are severe kidney damage.

Another medical neural network expert system possibility is described by Derek Stubbs, M.D.[15] This network would advise a critical care physician in optimizing patient process decisions. Input could consist of features of the patient: things like vital signs, blood gases, serum and urine chemistries, EEG and EKG readings, level of consciousness. The system could be trained on a number of examples to produce an appropriate output match for improving the state of the patient: altering the intravenous fluids, administering drugs, modifying the ventilator or other cardiopulmonary assist devices, and so on. Such systems could operate at lower cost than current methods and may soon become commercialized.

This sort of matching of input (data) to output (responses, diagnoses, decisions) could be used similarly for robot and process control in the manufacturing industry, for weather and financial forecasting, and for many other real-world problems. The knowledge is derived from the actual relationships implicit in the data.

Example: Handling Field Service Requests: Texas Instruments is one company taking advantage of this implicit knowledge within a database. Researchers are building a prototype for an expert system based on neural network technology to be used internally in the company's technical support areas of field service. The system is being designed to predict corrective action required to complete active service requests as well as to predict equipment assemblies required to restore faulty hardware to an operational state. This prediction is derived from a free-form textual description of the problem.

Parts prediction is important. Many of Texas Instruments' new products have assemblies costing thousands of dollars, and customers are understandably anxious regarding service. Additionally, not every customer response center can carry every part for every system. Predicting the spare parts required at the time of service call initiation will increase the probability that a center will have the parts necessary to resolve the system problem on the first on-site visit.

Previous similar efforts with traditional expert systems technology met with marginal success. They were found to require continual maintenance as the support environment for specific products changed over time. Rules numbered in the thousands, requiring a large investment in experts' time, rule development, and rule maintenance. Users quickly surpassed the knowledge of the expert system.

An adaptive, self-training system that learns by example on current data could eliminate the need for interviewing experts and writing rules to encode the knowledge; it could be self-maintaining.

Texas Instruments sees neural networks as a reusable technology. Retraining of the network to adapt to changes in the operating environment requires only processing time and new data. Periodic scheduled retraining can be automated; no reprogramming is required. Further, the network model can be exported as a self-contained ANSI C module for embedding into other applications. Other viable applications include database querying, predictive maintenance, service call categorization, service call forecasting, and service call assignments (hardware and software).

Managers found themselves wondering whether a conventional approach could replace the neural network. In one example, the prototype selected part #2535860–8000 by recognizing the words "process" and "memory." These two words in combination and individually were also associated with other part numbers. The selected part number was associated with words other than "process" and "memory"; it was also associated with word phrases containing one word or the other, but not both. They decided that developing rules for these complex associations would be a divergent exercise that would never end.

In current handling of service requests, humans are 60 to 70 percent accurate, and there is little opportunity for improvement. The network prototype is 70 to 90 percent accurate, can predict one or multiple parts, and includes significant opportunity for improvement.

Figure 6.5 (a conceptual block diagram) and figure 6.6 (a graphic illustration) depict the knowledge recall process.

Whole Brain Approach

Generalizing, expert systems are essentially a left-brain approach, and neural networks have more similarities to right-brain activities (see figure 6.7). Contrasts could look at symbols versus patterns, heuristics versus dynamics, serial versus parallel processing, *what* we know versus *how* we know.

Expert systems are typified by logical functions such as rules, concepts, and calculations. Neural networks embody gestalt functions such as the understanding of images, pictures, and graphic

A Practical Guide to Neural Nets

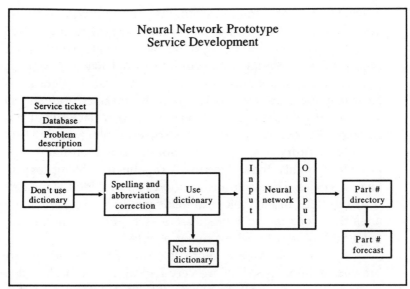

FIGURE 6.5 CONCEPTUAL BLOCK DIAGRAM—KNOWLEDGE RECALL

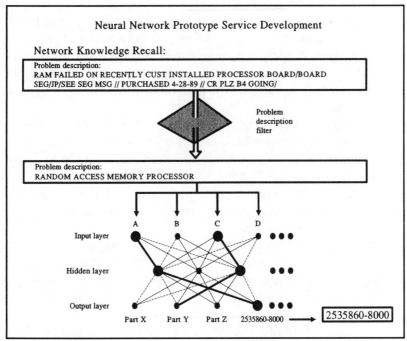

FIGURE 6.6 KNOWLEDGE RECALL GRAPHIC

How Do Neural Networks Relate to Other Technologies?   93

information.[16] The inference engines of expert systems are an appropriate contrast to the perceptual skills of neural networks. Further, note that expert systems work sequentially (although many AI researchers are trying to parallelize this approach), whereas true neural networks process in parallel. Algorithms are hard to parallelize, especially when the number of details being considered gets large. Expert systems learn didactically, by rules; neural networks learn Socratically, by example. (See figure 6.8.)

Our century has, up to this point, valued left-brain capabilities more highly than right-brain capabilities. Being logical has been a virtue. The scientific method has provided standards for research. Jobs in technological fields generally receive higher salaries than jobs in the human services sector. Having power has been an important goal for many people.

Some people take a more left-brained view of this right-brained technology. They are very logical, methodical, and pragmatic in their approach to neural networks. Others have a more right-brained style, emphasizing the potential for intuitive approaches and uses that may expand our horizons in ways we haven't yet considered. There are at least two other categories: a left-brained approach to left-brain technologies, perhaps exemplified by those who disregard neural networks altogether; and a right-brained approach to left-brain technologies, those who are still working on traditional AI logic systems to achieve right brain functions. The examples are generalizations, but the four divisions are real.

We are beginning to see significant signs of restoring a balance to this overemphasis on left-brain skills. One instance of this comes from Japan's Ministry of International Trade and Industry (MITI), which has formed a top-level committee of 100 people to study right-brain information processing.[17] Included in the study will be bio devices, pattern recognition, neural networks, intelligent control, and other technologies related to intuitive, nonlogical information processing. This committee may decide to recommend a companion project to the current, basically left-brain-approach national research project called ICOT (Institute for New Generation Computer Technology), also sometimes called the Fifth Generation computer project.

Many individual Japanese companies are following the same

A Practical Guide to Neural Nets

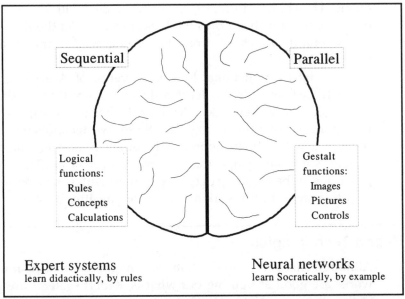

Sequential

Parallel

Logical
functions:
  Rules
  Concepts
  Calculations

Gestalt
functions:
  Images
  Pictures
  Controls

Expert systems
learn didactically, by rules

Neural networks
learn Socratically, by example

FIGURE 6.7   LEFT BRAIN VERSUS RIGHT BRAIN PROCESSING (ADAPTED FROM *EXPERT SYSTEMS STRATEGIES NEWSLETTER*, VOL. 3, NO. 12, © 1987 HARMON ASSOCIATES. ALL RIGHTS RESERVED.)

Consider . . .
  Where you learn by experience:

    Is X True?
    (Problem: Identify a forgery)

  Where you learn by reading the manual
  and following the rules:

    If X, Then Y
    (Problem: Apply relevant laws)

  Combining technologies can provide a
  whole brain approach.

FIGURE 6.8   A WHOLE BRAIN APPROACH

theme. Hitachi has a project on "how we deal with the left [lobe of the] brain, which controls the logical world, and the right [side of the brain], which controls the analog world, and how we integrate both."[18]

The 1989 International Joint Conference of Artificial Intelligence (IJCAI) included at least a dozen papers that specifically addressed neural networks. About half that many papers dealt with genetic algorithms. Together these two technologies could provide a whole brain approach to problem solving. Many researchers are suggesting that the real power of artificial intelligence lies in the blending of expert systems with neural networks. It's one way to begin working on a more healthy balance.

Hybrid Technologies

Although this is a simplification, you might say that neural networks are good at figuring out what is, expert systems are good at figuring out what to do about it, and conventional programs are designed to do it. For example, a neural network, good at modeling empirical data, could "decide" that a particular investment had peaked. An expert system could look at the investor's profile and apply rules to determine preferences. And an application could generate the paperwork for selling the investment. Combining all three technologies and adding a wide variety of supporting resources could provide a powerful approach to problem solving, as depicted in figure 6.9.

Many possibilities for technology integration exist. You can imagine, for instance, a hybrid tool in which a neural network would recognize speech and a conventional word processor would be used to format, spell-check, etc, and print out perfect copy. It's more than imaginary, however; hybrid tools are real.

In conventional *kanji* word processors, the phonetic spelling is entered and all possible matching characters are displayed. Many symbols have the same sound but different meanings, and there are thousands of characters. The user must manually select the appropriate character. Toshiba has recently developed a system that uses a neural-network simulation and senses sentence context to help in the selection, thereby reducing the manual choice task by 40 percent.[19]

The state of New York recently awarded a contract to Arthur

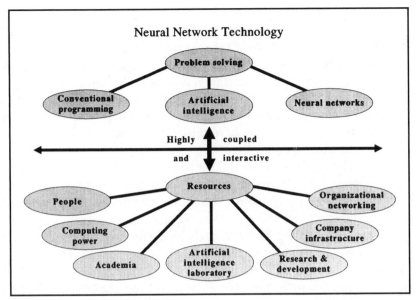

Neural Network Technology

FIGURE 6.9   PROBLEM-SOLVING APPROACH

D. Little Company to help reduce tax evasion. The proposed system will integrate conventional computing, expert systems, and neural network methods.

ARCO Oil and Gas Company foresees a combination of expert systems and neural networks for increased productivity in nearly every aspect of its business.[20] Expert systems provide a means for managing structured knowledge; neural networks supply enhanced pattern recognition. ARCO is particularly interested in the ability to recognize patterns that have previously gone undetected using traditional techniques.

For example, before ARCO "fractures" a field, injecting fluid into well holes at high pressure to crack rock formations and improve the flow of oil, huge computer models help engineers interpret data from sensors in the ground, informing them about how the fracture is proceeding. Previous models have taken hours to run; if a problem develops while fracturing is in progress, the model is almost useless. Using data stored in a mainframe, a neural network trained on the characteristics of an oil field can retrieve answers almost instantly. The network identifies some patterns better than the production engineers can.

The TNA system (SNOOPE) described in chapter 1 did not contain neural networks in the initial project design. Instead, a linear discriminant method was used to classify threats based on the neutron profile from the sealed baggage.[21] Specifications included accuracy and reliability, affordability, safety for passengers and belongings (including film and magnetic media), and speed (processing ten pieces of luggage per minute). The system had to handle all of this and determine "threat/no threat" by the time the bag exited the system.

The addition of neural network methods came about because of several problems. For one, the bags all had to be grouped by size before the machine could analyze them. That meant first setting up the machine for small bags and processing all the small bags; then setting the machine's mode for medium-sized bags and processing them, etc. Now add to this scenario impatient fliers who don't like airport delays anyway, and you get the picture.

The FAA deadline for a demonstration of the prototype was near. What to do? SAIC decided to integrate a neural network approach. Preclassification of bags was no longer necessary. The new system began to outperform the decision analysis method by a few percentage points. Fewer bags had to be reanalyzed by alternate means. An additional advantage was that the TNA with neural network methods reduced the set-up and calibration time, both in terms of required human supervision and computer time. Integrating technologies resulted in a successful field test.

Database management systems are currently host-resident on conventional computers. Just as knowledge-based processing and database processing are complementary technologies, neural network processing will likely find its particular niche within the overall information processing picture.

The future might bring shared processing, with neural networks performing the data analysis or serving as pattern processing front ends for knowledge-based systems. Neural networks may be used for algorithm development as well. First impressions are that both tasks could be done more rapidly using neural networks than using current conventional methods, but that remains to be seen. Training times for neural networks can be lengthy, and the development of suitable neural net architectures may rival the time required for algorithm development.

This sort of hybrid system, however, does show a great deal

A Practical Guide to Neural Nets

of promise. Neural networks could provide an interface between real-world data that is fuzzy and digital computers. Certainly, neural networks could add a degree of robustness relative to the hardware, as well as being good at handling uncertain or conflicting data. Expert systems (AI or neural network) could perform the higher, cognitive level tasks. AI knowledge-based systems could manipulate symbols and apply logic. Neural networks could perform the lower, signal-processing or data-level tasks, as well as the higher adaptive tasks involving learning. Conventional systems are still best at high-speed numeric processing. Problem/solution methodologies will encompass a wide variety of techniques in creating successful applications to solve problems (see figure 6.10).

Tom Schwartz points out that neural networks are not a replacement technology for procedural processing and expert systems.[22] "Each technology is different and each has its strengths. . . . in the future we will see software which uses procedural pre- and post- processing, in series or in parallel, with expert systems, neural networks, genetic algorithms and fuzzy logic."

Neural networks and conventional computers could be combined in a number of ways. Or, neural networks could be used to teach other neural networks. For the present, we need hybrids because the individual technologies can't address the same issues.

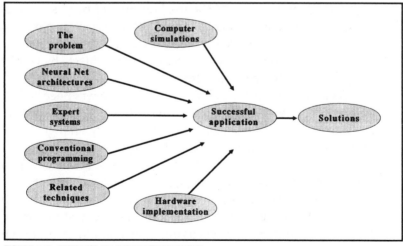

FIGURE 6.10   PROBLEM-SOLUTION METHODOLOGY

But the interplaying and controlling of each other by these hybrids also seems to be where the future lies.

Summary: A Maturation

Although neural network technology is in its infancy, it is not a revolution nor a reformation that will make conventional computers obsolete. It is a maturation of forces already in progress. The ways in which it may be combined with conventional computers and conventional and AI applications are potentially very useful. Jasper Lupo, in his introduction to the *DARPA Neural Network Study*, says, "my personal view is that neural networks will provide the next major advance in computing technology."[23] He points out that high-speed numerical processing and knowledge processing (artificial intelligence) have matured. "Neural networks seem to offer the next necessary ingredient for intelligent machines—namely, knowledge formation and organization."

Terrence Sejnowski, founder of the Salk Institute's Laboratory for Computational Neurobiology, predicts evolving working relationships between biomedical and artificial intelligence researchers will increase through the 1990s as work in each field stimulates work in the other.[24]

Hardware for neural networks is beginning to emerge. Even though there is still much to be done, researchers are more or less clear on what the hardware will need to do. Although current digital technology restricts the total number of processors that can be used in tandem, analog VLSI will allow massively parallel grids of simple, resistive elements to work as the human eye's retina does to detect orientation and movement of objects by comparing their positions in space and time.

As table 6.2 indicates, however, software will need to be quite different from what it has traditionally been. We have witnessed a progression of skills required as technology changes. Initially, there was only the hardware, and engineers made it work. Then there were software specialists: programmers, systems engineers, knowledge engineers, and now, neural network architects. This new professional will need to be much more familiar with statistics in order to choose and evaluate training and testing situations. Neural net software, the specifying of weights, transfer functions, learning laws, and the like, is seen by many as being one of the

A Practical Guide to Neural Nets

Table 6.2: Comparison of Traditional Software and Neural Networks

Traditional Software	Neural Networks
Distributive memory only	Both associated and parallel distributive memory
Computer is rendered useless by even a small amount of damage to memory	Neural computers are fault tolerant (graceful degradation) because information is distributed throughout the neural network system
Incomplete input produces no output	Incomplete input produces reasonable output results
Formalized structured programming is required	Neural networks are self-organizing

most difficult areas ahead. And this is beyond the software required for simulations.

Achieving a practical technology will be an evolutionary process rather than a revolutionary event. Even so, many areas, such as the design of control systems, could experience a revolutionary impact. Neural network technology is changing the way people think about AI and about statistical methods.

1. Halbert White, "Neural-network Learning and Statistics," *AI Expert*, vol. 4, no. 12 (December 1989): 52.

2. *Webster's New Collegiate Dictionary* (Springfield, MA: G. & C. Merriam Company, 1961).

3. *Webster's Ninth New Collegiate Dictionary* (Springfield, MA: Merriam-Webster, 1984).

4. Stanton Davis and Bill Illingworth, "Neural Network Simulation Applied to Statistical Process Control," (Dallas, TX: Texas Instruments, January 1989).

5. Franklin, Sutton, Anderson, Selfridge, and Schwartz, "Connectionist Learning Control at GTE Laboratories," Proceedings of the SPIE 1989 Symposium on Advances in Intelligent Robotics Systems, November 1989, Philadelphia, PA.

6. Franklin et. al., "Connectionist Learning Control at GTE Laboratories," p. 8.

7. A. Lapedes, C. Barnes, C. Burks, R. Farber, and K. Kirotkin, "Application of Neural Networks and Other Machine Learning Algorithms to DNA

Sequence Analysis," Computers and DNA, SFI Studies in the Sciences of Complexity, vol. VII, eds. G. Bell and T. Marr, Addison-Wesley, 1989.

8. The Human Genome Project. "Health and Environmental Safety Research Committee Advisory Report." Washington, D.C.: U.S. Department of Energy, 1987.

9. Lance B. Eliot, "Business Applications: You Can Bank On It," *Neural Network News* (newsletter), vol. 1, no. 4 (December 1989): 1.

10. White, "Neural-network Learning and Statistics," p. 52.

11. Jerry Smutz, "ARCO Foresees Productivity Increases With AI Technologies," *Oil & Gas Journal*, vol. 87, no. 2 (January 9, 1989): 43.

12. R. F. Stoisits, "AI is Vital Part of Production Computing," *Oil & Gas Journal*, vol. 87, no. 2 (Jan. 9, 1989): 48.

13. Alan Brody, "Artificial Intelligence Comes of Age," *Marketing Computers*, vol. 10, no. 1 (January 1990): 26.

14. James A. Anderson, *What Neural Nets Can Do*, Video Companion Manual, Lawrence Erlbaum Associates, 1988: 87–98.

15. Derek F. Stubbs, "Neurocomputers," *M.D. Computing*, vol. 5, no. 3 (1988): 14–24.

16. Paul Harmon, *Expert System Strategies Newsletter*, vol. 3, no. 12: 6–11.

17. *Electronic Engineering Times*, issue 556 (September 18, 1989): 4.

18. Shohei Kurita, "Expanding Neural Marketplace Challenges Japanese Engineers," *Electronic Business* (September 18, 1989): 79, 80.

19. R. Colin Johnson, "Japan Mounts Neural Push," *Electronic Engineering Times*, issue 572 (January 8, 1990): 20.

20. Jerry Smutz, "ARCO Foresees Productivity Increases with AI Technologies," *Oil & Gas Journal*, vol. 87, no. 2 (January 9, 1989): 43.

21. Tom J. Schwartz, "8 Parables of Neural Networks," *AI Expert*, vol. 4, no. 12 (December 1989): 54.

22. Tom J. Schwartz (president of Schwartz Associates, Mountain View, CA), "Neural Networks: Capabilities and Applications," IEEE Videoconference, September 27, 1989.

23. *DARPA Neural Network Study* (Fairfax, VA: AFCEA International Press, 1988), p. xxviii.

24. David A. Brown, "Neural Research May Benefit AI," *IEEE Software*, vol. 5, no. 6 (November 1988): 88.

How Many Ways Can You Organize a Neural Network?

To create consists precisely in not making useless combinations and in making those which are useful and which are only a small minority.
— *Henri Poincaré*

Poincaré's quote gets right to the heart of it. There are infinitely many ways to organize a neural network. Perhaps a couple dozen models are in common usage today. Before we look at several specific paradigms, or models, let's review the major variants (see figure 7.1).

Two general categories are used in describing neural network organization. *Neurodynamics* is a term that describes the properties of an individual artificial neuron: how it combines its inputs, handles its own internal transformations (such as adjusting weights), and produces its output. The term is also applied to the network as a whole—looking at the same properties just described, but on a system basis. The *architecture* defines the network structure: the number of nodes, number of layers, number and types of interconnections, and so on. These two aspects together dictate the specific characteristics of a given model, or paradigm.

Neurodynamics

We are accustomed to solving computational problems by breaking them down into steps and solving each small step. Neural networks don't work by developing an algorithm for each individual processing element. The knowledge is in the state of the

Factors: Numbers of processing elements

Number of interconnections

Number of layers

Possible weighting schemes

Possible transfer functions

Possible training methods

Neural nets are specified by the net topology, node characteristics, and training or learning rules.

FIGURE 7.1 HOW MANY DIFFERENT WAYS COULD YOU ORGANIZE A NETWORK?

whole network, not any one piece of it. Consequently, we have to think in overall terms of inputs, transformations, and outputs of the network—the network neurodynamics.

Even within a single processing element, these basic decisions about internal functions can become quite complicated. This fact somewhat models biology, because there are more than 100 different types of neurons in the brain. Considerable variation is possible in how we specify the activities of any given artificial neuron, or processing element.

Inputs

Typically, the input layer of a neural network serves only as a buffer, fanning out the inputs to the next layer. There are, however, several decisions to be made regarding the inputs. For starters, just exactly what will the inputs be? Visual images, audio signals, text, a pixel pattern, some other kind of signal (see figure 7.2)? Will signals be discrete (digital) or continuous (analog)? If digital, will they be limited to binary inputs of os and 1s? Will scaling or some other transformations of data be necessary? What if the inputs aren't numeric?

A Practical Guide to Neural Nets

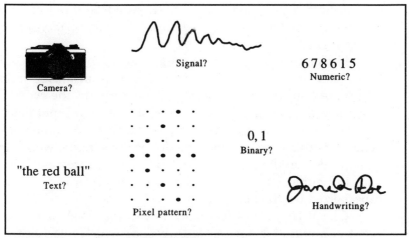

FIGURE 7.2 WHAT WILL THE NEURAL NETWORKS INPUTS BE?

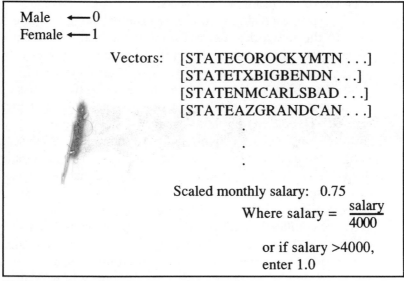

FIGURE 7.3 WHAT ENCODING OR SCALING WILL BE NEEDED?

Neural networks deal only with numeric input data. Therefore, you often must convert or encode data from the external environment. For example, as illustrated in figure 7.3, with inputs of male and female, one sex could be represented by a "1" and the other by a "0." Additionally, it is often necessary to scale data.

Monthly salary, scaled from 0 to 1, could be input as: "salary/4000, or if greater than 4000, set to 1." A salary relationship could be represented as a ratio: "net/gross."

Sometimes other preprocessing is necessary. Images could be converted from light or other radiation to an analog electrical signal. Again, there is a biological counterpart—the eye and the ear must do considerable preprocessing of their input data. The eye, for example, converts light signals to nerve impulses; light energy is transformed into a model of the external world. How? Our understanding is very limited. Visual processing is carried out in neural networks (located in the brain in higher animals) specialized for the task.

Global Holonetics (Fairfield, Iowa) has developed a quality-control application for the factory floor which relies heavily on preprocessing.[1] A neural network is used to classify objects such as candy bars, syrup bottles, sponges, tire treads, and batteries—over 100 different inspection tasks.

The preprocessing of the video-camera images is one of the keys to the network's ability to handle so many different tasks. Using spatial light modulators (SLMs) and lasers, a 65,000-pixel image is compressed into 32 numbers that contain information about an object's shape and orientation. Networks assign the number pattern to a category. Conventional statistical methods may also be able to do the task, but "we needed the system to be simple," said David Glover, Global Holonetics' chief scientist. "With a neural network a person on the factory assembly line doesn't have to be a programmer to train the machine to examine and classify new objects."

Even beyond the encoding methods mentioned above, there is the possibility of a different type of preprocessing. You might call it "weight pruning." By giving a network all the hints you can ahead of time, you will improve the solution space/error space ratio. Systems will be more efficient. Presetting of weights would comprise another type of input.

Inhibitory inputs are just as important as excitatory ones. Has the input scheme adequately allowed for both types? What actions should be given priority? Remember the Pac-Man example in chapter 5 where pain (inhibition) was more important than pleasure (excitation) and the symbol hid in the corner.

Some schemes make use of a constant-source input. This

A Practical Guide to Neural Nets

serves as an offset, or bias term, for the transfer function. Providing a mechanism for other influences attempts to model the fact that real neurons are affected by factors other than inputs. Additionally, sometimes dynamical, real-time models may use a "forgetting" term, or decay factor, so that outputs will not continue to be influenced by inputs that are no longer relevant over time.

This brings us to the matter of the history of the system inputs and outputs. The current state of a processing element will vary over time. How should the latest input combine with the current state of a processing element? Should they be treated equally? If not, should precedence be given to new inputs or to the accumulated current state?

The inputs are usually summed, taking the dot (or inner) product of the weighting factor and the input value (see chapter 4). However, even the summing function could be more complicated than just a simple summation. For example, the current sum could be added incrementally to the previous sum (useful in the traveling salesman problem). The minimum or maximum value of the weighted inputs could be used, or the number of weighted inputs above (or below) zero, and so on. Some networks require that inputs be normalized or scaled. Neural networks that use Kohonen learning are an example of this; you can find more about Kohonen networks later in this chapter. Further examples of inputs requiring scaling and other preprocessing appear in chapter 9.

Outputs

The output layer makes the network information available to the outside world. Like the input layer, this layer may be simply a linear transfer. Just as there may be a wide variation in the inputs, so may the outputs vary. Will the outputs be a pixel pattern, speech, a signal to some control device? How should the outputs be interpreted? Will scaling be necessary? Who makes use of the output data, and in what form does it need to be?

Transfer Functions

The relationship between inputs and outputs at any instant is specified by the transfer, or activation, function. The sum of the weighted inputs becomes the input to the transfer function, which specifies the output from the particular processing element. A number of transfer functions are commonly used. Typically they are nonlinear in the hidden layer(s). Figure 7.4 reviews the transfer functions we saw in chapter 3.

Example A in figure 7.4 is simple. Positive (including 0) inputs produce an output of 1; negative inputs produce an output of -1 (or 0). This is an example of a hard limiter function that produces binary output.

Example B is still quite simple. It typifies a ramping function. Inputs between 0 and 1 are mapped to output within the same range (or could be biased), and inputs less than 0 or greater than 1 work as in example A.

The sigmoid function in example C is used frequently. Variations can be made for adjusting the slope of the curve, and its derivatives are relatively easy to compute. However, the function itself may be more complicated than desirable for some networks, and example D presents a similar function that does not use logarithms. The sine function, hyperbolic tangent, and other nonlinear variations on these basic ideas have also been used.

This transfer function serves as a dynamic range limiter. If inputs are managed within some appropriate range, discrimination of inputs becomes feasible. Without such limitation, most of

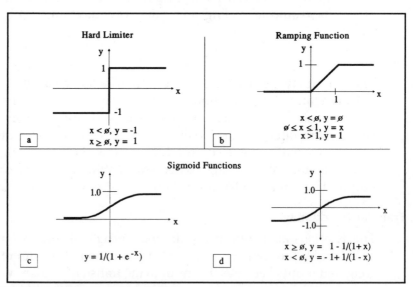

FIGURE 7.4 SAMPLE TRANSFER FUNCTIONS

the input data could produce outputs at the extremes of the range and it would be difficult to tell one output from another. This would be true in example D for inputs where $x < -1$ or $x > +1$. Output values for $x = 10$ would be about the same as the output for $x = 100$. Similarly, major trends could be lost because of focusing on minor perturbations, or vice versa.

Weighting Schemes

The transfer function is part of what determines the dynamic state of a neural network system. The other part is the memory state, usually local to a given processing element. In a nonlearning network, all the weights are fixed and do not change. However, the ability to change the weights enables the system to adapt so that similar initial conditions at different times give different results.

Initial weights may be set by an algorithm or set at random. How the interconnection weights are changed is the function of the learning algorithm. The objective is to adjust weights so that the error in the output layer is reduced. Back propagation of errors (commonly referred to simply as "back propagation") is currently the most popular of the learning algorithms for multilayer networks. Back propagation algorithms first adjust weights connected to the output layer. Then, working backward toward the input layer, such algorithms adjust weights in each successive layer to reduce the errors at each level.

A number of other variations are in use. Weights could be made irreversible to account for the causality of time. Weights could be correlational, relating input to output, or correctional, adjusting output to desired output (as in back propagation). Weights could be modified to cluster similar input patterns into distinct classes.

Architecture

Once the dynamics of an individual processing element are decided, the next step in specifying a neural network is to determine how the individual processing elements are combined. How many nodes should you put in a given layer? How many layers should there be? Where should the output from a given node be channeled? The number of possible variations is infinite.

Number of Processing Elements

The number of elements needed for the input and output layers will depend on the number of inputs and outputs for the system. For example, NETtalk needed to represent 203 inputs: $7 \times 29 =$ 7 character positions in the window, multiplied by 29 characters (alphabet, comma, space, and period). Similarly, NETtalk required 26 neurons for outputs: 1 for each of 23 distinct sounds and 3 for stress.

One experimental statistical process application done by a colleague used only five processing elements in the input layer and ten in the output layer. The inputs corresponded to actual statistical data for thin-film processing thicknesses taken at five different time intervals during a day. The outputs represented a prediction of the next ten thicknesses (or two days' worth of data).

The number of elements to use in the inner, or hidden, layers is less obvious. NETtalk used 80 neurons for continuous speech; the statistical process control example used 40 neurons organized in two inner layers of 20 neurons each. At this point, it seems to be mostly a matter of experimenting to find out what gives the best results. Simply adding extra hidden units may not provide any visible improvement in the system. The statistical process control network used a 4-to-1 ratio of first-hidden-layer units to input units. Experimentation with an 8-to-1 ratio provided very little improvement over the 4-to-1 ratio, while convergence was hard to achieve with a lower ratio.

Number of Layers

The examples above used totals of three and four layers. Some models use only two layers, directly mapping input patterns to a set of output patterns. This suffices when there is good similarity of input to output and the encoding provided by the external environment alone can perform the mapping.

However, whenever the structure of the input pattern is quite different from that of the output pattern, hidden units are needed to create an internal representation from the input signals. The ability to process information increases in proportion to the number of layers in the network. This is a powerful feature. Input patterns can always be recoded for suitable output if there are enough hidden units.

Example: The XOR Problem: Just for fun, let's take the eXclusive OR (XOR) function and look at the net requirements. The inputs will be binary (0 or 1) and we'll look at two inputs at a time. That means we'll need two nodes in our input layer. If the inputs are the same (both 0 or both 1), we want to output a 0. If the inputs are different (one 0 and one 1), we want to output a 1. That's what XOR is for—to tell you whether *one or the other* input is true (1 = TRUE; 0 = FALSE), but *not both*. So, one output node will be enough; it can either fire or not fire. So far so good.

Now, suppose we have the network connected as shown in Figure 7.5, where $w1$ and $w2$ are weights. We'll need the following equations to be true:

$0 * w1 + 0 * w2 = 0$ (0 * anything = 0, so this is all right)

$0 * w1 + 1 * w2 = 1$ ($w2$ must = 1 for this to work)

$1 * w1 + 0 * w2 = 1$ ($w1$ must = 1 for this to work)

$1 * w1 + 1 * w2 = 0$ (oops! can't be done.)

Let's try adding a hidden layer. (This has been done in a number of different ways, and we're just picking one of them.) Each node will have a threshold of 1, which means that the node will "fire" only if the sum of the inputs totals 1 or more. The weights along the connections will be as shown in figure 7.6. Try

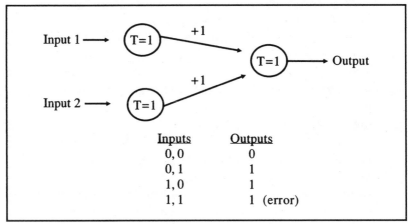

FIGURE 7.5 XOR (FIRST TRY)

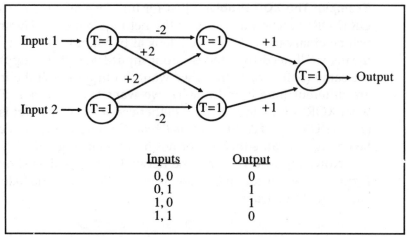

Inputs	Output
0, 0	0
0, 1	1
1, 0	1
1, 1	0

FIGURE 7.6 XOR (SECOND TRY)

inputs of 1 and 1. The threshold is achieved on both input processing elements, so both elements fire and pass signals on to the middle layer. Here, for each node, the total weighted signal is zero (+2 −2), and neither middle layer unit fires. Therefore, there is no signal passed on to the output layer, resulting in a 0, the correct output. You can see how the middle layer acts to inhibit firing in this situation.

Number and Type of Interconnections

How output from one processing element is fanned out to become input for another processing element is the next issue. If output from a single processing element is channeled to every node in the next layer, the network is said to be fully connected. Being connected locally to close neighbor nodes only is another option. Some networks (such as the Hopfield network) are sparsely connected to a few distant nodes, with only a small percentage of the nodes receiving input randomly from an element in the preceding layer.

If a network can pass outputs only to the next layer, it is termed a *feedforward network*. A *feedback network* would allow outputs to be input to preceding layers and *feedlateral connections* would send some inputs to other nodes in the same layer. Networks with closed loops are called *recurrent networks*.

Feedforward networks are faster than feedback nets, because

A Practical Guide to Neural Nets

you can set a solution with only one pass. In addition, feedforward nets are guaranteed to reach stability. On the other hand, feedback networks must iterate over many cycles until the system stabilizes. Even then the system may not be stable. It could oscillate between values, vary wildly, or lock up. The capacity of networks with feedback is more limited, too. You might ask, "Then why use recurrent networks?" The answer is fairly straightforward: they can do things that other networks cannot do. Feedback loops permit trainability and adaptability. Recurrent networks can perform functions such as automatic gain control or energy normalization and selecting a maximum in complex systems. Linear networks are limited; recurrency provides necessary nonlinearity. Hopfield networks and Kohonen networks, both presented later in this chapter, provide a couple of good examples of recurrent networks.

As if all this weren't enough flexibility, you could have a network develop new connections, lose existing connections, or modify the strength of existing connections.

Other Implementation Variables

One of the initial decisions is the choice between doing a software simulation and a hardware implementation. Should software be used only until the design is set, at which point the design will be cast in hardware? Will a single neural network be adequate, or is there a requirement for a number of networks to work together? What special-purpose hardware would be needed? This area will be addressed further in the section on implementation options in chapter 10.

Data representation is a major issue, as it is in conventional programming and AI. A notable amount of the research work being done in neural networks concerns representation. A good representation can reduce training time significantly. In addition to deciding whether information should be analog, digital, or symbolic data, you must decide how it should physically map to various parts of the network. Should variables be represented by many nodes over a wide region (a distributed representation), or should they be represented by only a few nodes (a local representation)? Should the value of a variable be represented by the amplitude of the output or by the location of nodes? Again, there's more than one way to solve a problem.

Most current neural network paradigms deal only with stationary patterns. (Grossberg's Avalanche, discussed briefly in chapter 8, is one exception; Dawes' Parametric Avalanche in chapter 11 is another.) Text-to-speech is an example of a stationary mapping; written words map to the same sounds, and don't vary over time (at least, not within the time frame we're considering here). The world is full of continuous change, however, and predictive networks will need to handle time-varying data. Process control nets will need to respond to changes in the process. A given parameter that is outside normal limits may be acceptable in one instance if it is just an aberration and the system comes back into acceptable tolerances. On the other hand, if the parameter is representative of a developing trend, it may be totally unacceptable. Further, for any network, what about the order of execution, or flow, through the network? And a scheduling function will be needed to determine how often a processing element should apply its transfer function.

A further variable is the learning rate. Generally you want a fast learning rate, but you want convergence, too. The issue is speed versus accuracy and accurate predictive capability. Will slower learning be needed to provide adequate granularity for accuracy? Should the learning rate be a constant or should it fluctuate? For some models, a constant learning rate is not efficient. Back propagation models, for example, may not converge unless the learning rate eventually declines to 0. On the other hand, dynamic models that are continually changing would be severely limited if they could not continue to learn. Should the learning rate be a scalar or a matrix form? What training methods should be used? There are significant tradeoffs.

The Right Paradigm

Different paradigms are good at solving different types of problems. When neural network technology is applied to a particular problem, the first tasks are selecting the right paradigm, deciding on the number of processing elements, and deciding on the training data to be used. The second task involves experimental "tweaking" to achieve better network performance; this is currently much more of an art than a science. The next few paragraphs discuss some of the early important paradigms, noting information on structure, applications, strengths, and limitations.

A Practical Guide to Neural Nets

What Are Some Neural Network Paradigms?

You could easily argue that other models should be included in this section. In fact, we do talk about several additional paradigms in chapter 8. We do not intend that what follows be interpreted as a complete set; there are lots of ways to do learning, and this is just a start. These particular paradigms were chosen because of their historical significance, their value in illustrating some of the concepts we have talked about in the first portion of this chapter, or simply on the whim of the authors. At any rate, a more comprehensive examination of some of the models and some of the mathematics involved will follow in the next chapter.

Perceptron

The Perceptron (see figure 7.7) is the earliest of the neural network paradigms. Frank Rosenblatt, a neurophysicist who had previously been a psychologist, built this learning machine device in hardware in 1958 and caused quite a stir. Controversial, overstated, known to have limitations, it was nevertheless a pioneering effort that intrigued physicists and engineers with its adaptive response potential. Here was a computational model for the

Computational model for the retina to show
pattern-recognition capability of visual system

Built by Frank Rosenblatt, neurophysicist

Applications:
Classification of shapes
Character recognition
Robot vision system

Minsky-Rosenblatt competition,
classifies only linearly separable patterns,
no XOR capability

FIGURE 7.7 PERCEPTRON

retina, a learning associator that showed the pattern-recognition capabilities of the visual system.

Anatomically, it was a three-layer network that was randomly, but locally, connected. The input layer was like a retina that gathered the sensory data and projected it to the next layer. Layer two was an association unit reciprocally connected to layer three, a response unit. Outputs were 0 or 1. Because the transfer function was linear, later researchers showed that the three layers could actually be collapsed to a single layer.

Rosenblatt believed the system should be able to handle noisy and variable inputs, as do biological systems, and self-organize to associate stimulus with response. To its credit, Perceptron could generalize and appropriately respond to stimuli it had never seen if the new data were similar to previously learned patterns. The patterns, however, had to be linearly separable in order to be classified. Remember the XOR example? Perceptron could not handle this type of problem. For this failure and others, it was criticized for being inflexible and literal and was termed a "brain-damaged" network that could not do anything interesting. Minsky and Papert's book *Perceptron* highlighted the flaws, and research funds began to dry up.

Nevertheless, the Perceptron can handle certain classes of problems well. Applications include classification of shapes, character recognition, and use in robot vision systems. The Perceptron has been a foundational building block for more powerful models, such as the ADALINE (discussed next), and it also provided the inspiration for Nakano's robots, which were mentioned in chapter 5.

ADALINE/MADALINE

ADALINE stands for ADAptive LINear Elements, and MADALINE is for Multiple ADALINEs in parallel. This model (see figure 7.8) was built by Bernard Widrow and Marcian Hoff. Widrow, then an EE Professor at Stanford, was one of the participants at the 1956 Dartmouth Conference who did not jump on the AI bandwagon. Recently, he demonstrated to delighted conference attendees one of the original ADALINEs, which has worked perfectly for 25 years. Widrow remains in the forefront of this technology, serving in 1988 as study director for the *DARPA Neural*

ADAptive LINear Elements and Multiple ADALINEs . . .

Built by Bernard Widrow, EE professor at Stanford

Contributions:
- Broomstick balancing
  (classic test in adaptive control)
- Adaptive noise cancelling in telecommunications
  (received Alexander Graham Bell award)
- Adaptive antenna arrays
- Adaptive blood pressure regulation
- Adaptive filtering
- Seismic signal pattern recognition
- Speech recognition
- Weather forecasting

FIGURE 7.8 ADALINE/MADALINE

Network Study and in 1989 as the president of the International Neural Network Society (INNS).

Widrow and Hoff were after an adaptive system that could learn more quickly and accurately than the Perceptron. They brought in the idea of the threshold in their three-layered network. An individual neuron computed a weighted sum of its inputs multiplied by corresponding weights plus a bias term. If the sum was greater than 0, the output was +1; if the sum was less than or equal to 0, the output was −1.

Their learning rule was simple, yet elegant. It required a teacher. Even when the output was correct, weights were adjusted to improve "reaction time." Compare that to your learning a new skill—say water skiing. Even after you've learned to stay up, a lot more learning takes place to improve balance and agility. The error-correction algorithm is sometimes known as the Widrow-Hoff Rule, or the LMS (Least Mean Squares) algorithm. (See chapter 5 for an explanation of LMS.)

Many applications control input voltages automatically using an error-correcting feedback signal. Pole balancing, the classic test in adaptive control, is one such example. Think for a minute about how you might try to balance a pole on your palm. You would sense the direction in which the pole is leaning, and try to compensate by positioning your hand under the center of gravity to maintain the balance. A computer program that attempts to have a robot duplicate your efforts would get very complex.

Figure 7.9 shows a sketch of a system controlled by a neural network.[2] The network receives feedback from a camera that monitors a point on the end of a broomstick. The objective of this system is to keep that point at a certain location in space. During trial-and-error learning, the system uses the feedback to control the movement of the balancing platform. As errors are corrected, the system learns to balance the broom very well, even if someone

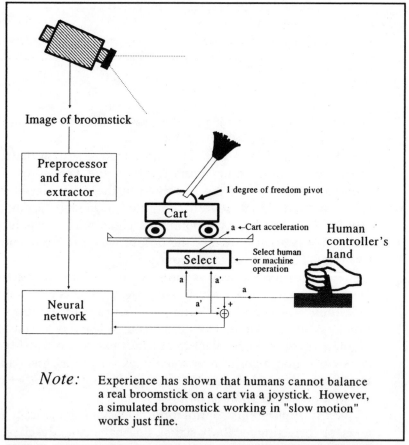

FIGURE 7.9 BROOM-BALANCER WITH VISION FEEDBACK (USED WITH PERMISSION OF HNC, INC.)

A Practical Guide to Neural Nets

comes along and taps it! Other pole-balancing experiments exist. Generally the objective is simply to balance the pole, which is attached to a cart running on a bounded track.

The modem noise canceling application featured in chapter 1 is based on an ADALINE; the weather example we mentioned in chapter 2 was also based on an ADALINE. Other adaptive systems include ones that cancel jamming signals in antenna arrays, blood pressure regulation, filtering, seismic signal pattern recognition, speech recognition, and weather forecasting.

Brain-State-in-a-Box (BSB)

James Anderson, a cognitive psychologist whose early works were neurophysiologically oriented, built a model that extends our own understanding of the brain and how it works (see figure 7.10). The clever name has to do with stabilizing the network within a "box" of limits, or a hypercube. (What is a hypercube? Let's start with something most of us understand. A square has 2^2 vertices and exists in two dimensions. A cube has 2^3 vertices and exists in three dimensions. A hypercube carries the pattern farther, to more than three dimensions in what has been called hyperspace, a space of more than three dimensions. So, a hypercube could have 2^n vertices in n-dimensions.) Therefore, Anderson's network would converge, or stabilize, at one of the corners of this "box."

Like the ADALINE, BSB uses feedback with error correction. This auto-associative network is not fully connected, and, as we

---

A model which extends our own understanding of
the brain and how it works

Built by James Anderson, cognitive psychologist

Puts feedback with autoassociative error correction and
guarantees convergence to one corner of a hypercube

Applications:
"bird" classification database
medical diagnosis (trained on diseases/symptoms)

FIGURE 7.10   BRAIN-STATE-IN-A-BOX (BSB)

said, utilizes feedback. Inputs are in the form of a vector that represents a partial pattern filled in. For example, a 25-ASCII-character vector with 8 bits per character would require a 200-bit (25-by-8) vector for input. The network would then try to complete the pattern. (Chapter 6 has examples of vectors in a medical system.)

The output is limited with a ramping transfer function or a bounded linear function (see figure 4.11b). Output is clipped to the limit levels. This guarantees convergence to one corner of the box and minimizes the error in response to a training set. The BSB model is fault- and noise-tolerant but requires time and supervision for the encoding.

Applications are more experiments than products. For example, you could use this network to extract knowledge from databases. This has been demonstrated with a bird classification system. Or, there is the medical diagnosis system. After training on diseases and symptoms, the network can suggest possible treatment when you provide it the symptoms for a disease it doesn't know.

Hopfield Network

Out of research on the neurophysiology of garden slugs comes a model built by John Hopfield, a physicist at Caltech and AT&T Bell Laboratories (see figure 7.11). He conceptualizes a network in terms of its energy and the physics of dynamic systems. A processing element will change state if doing so will reduce the "frustration level" of the network.

The output of each processing element in the binary, symmetrically weighted model is fully connected by weights to the inputs. This recurrency provides the nonlinearity. Positive weights are excitatory and will strengthen connections; negative weights are inhibitory, weakening connections. In Hopfield's own abstract, "The collective properties of this model produce a content-addressable memory which correctly yields an entire memory from any subpart of sufficient size." However, storage capacity is limited to approximately 15 percent of the number of elements, which is sometimes an important limitation of the model.

One of the reasons Hopfield's model was so well received was that it could be implemented readily by integrated circuit hardware. Neural network chips soon followed. Possible appli-

Out of research into neurophysiology of garden slugs

Built by John Hopfield, physicist

Conceptualizes network in terms of energy
   and the physics of dynamic systems

   Positive weights are excitatory;
      connections are strengthened
   Negative weights are inhibitory;
      connections are weakened

Lends itself to analog and optical implementation . . .
Potential for dense network — on a chip

Possible applications:
   Robotic control systems (in space!)
   Military target/friend-or-foe identification

FIGURE 7.11   HOPFIELD NETWORKS

cations are in robotic control systems and military target/friend-or-foe identification. The former, implemented on dense chips, would have a high radiation immunity and would be suitable for use in space. The latter show promise in optical system implementations. This network also does well with np-complete problems, such as the traveling salesman problem, and the retrieval of complete data from fragments.

Back Propagation

Back propagation of errors (see figure 7.12) appears to be a case of an algorithm whose time had come. It arrived on the neural network scene at approximately the same time from several independent sources (Werbos; Parker; Rumelhart, Hinton, and Williams). This timing is not too surprising, however, when you find out that many of the researchers talked with one another and shared their ideas. Currently back propagation is the most popular, effective, and easy-to-learn model for complex, multilayered networks. Although work is continuing on ways to speed it up, it is still faster than some other models.

Simultaneous, independent development:	Werbos
	Parker
	Rumelhart, Hinton, Williams

Refinement of Widrow-Hoff:
        Output - Desired Output = Error

1 Cycle = 2 Passes: Forward pass to determine error
                      Backward pass to modify weights &
                          correct errors

Applications: Speech from text
              Robot arms
              Bank loans
              Knowledge representation
              Multitarget tracking

FIGURE 7.12   BACK PROPAGATION

Essentially this feedforward network uses a refinement of the Widrow-Hoff technique, which calculates the difference between actual outputs and desired outputs. Using this error, weights are changed in proportion to the error times the input signal. Doing this for an individual node means that the input, the output, and the desired output all have to be present at the same "synapse." This is a bit hard to do with hidden units. How can you tell how much "blame" to assign a particular element unless you know how much input came into that node? An inactive node wouldn't contribute to the error and would have no need to change its weights.

To solve this problem, the synapses are run backwards so you can tell how strongly that particular synapse is connected. Each hidden processing element's error is a weighted sum of the errors in the successive layer. The whole sequence involves two passes: a forward pass to estimate the error, then a backward pass to modify weights so that the error is decreased.

This is *not* the way nature does it. Obviously, then, modeling biology is not the goal here (true with most models, though not all). Instead, one of the strengths seems to be in developing good representations. Imagine an example using a hidden layer that had fewer nodes than either the input or output layers. If the

A Practical Guide to Neural Nets

inputs could map correctly to the outputs, then the hidden layer would provide a good model for data compression.

Unlike the Hopfield model, this network can store many more patterns than the number of dimensions. It generalizes well and can perform arbitrary nonlinear mappings. There are limitations. Back propagation requires lots of supervised training, with lots of I/O examples. Additionally, the mapping procedure is not well understood, and there is no guarantee the system will converge.

Applications include speech synthesis from text, robot arms, evaluation of bank loans, image processing, knowledge representation, forecasting and prediction, and multitarget tracking.

Self-Organizing Maps

Tuevo Kohonen, an electrical engineer at the Helsinki University of Technology, has built a self-organizing network that "learns" without being given the correct answer for an input pattern (see figure 7.13). It models neurobiological systems fairly closely. For example, our visual system maps visual space onto the surface of

---

A self-organizing network that "learns" without
being given the correct answer for an input pattern . . .
closely modeled after neurobiological systems

Built by Teuvo Kohonen, Helsinki U. of Technology

A single layer, highly connected
  Weights must be initialized;
    weights and inputs must be normalized
  Neurodes compete for privilege of learning;
    "winner takes all" and nearest neighbors adjust

Good for statistical/topological modeling,
  inputs could be frequency, spatial location, etc.

Advantages:
  Potentially very fast (real-time)
  Can learn continuously (adapt to changes over time)
  Capabilities unmatched by other neural networks

FIGURE 7.13 SELF-ORGANIZING MAPS

---

our visual cortex. Similarly, this network maps analog signal representations onto a set of output responses (classes).

This auto-associative network is a single layer, recurrent and highly connected. Weights must be initialized, and both weights and inputs must be normalized or adjusted to some standard reference. Processing elements compete for the privilege of learning. In a "winner-takes-all" learning rule, the node with the highest response and its nearest neighbors all adjust their weights. As time passes, the size of the neighborhood may be reduced. Neighborhoods become similar in their response properties, and a global organization begins to take shape.

Topology is a branch of mathematics that studies properties of geometric configurations that do not change when the configurations are mapped in a one-to-one continuous transformation. Because the connection weights in a Kohonen network vary over time to approximate the density of the input patterns, this network could plot its inputs on a grid and create a graphical picture of the input distribution. As mentioned earlier, many kinds of maps in the brain relate sensory inputs to some organized pattern. Our ears, for example, can distinguish higher pitches from lower frequencies.

Kohonen networks have capabilities unmatched by other neural network models. Their ability to map a statistical distribution, however, works well only with large networks. Although they require considerable self-training, such networks are potentially very fast and can work in real time. This means the network could learn continuously and adapt to changes over time. In applications for statistical or topological modeling, for example, inputs could be frequencies, spatial locations, and so on. Self-organizing maps are more effective than many algorithms for performing calculations such as those for aerodynamic flow.

Summary

These models, and many we haven't yet introduced, all have several things in common. Although the pieces of the puzzles are put together in a variety of ways, the pieces are all simple processing elements—the lowly but powerful artificial neuron. The functions of these artificial neurons are the ones we detailed in chapter 4. They take their many inputs, multiply by the corresponding weights, sum all these products, and pass this sum to a transfer function that produces an output. This output is then fanned out to other nodes.

The processing elements are arranged in layers. Some models are composed of a single layer; more are multilayered. Processing elements may be fully connected, sparsely connected, or randomly connected. The connections may be strictly feedforward or they may be feedback, feedlateral, or even self-feed.

Transfer functions vary. Learning rules vary. Strengths and limitations vary. Different models are good at different things. Table 7.1, adapted from Robert Hecht-Nielsen,[3] lists 13 well-known neural network models (while over 50 different models are being explored).

Much depends on what you want to do with the model. If you are still involved in research, it may well be important to have the flexibility offered in some software models. Then you can experiment, try a variety of functions, alter the structures, and evaluate the differing results. When an application is approaching commercialization, however, other values such as speed and cost become paramount.

This is a rapidly changing technology. New and better models are already in the works and limitations of some of the "old" models are being chipped away. The needs of commercial applications will drive the direction of some model-building. Alongside this, other models will be built in attempts to better duplicate the structures and functions of biological models, as we understand them. Each approach can learn from others. It would be a mistake to close off experimentation too early; there is so much to be learned.

1. June Kinoshita, "Neural Networks at Work," *Scientific American* (Science and Business Section), vol. 259, no. 5 (November 1988): 134.

2. Douglas A. Palmer, "Neural Networks: Computers That Never Need Programming," *I&CS*, vol. 61 (April 1988): 77. See also Tom Inglesby, "No Clowning Around, Neural Networks Can Help Manufacturing," *Manufacturing Systems* (October 1988): 26.

3. Robert Hecht-Nielsen, "Neurocomputing: Picking the Human Brain," *IEEE Spectrum*, vol. 25, no. 3 (March 1988): 39.

Table 7.1: Well-known Neural Networks

Network	Inventor/Developer	Years	Applications	Limitations	Comments
Adaptive resonance theory	Gail Carpenter, Stephen Grossberg	1978–86	Pattern recog, (radar/sonar, voiceprints)	Sensitive to translation, distortion, scale	Sophisticated; not applied much yet
Avalanche	Stephen Grossberg	1967	Continuous-speech recog; commands to robot arms	No easy way to alter speed or interpolate mvmt	Class of networks; no single net can do all this
Back propagation	Paul Werbos, David Parker, David Rumelhart	1974–85	Speech synthesis from text; robot arms; bank loans	Supervised trng only—needs lots of I/O examples	Most popular net; works well, easy to learn, powerful
Bidirectional associative memory	Bart Kosko	1985	Content-addressable associative memory	Low storage density; data must be coded	Easiest to learn; assoc frag pairs w/ complete pairs
Boltzmann & Cauchy machines	Jeffrey Hinton, Terry Sejnowsky, Harold Szu	1985–86	Pattern recog for images, sonar, radar	Long trng time, gen. noise in statis distrib.	Simple nets; noise function used to find global min.
Brain State in a Box	James Anderson	1977	Extraction of knowledge from data bases	One-shot decisions—no iteration	Similar to bidirect in completing fragmented inputs
Cerebellatron	David Marr, James Albus, Andres Pellionez	1969–82	Control motor action of robotic arms	Requires complicated control input	Like Avalanche; can blend cmds w/diff wts for smoothness

Name	Inventor	Year	Application	Limitation	Comment
Counter-propagation	Robert Hecht-Nielsen	1986	Image compress; stat analysis; loan appl score	Many PEs and connections for high accuracy	Self-prog look-up table; similar to back-propagation
Hopfield	John Hopfield	1982	Retrieval of complete data from fragments	Does not learn; weights must be set in advance	Can implement on a large scale
MADALINE	Bernard Widrow	1960–62	Nulling of radar jammers; modems; phone equalizers	Assumes linear relationship between I & O	In commercial use >20 yrs; powerful learning law
Neocogni-tron	Kunihiko Fukushima	1978–84	Handprinted char recognition	Requires many PEs and connects	Most complicated; insensitive to scale transl, rotation
Perceptron	Frank Rosenblatt	1957	Typed-character recognition	Cannot recognize complex chars; sensitive to scale, distortn	Oldest net; was built in H/W, rarely used today
Self-organizing map	Teuvo Kohonen	1980	Maps 1 geometric region (grid) to another (aircraft)	Requires much training	More effective than many algorithms for aerodyn flow calcs

Used with permission of HNC, Inc. and IEEE. © 1988 IEEE.

How Do Neural Networks Learn?

Learning is kindled in the mind of the individual. Anything else is mere schooling. . . . The greatest learning disability of all may be pattern blindness—the inability to see relationships or detect meaning.

—Marilyn Ferguson

Funk and Wagnall's *Britannica Dictionary* gives the following definition for learning: "The modification of behavior following upon and induced by interaction with the environment and as a result of experiences leading to the establishment of new patterns of response to external stimuli."

This definition was written many years prior to the technology of neural networks and yet applies almost in its entirety for the learning processes used by neural networks today. Learning is so fundamental that we seldom stop to analyze exactly what takes place. In fact, researchers are still trying to figure out how learning happens.

From the very start of the computer era, we have dreamed of making computers that can learn and think. Pamela McCorduck's book, *Machines Who Think*,[1] details much of this effort. To date, a lot of energy has been expended but successes have been limited. Into this milieu comes now the neural network approach to artificial intelligence, where learning is built into every system.

In this chapter, we will address the following basic questions:

- What is the basic learning mechanism in neural networks?
- What are supervised and unsupervised learning?

A Practical Guide to Neural Nets

- What are the most common learning rules?
- What architectures and learning paradigms are employed in neural networks?
- What type of equations are typically used in neural networks?

The Basic Learning Mechanism

As we saw in chapter 4, a neural network consists of many simple interconnected processing elements. These processing elements, or PEs, are usually grouped into linear arrays called *layers*. Each PE has a number of inputs (Xi), each of which must store a connection weight (Wi). As we have seen, the processing element sums the weighted inputs ($WiXi$) and computes one and only one output signal (Yj). This output is a function (f) of that weighted sum. Figure 8.1 summarizes how a PE works.

We refer to the function (f) as the transfer function. As we noted previously, a number of transfer functions are in current

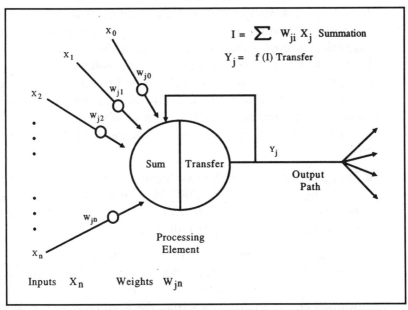

FIGURE 8.1 HOW A PROCESSING ELEMENT WORKS (REPRINTED FROM *DARPA NEURAL NETWORK STUDY*, AFCEA INTERNATIONAL PRESS, 1988.)

How Do Neural Networks Learn?

use. These include, but are not limited to, the sigmoid function, sine function, hyperbolic tangent, and various threshold and linear functions. The function (f) remains fixed for the life of the processing element. It is generally decided upon as a part of the design, and it cannot be changed dynamically. In other words, the transfer function currently cannot be adjusted or modified during the operation or running of the neural network.

However, the weights (Wi) are variables. They can be dynamically adjusted to produce a given output (Yj). This dynamic modification of the variable weights (Wi) is the very essence of learning. At the level of a single processing element, this self-adjustment is a very simple thing; when lots of PEs do it collectively, we say it resembles "intelligence." The meaningful information is in the modified weights. The ability of an entire neural network to adapt itself (change the Wi values) to achieve a given output signal (Yj) is its uniqueness. Uniqueness, that is, for a nonliving entity.

We have considered many examples to illustrate the "learning ability" of neural networks, but none suits our purpose better than the "single neuron learning" example found in the *DARPA Neural Network Study*.[2] Figure 8.2 illustrates how the training, or learning, of a supervised neural network is conducted. In this example we desire that a single neuron be trained to turn the light bulb on when the sum of two input voltages is greater than 0.5. Conversely, we want the light to be turned off when the two input sums are less than 0.5. The neuron will be trained by adjusting only the two weights $W1$ and $W2$.

The supervised training process utilizes the following training trials.

- First trial: The sum of the two inputs is less than 0.5. Therefore, the light bulb should be OFF. However, the light bulb is ON because of the initial weight values. Now the supervisor adjusts the weights until the light bulb turns OFF.

- Second trial: In the second trial, the sum of the two inputs is greater than 0.5. Therefore, the light bulb should be ON. Because the supervisor overcorrected the weights and threshold adjustment on the previous trial, the light bulb is OFF. We now adjust the weights and threshold until the light turns ON.

A Practical Guide to Neural Nets

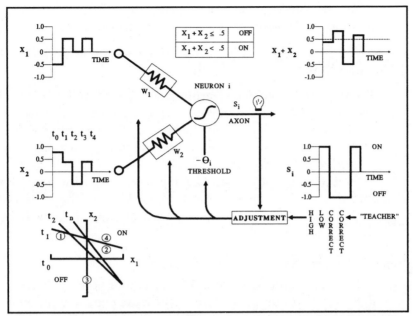

FIGURE 8.2 SINGLE NEURON LEARNING (REPRINTED FROM *DARPA NEURAL NETWORK STUDY*, AFCEA INTERNATIONAL PRESS, 1988.)

- Third trial: The third set of inputs sum to less than 0.5 and the light bulb is OFF, as it should be. No corrections are required by the supervisor.

- Fourth trial: The fourth set of inputs sum to greater than 0.5 and the light turns ON, which indicates that the neural network is trained.

We can now conclude that in this simple single-neuron exercise the network has "learned" to identify a line in two-dimensional space, as shown in the lower left corner of figure 8.2 and given by the equation $X_1 + X_2 = 0.5$. The more important lesson here is that we may teach neural networks to "learn" two, three or n-dimensional equations.

Learning is the process by which a neural network modifies its weights in response to external input. The equation that specifies this change is called the *learning law*, or *learning rule*. Before we look at various learning rules, there are a couple of other things to consider, such as learning modes, learning rates, and training techniques.

Learning Modes

There are two types of learning: supervised and unsupervised. As you might guess from your own experience, supervised learning requires a teacher. The teacher may be a training set of data or an observer who grades the performance (such as rating the next play in a chess game or evaluating the quality of parts on an assembly line). Either way, having a teacher is learning by reinforcement. When there is no external teacher, the system must organize itself by some internal criteria designed into the network; this is learning by doing.

Supervised Learning

In this mode, the actual output of a neural network is compared to the desired output. Weights, which are generally randomly set to begin with, are then adjusted by the network so that the next iteration, or cycle, will produce a closer match. The goal of all learning procedures is ultimately to minimize the error between the desired output and the current output sample by continuously modifying the weights.

With supervised learning, it is necessary to "train" the neural network before it becomes operational. Training consists of presenting input and output data to the network. This data is often referred to as the *training set*. That is, for each input presented, the corresponding desired output is presented as well. In many applications, actual data are used. The training phase can consume a lot of time. It is considered complete when the neural network produces the required outputs for a given sequence of inputs. When no further learning is to occur, the weights are "frozen."

Using this technique, a network could do things like make decisions, map associations, "memorize" information, or generalize.

Unsupervised Learning

Unsupervised learning is sometimes called *self-supervised learning*. Here, networks use no external influences to adjust their weights.

Instead there is an internal monitoring of performance. The network looks for regularities or trends in the input signals, and makes adaptations according to the function of the network. Even without being told whether it's right or wrong, the network still must have some information about how to organize itself. Here's a possible example: a network could learn to track a moving object by coordinating a spot on its simulated retina with the center of the retina.

An unsupervised learning algorithm might emphasize cooperation among clusters of processing elements. In such a scheme, the clusters would work together and try to stimulate each other. If external input activated any node in the cluster, the cluster activity as a whole could be increased. Likewise, if external input to nodes in the cluster was decreased, that could have an inhibitory effect on the entire cluster. Clusters could then compress data for the next layer.

Competition between processing elements could form the basis for learning, also. Training of competitive clusters could amplify the responses of specific groups to specific stimuli and associate those groups with each other and with a specific appropriate response. For example, processing elements could be organized to discriminate between various pattern features, such as horizontal or vertical edges or left-hand and right-hand edges. Figure 8.3 is one of the screens from the Brain Simulator software package; it shows an example of edge detection.

At the present state of the art, unsupervised learning is not well understood and is still the subject of much research. It is of great interest to the government, for one, because many military situations don't have a data set available until a conflict arises. Supervised learning procedures, on the other hand, have achieved a reputation for producing good results in practical applications and are gaining in popularity.

Learning Rates

How fast should learning occur? That depends on several things. There are trade-offs in the rate of learning. Obviously, a slower rate means a lot more time is spent in accomplishing the off-line learning to produce a trained system. With the faster rate, however, the network may not be able to make the fine discriminations

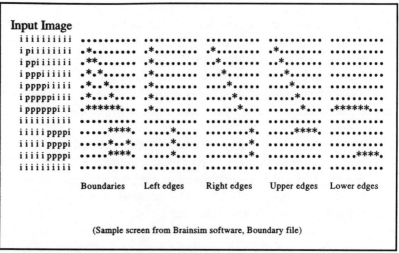

FIGURE 8.3   DETECTING PATTERN FEATURES (COURTESY ABBOT, FOSTER & HAUSERMAN CO. FROM THE BRAIN SIMULATOR.)

possible with a system that learns more slowly. Researchers are working on giving us the best of both worlds.

In chapter 9 we compare five actual networks with respect to off-line training time, number of training cycles, and the overall accuracy of the fully trained neural network. Generally, it is much simpler to train (off-line) pattern classifier networks. Several factors besides time have to be considered when discussing the off-line training task, which is often described as "tiresome." We must consider network complexity, size, paradigm selection, architecture, type of learning rule or rules employed, and desired accuracy. These factors play a significant role in determining how long it will take to train a network. Changing any one of these factors may either extend the training time to a completely unreasonable length or result in an unacceptable accuracy.

For example, in an optimization network where many curves of various degrees represent the training data, the training time could be as long as 24 hours with an overall accuracy of only 88 percent. Compare this with an image or pattern classifier that uses as many as several hundred inputs, with a hidden layer of 50 to 100 neurons, and that requires only three minutes or less to fully "learn" a complex image represented in a matrix of 256 shades of gray.

A Practical Guide to Neural Nets

Consider accuracy and speed with the following illustration. Once a system had learned a 500 matrix image consisting of 500 three-digit decimals ranging from .000 to 1.000 in less than three minutes, we purposely altered one digit of a three-digit decimal. Upon recall, the neural network detected this change every time. This is analogous to learning the image of a dollar bill in pixel form. Now we alter one pixel in George Washington's eye, and by George, the neural network will detect it (in less than a wink).

Finally, the learning rule and the modification of the weights play a smaller but sometimes lengthy role in the training effort. Again, it depends on the particular problem for which the network was developed. We do find that, as before, imaging or pattern classification networks are several orders of magnitude simpler to train. Little or no adjustment to the weights is required and learning rules do not have to be changed.

Most learning equations have some provision for a learning rate, or learning constant. Usually this term is positive and between 0 and 1. If the learning rate is greater than 1, it is easy for the learning algorithm to "overshoot" in correcting the weights, and the network may oscillate. Small values of the learning rate will not correct the error as quickly, but if small steps are taken in correcting errors, there is a good chance of arriving at the minimum error and thus the optimum weight settings. The learning rate is, then, a measure of the speed of convergence of the network.

Training Techniques

In traditional programming, where highly structured programs such as FORTRAN are used, the programmer will be given the inputs, some type of processing requirements (what to do with the inputs), and the desired output. The programmer's job is to apply the necessary, minute, step-by-step instructions to develop the required relationship between the input and output.

Knowledge-based programming techniques (expert systems) use even higher-level concepts to specify relationships between inputs and outputs. These higher-level concepts are referred to as *heuristics*, or more commonly, *rules*.

In contrast, neural networks do not require any instructions, rules, or processing requirements about how to process the input data. In fact, neural networks determine the relationship between input and output by looking at examples of many input-output pairs. This unique ability to determine how to process the data is usually referred to as *self-organization*. The process of self-organizing is called *adaptation*, or *learning*.

Pairs of inputs and outputs are applied to the neural network. These pairs of data are used to teach or train the network, and as such are referred to as the *training set*. Knowing what output is expected from each input, the network learns by automatically adjusting or adapting the strengths of the connections between process elements. The method used for the adjusting process is called the *learning rule*.

You can imagine that the training set needs to be fairly large as well as to contain all needed information if the network to "learn" the features and relationships that are important. How to represent, or encode, the data is an important decision we talked about earlier (chapter 7).

Suppose you tried to teach a neural network one thing at a time before going on to something new. That approach doesn't work. All the weights set so meticulously for one fact could be drastically altered in learning the next fact. The previous facts could be "forgotten" in learning something new. As a result, the system has to learn everything together, finding the best weight settings for the total set of facts. In teaching a system to recognize pixel patterns for the ten digits, where you had, say, 20 examples of each digit, you would not present all the examples of the digit 7 at the same time.

After a supervised network performs well on the training data, then it is important to see what it can do with data it has not seen before. If a system does not give reasonable outputs for this test data, the training period is not over.

Learning Laws

Many learning laws are in common use. Most of the common ones are some sort of variation of the best known and oldest learning law, Hebb's Rule, or the Hebb synapse. Research has continued, however, and new ideas are being tried. Some researchers have the modeling of biological learning as their main objective; others are experimenting with adaptations of their perceptions of how nature handles learning. Unfortunately, there is still a great deal we don't know about how learning happens, and experimental evidence is not easy to obtain. Learning is certainly more complex than the simplifications represented by the laws we have developed.

Hebb's Rule

The first, and undoubtedly the best known, learning rule was introduced by Donald Hebb. The description appeared in his book *The Organization of Behavior* in 1949. His basic rule, simply stated, is this: If a processing element receives an input from another processing element, and if both are highly active (mathematically have the same sign), the weight between the processing elements should be strengthened.

The Delta Rule

This commonly used rule is based on the simple idea of continuously modifying the strengths of the connections to reduce the difference (the delta) between the desired output value and the current output value of a processing element. This rule is also referred to as the Widrow-Hoff Learning Rule (Widrow and Hoff used it in their ADALINE model) and the Least Mean Square (LMS) Learning Rule, because it minimizes the mean squared error.

Gradient Descent Rule

Here we have a mathematical approach to minimizing the error between actual and desired outputs. The weights are modified by an amount proportional to the first derivative of the error with respect to the weight. This rule is commonly used, even though it converges to a point of stability very slowly.

Pictorially, you could think of this procedure as descending along the curve to the bottom of a basin (see figure 8.4). Once you reach the bottom, the error is at its minimum; you would be at the lowest point on the basin. The Delta Rule is one example of a gradient descent rule.

Kohonen's Learning Law

This procedure, developed by Teuvo Kohonen, was inspired by learning in biological systems. It is employed only in unsupervised learning network applications. In this procedure, the pro-

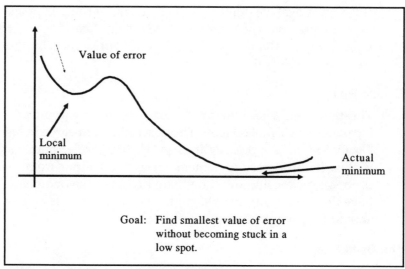

Goal: Find smallest value of error
without becoming stuck in a
low spot.

FIGURE 8.4   LOCAL MINIMUM VERSUS ACTUAL MINIMUM

cessing elements compete for the opportunity of learning. The processing element with the largest output is declared the winner and has the capability of inhibiting its competitors as well as exciting its neighbors. Only the winner is permitted an output, and only the winner plus its neighbors are permitted to adjust their weights.

Further, the size of the neighborhood can vary during the training period. The usual pattern is to start with a larger definition of the neighborhood, and narrow in as the training proceeds. Because the winning element is defined as the one that has the closest match to the input pattern, Kohonen networks model the distribution of the inputs. This leads to the feature mentioned in chapter 7, topology-preserving maps.

Back Propagation Learning

The back propagation of errors technique is the most commonly used generalization of the Delta Rule. This procedure involves two phases. The first phase, called the *forward phase*, occurs when the input is presented and propagated forward through the network to compute an output value for each processing element. For each PE, all current outputs are compared with the desired output, and the difference, or error, is computed.

A Practical Guide to Neural Nets

In the second phase, called the *backward phase*, the recurring difference computation (from the first phase) is now performed in a backward direction. Only when these two phases are complete can new inputs be presented.

Generally this technique is applied to hierarchical networks of three (or more) layers. At the output layer, there's no problem; you know the actual output from each node and also the expected output. The trick comes in adjusting the weights on hidden layers. What is the "desired" output for a hidden-layer PE? How do you tell how much each individual node from a preceding layer contributed to the total error at a given node? The information from the forward phase tells you how much each input influenced the error at that node. With two phases, all the weights can be appropriately adjusted.

So far there doesn't appear to be any evidence that this method is used in biological systems. Additionally, there are several important drawbacks: back propagation is very slow, requires much off-line training, exhibits temporal instability (can oscillate), and has a tendency to become stuck at local minima. This last item occurs when the system finds an error that is lower than the surrounding possibilities but does not finally get to the smallest possible error. Often, researchers will add a term to their computations to "bump" weights past barriers and find the actual minimum rather than a temporary "pocket." (See figure 8.4.)

Grossberg Learning

Stephen Grossberg has done neural network research for many years. He read the work of Donald Hebb and studied biological models and Pavlovian conditioning. (You probably took a psychology class somewhere along the line that highlighted Pavlov's famous experiment in teaching a dog to salivate at the sound of a bell.) Grossberg's learning law combines Hebbian learning with biological forgetting. The mathematical calculations are not easy, but the concepts are relatively familiar.

In Grossberg's model, every neural network is made up of *instars* and *outstars*. An instar is a processing element receiving many inputs; an outstar is a processing element sending its output to many other PEs. (This terminology could be applied to components of any network.) Here, the connections allow recall of a concentrated image from a single outstar node; the pattern is stored distributively. If both the input and output activity of a node are high, the weights change significantly. If either the total input or the output is small, however, the change in weights is very small, and weights could approach o on unimportant connections.

Time is important in Grossberg learning. If an input stimulus is removed, over time there is less output response as forgetting sets in. The threshold is important. If it is set too high, the network responds to every little nuance; if it is set too low, the network ignores too much. Learning must be separate from observation. During recall, learning is turned off. There also needs to be a term in the equation to control the rate of learning.

Grossberg's Avalanche model uses the above concepts in a sort of moving picture implementation. Each "frame" in time records the relationships of inputs to output. As a result, different outputs could result from activating the same node at different points in time. Possible applications are continuous speech recognition and commands to robot arms.

Drive-Reinforcement Theory

Drive-Reinforcement Theory (DRT), developed by Harry Klopf, is more of a learning model than a neural network model. To understand the name, think about your own biological drives, such as hunger, thirst, sexual desire, and fear. You experience positive drives when the stimulation is excitatory and negative ones when the stimulation has an inhibitory effect. DRT has similarities to Grossberg learning in that it also attempts to model classic Pavlovian conditioning behavior in animals; however, DRT is even more biologically rigorous.

In this scheme, processing elements can be conditioned by certain types of inputs that serve as rewarding stimuli and others that act as punishing stimuli. The PE learns how to attain some inputs and avoid others by adjusting its weights. Unlike in Hebb's rule, in DRT, the change in strength of an input is proportional to the product of changes in output and input. Moreover, the current output depends on the previous input rather than the current input.

The timing sequence in presenting the conditioning stimulus (such as the bell) *before* presenting the unconditioned stimulus (such as the food) becomes very important. The strength of the response (which would be the salivation of the dog in the Pavlovian example) is measured by the frequency with which the processing element fires. This, too, models biological systems and is different from most implementations, which measure the response by the size of the output rather than the frequency.

AT present, DRT is used as a research tool. There are few applications so far, though the Pac-Man example in chapter 5 is an example of the type of unsupervised learning that is possible with this learning law. Experiments have demonstrated the ability to reproduce classical conditioning phenomena and robot control simulations. Possibilities for applications include forecasting and control.

Other Learning Techniques

Boltzmann and Cauchy machines both use stochastic learning procedures rather than deterministic ones. (Stochastic means involving chance, probability, or a random variable.) This is rather like learning by a "throw of the dice." A processing unit can assume a new state even if the result is an overall increase in energy. Referring back to figure 8.4, a node stuck in a local minimum might be able to get out by initially going uphill. Then there is a good chance of finding the global energy minimum.

An introduction to a paper on "Learning Algorithms for Boltzmann Machines" gives this definition of the model: "All states of the network are possible at thermal equilibrium, with their relative probabilities given by the Boltzmann distribution. If the probability of the states in the network are the same as the probabilities of states in the environment, then the network has an accurate model of the environment. This is a strange definition of learning, but useful in many situations."[3]

The Neocognitron model of Fukushima assumes the builder of the network knows roughly the features that will be required, and it uses this to solve the credit assignment problem of hidden layer nodes. More complex PEs in one layer respond to features picked up by simpler nodes in the previous layer. Learning progresses sequentially up a hierarchy. Further, the complex PEs also direct inputs and can respond before simpler nodes do. Stages of response and abstraction follow each other. (One of the applications of Neocognitron networks is the recognition of handwritten characters. Japan, not surprisingly, has a large commercial market for this because of its written language.)

Simulated annealing techniques are being applied to such practical problems as the layout of computer chips, routing of wires on a printed circuit board, and the famous traveling salesman problem. This type of learning, a statistical mechanics method for solving complex optimization problems, has its basis in physics. When a system is started at a high temperature and gradually cooled, the process is referred to as annealing. Examples would be the growing of a crystal or the cooling of a metal. (A crystal is the lowest energy state of many solids. Crystals can be grown by melting a solid and then cooling the system very gradually so that the system can reach this lowest energy state. The slower the cooling, the larger and more regular the final crystal is liable to be.)

Many other learning rules are available. We recommend the *DARPA Neural Network Study* and the collection of papers in Anderson and Rosenfeld's *Neurocomputing: Foundations of Research* for further information (see appendix B).

Architecture and Learning Paradigms

Neural networks have unique characteristics attributable to their particular architecture and neurodynamics. How the processing elements are connected plays a big part in this. Connections may use feedback or feedforward techniques; networks may have partial or full connectivity. The result of combining the processing elements, the neurodynamics, and the architecture in a particular manner is a neural network *paradigm.*

Many neural network paradigms have evolved over the past decade. Each is specifically designed to solve a particular type of problem. For example, back propagation is good for approximating functional relationships, and other network paradigms are better at combinatorial optimization problems. Some paradigms are intended especially for signal processing applications.

Tables 8.1 through 8.4 present the most generally used and best known neural network paradigms. The horizontal headings show the acronym or abbreviation for each paradigm represented, the type of problem it is best at solving, if on-line or off-line training is required, whether the paradigm is a "pattern matcher,"

Table 8.1: Unsupervised Learning: Feedback Recall Artificial Neural Systems

Paradigm	Problem Type Solved	On-line Learning	Off-line Learning	Pattern Matching	Type Learning	Limitations	Implementation
AG	Unsupervised data classification	Yes	No	Yes	Hebbian	Limited storage	Optical and electronic
SG	Human information processing	Yes	No	Yes	Hebbian	Limited storage	Electronic
ART1	Classify complex patterns	Yes	No	Yes	Competitive decay	Restricted to binary	Neural computer
DH	Speech processing	No	Yes	No	Hebbian	Restricted to binary	Optical electronic VLSI
CH	Combinatorial optimization	No	Yes	Yes	Hebbian or competitive	Limited storage	Optical electronic VLSI
BAM	Image recognition	No	Yes	Yes	Hebbian	Extensive off-line learning	Optical and neural computer
TAM	Store spatial-temporal patterns	No	Yes	No	Hebbian	Extensive off-line learning	Computer simulation
ABAM	Process analog patterns in continuous time	Yes	No	Yes	Hebbian	Limited storage	Neural computer
CABAM	Combinatorial optimization	Yes	Yes	Yes	Hebbian	Limited storage	Computer simulation
FCM	Combinatorial optimization	Yes	Yes	No	Hebbian	Extensive off-line learning	Computer simulation

Table 8.2: Unsupervised Learning: Feedforward Recall Artificial Neural Systems

Paradigm	Problem Type Solved	On-line Learning	Off-line Learning	Pattern Matching	Type Learning	Limitations	Implementation
LM	Process Monitoring	No	Yes	Yes	Hebbian	None reported	Mechanical electronic magnetic
DR	Prediction	No	Yes	Yes	Hebbian	Restricted to discrete time	Robot simulations
LAM	System control	No	Yes	Yes	Hebbian	Limited storage	Computer simulation
OLAM	Signal processing	No	Yes	Yes	Hebbian	Extensive off-line learning	Optical
FAM	Knowledge processing	Yes	No	Yes	Hebbian	Limited storage	Computer simulation and silicon chip

Table 8.3: Supervised Learning: Feedforward Recall Artificial Neural Systems

Paradigm	Problem Type Solved	On-line Learning	Off-line Learning	Pattern Matching	Type Learning	Limitations	Implementation
BSB	Real-time classification	No	Yes	Yes	Error correction	Extensive off-line learning	Computer simulation

Table 8.4: Supervised Learning: Feedback Recall Artificial Neural Systems

Paradigm	Problem Type Solved	On-line Learning	Off-line Learning	Pattern Matching	Type Learning	Limitations	Implementation
Perceptron	Prediction	No	Yes	Yes	Error correction	None reported	Mark I perceptron machine
ADALINE/MADALINE	Prediction noise-canceling	No	Yes	Yes	Error correction	Extensive off-line learning	Magnetic optical
BP	Crypting character-recognition	No	Yes	Yes	Error correction	Extensive off-line learning	Optical electronic VLSI
AVQ	Self-organization of data	No	Yes	Yes	Error correcion	Extensive off-line learning	Neural-computer VLSI
CPN	Self-programming	No	Yes	Yes	Hebbian	Lack of control w/o star mapping	Neural computer
BM	Combinatorial optimization	No	Yes	Yes	Hebbian and simulated annealing	Extensive off-line learning	Optical electronic VLSI
CM	Combinatorial optimization	No	Yes	Yes	Hebbian and simulated annealing	Extensive off-line learning	Optical
AHC	Prediction control	Yes	No	No	Error correction and reward/punish	Restricted to bipolar inputs	Computer simulation
ARP	Pattern-matching control	Yes	No	Yes	Stochastic reinforcement	Extensive off-line learning	Computer simulation
SNMF	Speech-image-recognition	No	Yes	Yes	Hebbian	Extensive off-line learning	Computer simulation

the type of learning equation used, known limitations with this paradigm, and how the paradigm has been implemented. The following list defines the abbreviations used in the tables:

Acronym	Definition
AG	Additive Grossberg
SG	Shunting Grossberg
ART1	Binary Adaptive Resonance Theory
DH	Discrete Hopfield
CH	Continuous Hopfield
BAM	Discrete Bidirectional Associative Memory
TAM	Temporal Associative Memory
ABAM	Adaptive Bidirectional Associative Memory
CABAM	Competitive ABAM
FCM	Fuzzy Cognitive Map
LM	Learning Matrix
DR	Drive Reinforcement
LAM	Linear Associative Memory
OLAM	Optimal Linear Associative Memory
FAM	Fuzzy Associative Memory
BSB	Brain-State-in-a-Box
PERCEP	Perceptron
ADALINE	ADAptive LINear Element
MADALINE	Multiple ADAptive LINear Element
BP	Back Propagation
AVQ	Adaptive Vector Quantizer
CPN	Counterpropagation
BM	Boltzman Machine
CM	Cauchy Machine
ARP	Associative Reward-Penalty
SNMF	Spatiotemporal Nearest-Matched Filter

Typical Equations Used in Neural Networks

Figure 8.5 shows some of the typical equations used in neural dynamics. Please refer to appendix C for a detailed treatment of the most common paradigm neural dynamic equations.

Research Areas

Learning constitutes one of the key features of a neural network. Most current models and applications use some form of supervised learning where the correct outputs are known ahead of time. These outputs are specific solutions for specific problems. This approach has limitations, because in many real-life situations a certain amount of novelty is present. It is impossible to predict and code rules for all eventualities.

One important research area emphasizes learning that builds an internal model of "the world." Learning is through interaction

INPUT: $X_i(t) = \sigma[a_j(t)]$ WHERE a_j IS A VECTOR

LEARNING: $\dfrac{d}{dt}\, a_j(t) = Q\, a_j(t) + \displaystyle\sum_{i=1}^{N}\sum_{j=1}^{N} W_{ij}\sigma[a_i(t)] + f_j(t)$MATRIX

MEMORY: $\dfrac{d}{dt}\, W_{ij}(t) = \Phi\, W_{ij}(t) + \bigwedge\; (X_{ij}\, a_{ij}\, w_{ij})$VECTOR NOTATION

ENERGY: $E_w(\overline{X}) = Q(\overline{X}, W)$

RECALL: $a_j(t+1) = f\left[a_j(t) + B \displaystyle\sum_{i=1}^{N}\sum_{j=1}^{N} W_{ij}\, a_i(t) \right]$

STABILITY: $L(A) = \dfrac{1}{2} \displaystyle\sum_{i=1}^{N}\sum_{j=1}^{N} a_i a_j W_{ij} - \sum_{j=1}^{N} a_i\, [a_i - f(a_i)]$

CONVERGENCE: $\dfrac{\partial}{\partial W_{ij}} = E[(d_j)^2]$

FIGURE 8.5 TYPICAL EQUATIONS USED IN NEURAL DYNAMICS

with the environment rather than being preprogrammed. Complex behaviors are built up over time. Once this is done, it would be possible to simulate the external environment and even to make predictions about possible interactions.

It would be fairly easy to have a network learn the path to the goal (G1) in the maze in figure 8.6. Suppose, however, you blocked off the usual path or moved the goal. If the network knew the entire maze environment, it would be relatively easy to find an alternative route, if one existed. That would be much different from having to start all over from scratch, and would undeniably provide much greater flexibility to a system. Robots operating in dynamic environments would need to have an internal model of their world.

Another area of great interest to researchers has to do with "attention." Humans can give attention to particular inputs in a field of many inputs. Most mothers, for example, seem to have a built-in selective radar to distinguish their baby's crying and tell the fussy from the serious sounds. Neural networks likewise will need to be able to distinguish significant inputs from similar but insignificant ones.

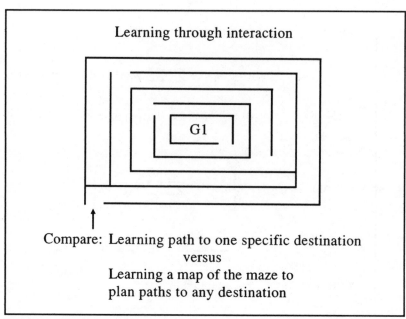

Learning through interaction

G1

↑
Compare: Learning path to one specific destination
versus
Learning a map of the maze to
plan paths to any destination

FIGURE 8.6 INTERNAL WORLD MODELS

The Neocognitron paradigm can pay selective attention to particular elements in visual pattern recognition.[4] The model automatically segments and recognizes individual patterns that are presented simultaneously. A momentary interruption of the backward signal flow allows the model to switch attention to another pattern. Further, it can restore imperfect patterns and eliminate noise from contaminated patterns. Most other paradigms that do the latter do not work well unless the stimulus pattern is identical in size, shape, and position to a training pattern. Fukushima's model works well even for deformed stimulus patterns, regardless of their position.

Robert Hecht-Nielsen calls attentional neurocomputers "a new theme for the 1990s" made possible by recent breakthroughs in neuroscience.[5] It may take the rest of the decade, or longer, says Hecht-Nielsen, to realize such machines, but "the payoff from their development will be substantial." Automatic target recognition, for example, will require an image or sound stream to be searched for objects with arbitrary combinations of attributes specified only moments before. If researchers accomplish this,

A Practical Guide to Neural Nets

other things will also be possible, such as searching text for passages with particular combinations of meaning attributes.

Hecht-Nielsen describes the recent discoveries of Grey and Singer (of the Max Planck Institute for Brain Research in Frankfurt, West Germany). Their findings may alter some of the existing theories of how brains carry out sensory processing. The Soviet government has also been studying models of biological attention (since the early 1970s) and recently established the International Center for Attentional Neurocomputers in Pushchino. Results from neurobiological research can lead to useful ideas for engineering—what Bart Kosko terms the "third wave" of neurocomputing, where such technology transfer will be commonplace.

The problem of attention is related to the problem of sensor fusion. Sensor fusion is the combining of data from several different sensors to better clarify a pattern or to perform more complete processing. An autonomous land vehicle (such as the NAV-LAB described in chapter 11) could fuse data from a video-camera and a laser range finder. This would allow it to determine the position and orientation of a road more accurately than would be possible with either sensor alone.

This approach is common in the animal kingdom. Sharks appear to have one of the most remarkable detection systems in all of nature, with a number of different sensors providing information for locating food. The sense of smell is good. In fact, sharks can't locate food when their nostrils are plugged. Odors allow them to zero in on a wounded fish from a quarter of a mile away or more. Using both taste and smell, sharks can home in on ounces of blood diffused in the sea. Then the eyes, which have poor visibility underwater, can take over. Or, extremely sensitive electroreceptors, sensory organs located in the head, help locate hidden prey buried beneath the sand (as well as orient the sharks in the open sea electromagnetically). Another sensor, a sonar-like apparatus, uses echolocation to detect both distant pressure disturbances and changes of flow patterns nearby. All of these different sensors work together to help the shark find a meal.[6]

Sensor fusion can be a complicated process. Data from both radio frequency and imaging infrared, for example, are used in target identification, where mistakes can be disastrous. Some researchers working on data fusion problems feel they can learn from nature's examples. Does nature preprocess the data? Are the data from the different sensors combined before processing, or are they processed separately and then combined? Suppose the sensors give contradictory information—what then? Neural networks have been shown to work well with partial and somewhat conflicting (erroneous) data, and to be applicable to sensor fusion problems.

Summary

A few water and dust molecules by themselves are not terribly impressive. Trillions of molecules together create the air patterns that we call weather. A few processing elements by themselves do very simple tasks. Collectively they can do impressive things— things we call "intelligent." They can adapt their "behavior" in response to varying inputs. Critics might say that neural networks just do a good job of keeping statistics. Whatever, there's no denying the ability of prototype artificial neural networks to perform responsively.

However, we don't wish to go overboard in our claims of what these systems can accomplish. They are still only machines. Their architecture is limited. Designers may implement architectures and learning rules that work well for specific types of generalizations but that don't work well at all for other types of tasks. We, though, can apply our common sense, make analogies, intuit beyond logic, and adapt to wonderfully different circumstances. Machines are not likely to replace us anytime soon.

We began this chapter with a definition of learning, and we'll end with another. Perhaps this is a definition fit for machines. "Learning can be defined as any deliberate or directed change in the knowledge structure of a system that allows it to perform better on later repetitions of some given type of task."[7] In a changing environment, it is impossible to anticipate all eventualities; "intelligent" systems must be able to adapt. Learning is clearly an essential component of intelligent behavior.

1. Pamela McCorduck, *Machines Who Think* (New York: W. H. Freeman and Company, 1979).

2. *DARPA Neural Network Study* (Fairfax, VA: AFCEA International Press, November 1988).

A Practical Guide to Neural Nets

3. David H. Ackley, Geoffrey E. Hinton, and Terrence J. Sejnowski, Introduction to "A Learning Algorithm for Boltzmann Machines," in *Neurocomputing: Foundations of Research*, Anderson and Rosenfeld, eds. (Cambridge, MA: MIT Press, 1988), p. 363.

4. Kunihiko Fukushima, "A Neural Network for Visual Pattern Recognition," *IEEE Computer*, vol. 21, no. 3, (March 1988): p. 65–75.

5. Robert Hecht-Nielsen, "Attentional Neurocomputing Deserves More Attention," *Electronic Engineering Times*, issue 575 (January 29, 1990): T28, T44 (special insert).

6. Edith Pavese, editor. *Jacques Cousteau: The Ocean World* (New York: Harry N. Abrams, 1985).

7. Martin A. Fischler and Oscar Firschein, *Intelligence: The Eye, the Brain, and the Computer* (Reading, MA: Addison-Wesley, 1987), p. 129.

How Do You Move from Theory to Applications?

I hear and I forget.
I see and I remember.
I do and I understand.
   —*Confucius*

This chapter tells a story. It represents the personal experience of one of the authors, Bill Illingworth, and one of his engineers, Bill Davis, in learning about neural networks by building them. It seems appropriate here to switch our writing style to first person and let Bill Illingworth share his experiences and his insights.

Getting Started: One Approach

The absolute fastest way to get started in moving from theory to an actual hands-on application is with specific simulation software. Our own experience can be used to best illustrate this most important method of getting started in neural networks.

After spending more than a year reading every paper that our library could find, including many on the neurobiological aspects of neurons, postsynaptic and presynaptic signals, and so on, I was becoming neural-net saturated. Perhaps even supersaturated! And I still didn't have the faintest idea how to design a neural network. I tried sketching network diagrams, writing input equations, summation equations, and transfer equations. I tried placing the results in circles, graphically building processing elements. I tediously completed the resulting calculations for each and every processing element output.

After many, many hours of laborious work, I reached a startling conclusion . . . I needed help! I had previously attended several workshops and had been introduced to several software packages. Looking to see what was available, I chose Neural-Works Professional II. Other packages could probably have produced similar results, but I particularly like NeuralWare's graphics capabilities and displays. (The graphics on the diskette included with this book are compliments of NeuralWare.) This software package eventually brought me closer to designing a neural network in several weeks than I had come in all my efforts for the previous two years.

Initially, my interest in the networks was only a hobby. I had many other pressing duties, so I gave the neural software to one of my engineers. He had no previous experience or knowledge relative to neural networks, but I asked him to investigate what it would require to actually design a specific neural network to solve a problem we were currently looking at in process control. This was mid-January of 1989. I didn't expect to hear from this engineer for six months.

Three days later, I was astonished when he successfully demonstrated on his PC a specifically designed neural network that indeed solved the particular manufacturing process problem. This young engineer had accomplished what appeared to be a minor miracle in just three days with the help of the neural network software package. He not only solved the process problem, but more importantly, he now had an equal, if not greater, understanding of neural networks than I had.

He continued developing and modifying the network until he was satisfied. This effort produced three additional networks, each utilizing different paradigms and requiring varying degrees of off-line training. He evaluated these three paradigms from every aspect, including convergence, training, accuracy, consistency and process predictability. He then wrote a paper on his efforts (which was immediately accepted by the Third Annual Parallel Computer Processing Conference at California State University in March of 1989).

His expertise in rapidly prototyping various neural networks was unbelievable. He could easily do a 96-process-element neural network, fully connected, in less than a day. It took an additional day to modify the weights and evaluate the network. Off-line training took approximately 24 hours and could be done unattended, overnight.

Summing up, I can state categorically that there is no substitute for hands-on experience. I have learned more neural network technology in developing networks on my PC in a few weeks than in all the previous literature searches over the previous two years.

In the following paragraphs, we will walk through several networks to illustrate how the input/output data are prepared, and how the training and testing sets are organized. We will also indicate the paradigm, the transfer function, the learning rule, number of network layers, how to randomize the weights and, finally, how to solve problems with neural networks.

Preparing the Network Data

Regardless of what network paradigm, architecture, transfer function, or learning rule you select when prototyping a neural network, the approach is always the same. Success depends upon a clear understanding of the problem. Try writing a brief narrative description of what you want the neural network to do. Then jot down the input data as you now understand it. Don't be concerned as to the format, units, or the range of the data. For example, you might have "degrees Celsius" for temperature and "feet per second" for belt speed in the same set of inputs. For now, all that is necessary is that you get a handle on the inputs as far as the range is concerned. Then write down what you desire as an output. If you are an experienced computer programmer, please try to forget your coding experience, because no programming is required. As is illustrated in figure 9.1, neural nets do not learn from a set of rules or from a series of structured instructions. Neural networks learn by example and cannot be programmed in the traditional sense.

Again, before walking through several examples, I want to remind you that a complete understanding of the problem to be solved by the neural network is paramount. It has been suggested that most of the "black magic" in neural networks comes in defining and preparing the training input set. Since neural networks are pattern matchers, the representation of the data contained in the training sets is critical to the successful solution by the neural

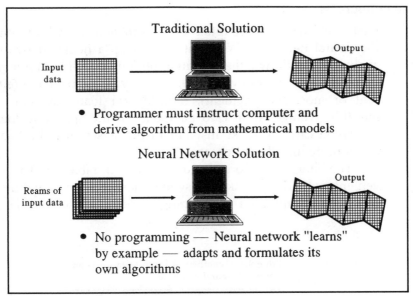

Traditional Solution

Input data • Programmer must instruct computer and derive algorithm from mathematical models

Neural Network Solution

Reams of input data • No programming — Neural network "learns" by example — adapts and formulates its own algorithms

FIGURE 9.1 TRADITIONAL VERSUS NEURAL NETWORK SOLUTIONS

network. The data sets in the input training set, as well as the desired output, should be as orthogonal as possible; that is, the variables contained in the data sets should be independent with no correlation. James Anderson said it best: "A good representation does most of the work. Neural networks no matter what kind, are weak computers, but a proper representation, coupled with the abstracting and cooperative effects of the network, can become extremely fast, powerful, and accurate."[1]

Once you have described the problem and listed the input data sets with the desired outputs, then the rest of the development of the neural network will simply fall into place.

Five Network Applications on a PC

As we proceed through five examples, you will note that we use different data representation schemes for different applications. The first step each time is to decide how to represent your information for presentation to the neural network. Do not be concerned about the mechanics or just how the neural network will process this information. Believe me, the neural network knows what to do and will take care of that problem nicely.

How Do You Move from Theory to Applications?   155

Loan Approval

First, we'll write a description of the problem we will present to the neural network: "We want to develop a neural network to analyze instantly whether a loan applicant is qualified for a loan, based on gross monthly income, monthly house payment (either rent or mortgage payment), monthly car loan payment, and monthly average credit card payments. If the applicant doesn't use credit cards to make installment purchases, use the total of all monthly installment charges."

The data may be organized as shown in table 9.1. This convenient method will make it easy for us to prepare many different hypothetical inputs for the training (or learning) set and the test set.

Table 9.1: Hypothetical Input Data for Loan Approval Neural Network

Monthly Income	House Payment	Car Payment	Plastic Payment	Qualified
10000	2500	500	300	Yes
9000	4500	900	900	No
8000	3300	900	1100	No
7000	1700	500	300	Yes
6000	1500	300	200	Yes
5000	2700	900	780	No
4500	1100	300	100	Yes
4000	1400	700	350	No
3500	800	300	100	Yes
3000	600	200	100	Yes
2500	500	250	50	Yes
2000	385	155	0	Yes
1500	600	250	50	No
1000	300	350	100	No
500	200	250	0	No

Networks can't get too many examples to train on. We use the data in table 9.1, which lists data that are both within and not within the following guidelines: "If the applicant's house payment is equal to or less than approximately 30 percent of gross income and the sum of all three payments is equal to or less than approximately 35 percent of gross income, then the applicant is qualified for a loan." (Source of guidelines: averaged from information from several local credit unions in Dallas, Texas.)

Table 9.2 illustrates how we put together the inputs and desired outputs required for the training of the neural network. Please note that inputs are scaled between 0 and 1. This is necessary because we will be using a sigmoid transfer function in all

Table 9.2: Example of Input Data Format for Loan Approval Neural Network Application

Item	Salary	House	Car	Plastic	Output
1	1.00	.50	.50	.2	1
2	.90	.90	.90	.6	0
3	.80	.66	.90	.7	0
4	.70	.34	.50	.2	1
5	.60	.30	.30	.1	1
6	.50	.54	.90	.5	0
7	.45	.22	.30	.1	1
8	.40	.28	.70	.2	0
9	.35	.16	.30	.1	1
10	.30	.12	.20	.1	1
11	.25	.10	.25	.0	1
12	.20	.08	.16	.0	1
13	.15	.12	.25	.0	0
14	.10	.06	.35	.1	0
15	.05	.04	.25	.0	0

our applications (figure 4.11 shows a graph of a sigmoid function). We will employ the most commonly used paradigm, the back propagation-cumulative network. See figure 9.2 for the criteria and other selections necessary to build our computer application for the loan approval neural network. An explanation of terms follows.

The diagram in figure 9.2 shows only the first two connections and implies the rest, a common network representation scheme. (In the next application, where we demonstrate imaging, we will explain in detail how we format the input data sets as well as how we print out and read the output test results.)

When we call up the development program we are first required to select the paradigm (for example, back propagation, Kohonen, Brain-State-in-a-Box, and so forth). We selected back propagation-delta-cumulative. The cumulative refers to the manner in which we will calculate the error. In this case, the error will be delta (the difference between actual and desired output) and will be collected cumulatively, as opposed to individually, at the processing element level prior to being acted upon.

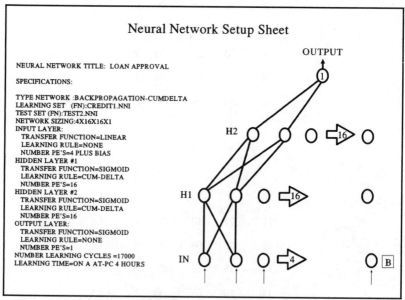

FIGURE 9.2 SPECIFICATIONS FOR LOAN APPROVAL NETWORK

The next requirement is to decide on the number of input nodes. We then select the number of nodes in the first hidden layer. In most cases, except for imaging, we use four or five hidden layer neurons to one input neuron. In imaging we use significantly fewer neurons in the hidden layers. The number of pixels in the image determine the exact size of the input layer. (For example, 100 pixels will require exactly 100 neurons.) We establish the size of the hidden layer by taking 10 percent of the input layer size. (For example, if the input layer is 100 neurons then the hidden layer is 10 neurons.) The output layer in imaging is almost always just one neuron.

The development program automatically will insert a bias node that is located graphically at the input layer and that is interconnected to each neuron, with the exception of the input nodes. The program requests a file name that we must assign to the network. On the same specification sheet, the development program requires the file name of our neural network input file (NNI). We are also requested to enter either a file name for the test file or the recall file. The NNI file is always the training set and will automatically generate an output (NNO) file immediately after the execution of either a test set or a recall of the training set. Many times we will train the network until recalling the original training set results in satisfactory performance as measured and determined by the neural network output report (NNO).

When we are ready to test the network with data never seen before by the network, we must indicate the file name of the new data file to the network by changing the specification window. Then we must copy the test file to the network directory. If we are concerned with imaging or pattern classification, we almost always eliminate the recall tests and go directly to a test set.

Image Processing

Imaging applications for neural networks seem to be a natural fit. One could conclude that neural nets love to do pattern classification. The supervised, off-line training is very fast and usually error-free. In the course of our work, we were able to classify and select solder joint images with an input image matrix of 30 by 30 pixels, containing 256 shades of gray, with little trouble.

Let's walk through a simple imaging, or pattern classifier, application. Our goal is to develop a neural network that can recognize the numerals 0 through 9. Each of these numerals can easily be represented and recognized in a four-by-seven matrix, using just two shades of gray, namely black and white. Alternatively, we may represent each numeral by a matrix of 1s and 0s. Each image, or numeral, then requires an input containing 28 digits made up of only 0s and 1s.

Experience has shown that when we prepare the input data for both the training set and the test set in image applications, much is gained by representing the data in matrix form, as in figure 9.3a.

In the numeral image for "2" in figure 9.3a, the 0 represents the absence of light and the 1 represents black. Figure 9.3b illustrates this pattern.

In order for the neural network software to recognize the input data, we must enter each image or number serially. For the numeral image "2", we would have:

```
I  1111000100011111100010001111
D  2
```

The I stands for input and the D is for desired output. Because we must represent ten numerals with desired outputs between 0

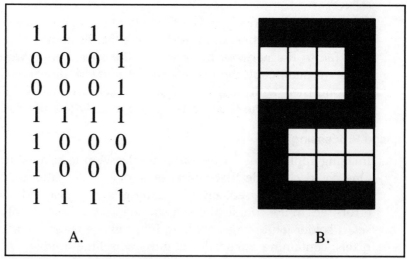

FIGURE 9.3 REPRESENTING THE NUMERAL 2

and 9, it is convenient to assign each numeral image its numeric value. That is, 0 = 0, 1 = 1, 2 = 2 . . . 9 = 9.

When the training set is constructed, it is necessary to train the network with the correct numeral image inputs; we will not be concerned with non-numerals during the training. Next we prepare the data for presentation to the neural network software development program. The following example shows a shortcut method of inputting image matrices. For the numeral "2" we first write the following:

```
I        1 1 1 1
               1
               1
         1 1 1 1
         1
         1
         1 1 1 1
D 2
```

Then fill in the zeros:

```
I        1 1 1 1
         0 0 0 1
         0 0 0 1
         1 1 1 1
         1 0 0 0
         1 0 0 0
         1 1 1 1
D 2
```

A non-numeral is illustrated for use in presenting test data never seen by the neural network before. Please note that we do not label desired output (D) as we must in preparing a training set. After all, when teaching a class of students, we drum into them the desired output (answers), but we do not reveal the answers when giving them a test.

Again, the "I" stands for input and always precedes the input data. Therefore, a typical non-numeral in a test set might appear as:

```
I        1 0 0 0
         0 1 1 1
         0 1 0 0
         1 0 0 0
         0 0 0 0
         0 0 0 0
         0 0 0 0
```

The training set is shown in figure 9.4. Again, notice that we do not have to train the network to recognize non-numerals, only numerals. In the test set, however, we will include non-numerals to test the network's ability to differentiate and recognize the ten numerals on which it was trained.

Constructing the test set will be similar to constructing the training set except that we will purposely try to confuse the network with mixed-up matrices, not unlike the noise present in an electrical circuit. We can experiment and place repeated numerals as well as almost-numerals in the test set. We will see that the network will generalize. For example, if we present the network with an almost-numeral two, it will report its results as almost a two. Figure 9.5 is a typical test set for a first trial. You will find it

```
D1              D2              D3              D4              D5
I 0 0 1 0       I 1 1 1 1       I 1 1 1 1       I 1 0 0 1       I 1 1 1 1
  0 0 1 0         0 0 0 1         0 0 0 1         1 0 0 1         1 0 0 0
  0 0 1 0         0 0 0 1         0 0 0 1         1 0 0 1         1 0 0 0
  0 0 1 0         1 1 1 1         1 1 1 1         1 1 1 1         1 1 1 1
  0 0 1 0         1 0 0 0         0 0 0 1         0 0 0 1         0 0 0 1
  0 0 1 0         1 0 0 0         0 0 0 1         0 0 0 1         0 0 0 1
  0 1 1 1         1 1 1 1         1 1 1 1         0 0 0 1         1 1 1 1

D6              D7              D8              D9              D10
I 1 0 0 0       I 1 1 1 1       I 1 1 1 1       I 1 1 1 1       I 1 1 1 1
  1 0 0 0         0 0 0 1         1 0 0 1         1 0 0 1         1 0 0 1
  1 0 0 0         0 0 0 1         1 0 0 1         1 0 0 1         1 0 0 1
  1 1 1 1         0 0 0 1         1 1 1 1         1 1 1 1         1 0 0 1
  1 0 0 1         0 0 0 1         1 0 0 1         0 0 0 1         1 0 0 1
  1 0 0 1         0 0 0 1         1 0 0 1         0 0 0 1         1 0 0 1
  1 1 1 1         0 0 0 1         1 1 1 1         1 1 1 1         1 1 1 1
```

FIGURE 9.4 TRAINING SETS FOR TEN NUMERALS

```
I 1111      I 1111      I 1111      I 1111      I 0000
  1001        0001        1111        1000        1110
  1001        0001        0000        1000        0000
  1111        1111        0111        1111        0100
  1001        1000        0000        0001        0001
  1001        1000        0011        0001        1001
  1111        1111        0000        1111        0010
```

FIGURE 9.5 FIRST TRIAL TEST SET

A Practical Guide to Neural Nets

most interesting to devise other test sets for experimental and instructional purposes.

Neural Network Output Interpretation: The output report found in figure 9.6 was printed by the neural network development software program.

In the imaging neural network that we developed specifically to gather data for this section, we interpreted the results as given in figure 9.6. It should be pointed out that different neural network architectures will generate different output results for the same problem. However, the results generated in the output file will logically be interpreted with the same results. That is, the output file for the problem shown in figure 9.6 might interpret an 8 as 7.9989 or 7.9999, provided that you use the same desired outputs. The important point is that it will be quite clear whether the neural network truly recognized the numerals 8, 2, and 5 as well as correctly recognizing the two non-numerals.

Specifications for our imaging neural network are shown in figure 9.7.

Comments on Interpreting the Imaging Network Output File: The interpretation of output values less than 0.8 as non-numerals is (within a range) arbitrary. We could have selected <.5, but experience has shown that pattern classification neural networks are extremely accurate. Selecting the wider range—even though 0.8 is very close to 0.99 (which is interpreted as the numeral 1)—will not affect the numeral 1 and will eliminate non-numerals that are

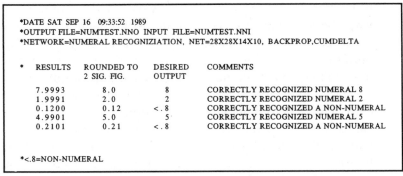

```
*DATE SAT SEP 16  09:33:52  1989
*OUTPUT FILE=NUMTEST.NNO  INPUT FILE=NUMTEST.NNI
*NETWORK=NUMERAL RECOGNIZIATION, NET=28X28X14X10, BACKPROP,CUMDELTA


*   RESULTS   ROUNDED TO   DESIRED    COMMENTS
              2 SIG. FIG.  OUTPUT
    7.9993    8.0          8          CORRECTLY RECOGNIZED NUMERAL 8
    1.9991    2.0          2          CORRECTLY RECOGNIZED NUMERAL 2
    0.1200    0.12         <.8        CORRECTLY RECOGNIZED A NON-NUMERAL
    4.9901    5.0          5          CORRECTLY RECOGNIZED NUMERAL 5
    0.2101    0.21         <.8        CORRECTLY RECOGNIZED A NON-NUMERAL


*<.8=NON-NUMERAL
```

FIGURE 9.6   RESULTS OF TEST SET PRESENTED TO IMAGING NEURAL NETWORK

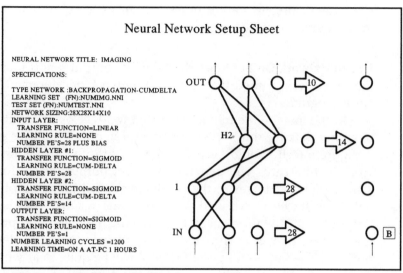

FIGURE 9.7 SPECIFICATIONS FOR IMAGING NEURAL NETWORK

almost a numeral 1. In other words, a perfect numeral 1 (as learned by the network) will always result in an output of 0.999xx. Similarly, a perfect numeral 4 will always result in an output of 3.999xx, and a perfect numeral 7 will always appear as 6.999xx. After all, we trained the network to give us an output of 1 for numeral 1, an output of 4 for numeral 4, and an output of 7 for numeral 7. Only an ideal, fully trained network with absolute zero error will yield the exact value of the desired numeral output. One must admit that 3.999xx is very close to 4. Again, the only way that there could be significant differences in the output file is when you train the network with the same ten numerals but use different desired outputs. However, a non-numeral will always be less than 0.50000. An almost-numeral 4 will be in the range of 3.00000 to 3.50000, but will never be 3.99900. The important interpretation is that rounding up to two significant figures will eliminate the non-numerals and almost-numerals.

It is interesting to note that in some instances where we are employing a neural network to read numbers, we then utilize the almost-numeral data to a considerable advantage. We can read part numbers that have been partially obscured quite accurately. Interpreting the NNO file results is a science all its own. One can be most innovative here.

A Practical Guide to Neural Nets

Some additional side notes on pattern classification. We have seen that the input requirements are equal to the number of pixels in the matrix. If we have a 900-pixel image where the area of interest is square, we have a 30-by-30 matrix. The input layer required for the 900-pixel image is then 900 processing elements. We have found that a single hidden layer node per about 50 input nodes will satisfy our requirements in imaging applications. In this case we will need a hidden layer of 18 nodes. Allowing one unit for the output, we end up with a network of 919 processing elements plus a bias. The number of interconnections required is calculated as: 900 x 18 x 1 plus the bias connections to the hidden layer and the output of 19 interconnects. This gives a grand total of 16,219 interconnections.

If the training set consists of 50 images, the off-line training time could easily take six hours. In most cases the computer will not have sufficient RAM (memory) to accommodate such a large network. We run into this problem every day. A simple solution is to subdivide the 900-pixel matrix into nine 10-by-10 matrices. Now we can feed 100 inputs into a 100-by-2-by-1 network that can be trained in 3 to 4 minutes. Even allowing that we must do this for nine networks, our total image processing training time still will be well under an hour. More importantly, we do not require more than the usual 640K RAM memory found in most AT computers. This, of course, is an example of data compression. This technique is completely reversible, because we can start with the compressed data and reverse it back to the original image.

Another data-compression technique requires taking, for example, a 30-by-30 matrix and averaging all the pixels in one horizontal line, resulting in a matrix compressed to 1-by-30 to represent the original 30-by-30. This works satisfactorily where you are only required to inspect the image and classify it as "good" or "bad," as in parts inspection. We refer to this method as obtaining a "pixel signature" of the area of interest. We used this technique in classifying solder joints and speeded the training process from an off-line session requiring six hours to an on-line training session requiring less than six minutes. It is important to note that this procedure is not reversible, nor does it allow for post-inspection audit. Traceability in this instance is generally not a problem, because classification by humans is not easily reconstructed either.

If you desire instant success with initial hands-on experience in the design of neural networks, we recommend that you confine your first activities to pattern classification. Such networks are relatively easy to construct because they require fewer nodes and interconnects than other networks. They are extremely accurate and lend themselves to many manipulation techniques. Preparing both training and test input files will not depend on historical data sets, which are usually controlled by someone else. Indeed, you can design your own input sets right on your computer. Here are a few suggestions for those who wish to try their hand at neural network design in imaging:

1 Construct an alphanumeric imaging neural network (presenting ABCs or numerals).

2 Train an alphanumeric neural network and test the network with several different tests. Try to confuse the network!

3 Construct an alpha neural network that can recognize several simple three- and four-letter words.

4 Construct a network that can process a 16-pixel image requiring a matrix of 4-by-4 with an input layer of 16.

5 Compress the 4-by-4 to four 2-by-2 matrices and actually witness the training speed efficiency without compromising accuracy.

6 Try reversing the four 2-by-2 matrices back to the original 16-pixel matrix.

Semiconductor Etch Process

In most neural network applications we "tune" networks by randomizing weights, jogging the weights, or even changing learning rules for each layer. However, this application will illustrate in detail other techniques you can adopt in developing an application-specific neural network.

Description of the Process: A standard process employed in the production of semiconductors is to adjust the gate current to a desired value by etching a moat through the volumetric path of the current. That is, taking away material will increase the resistance to the current flow (see figure 9.8).

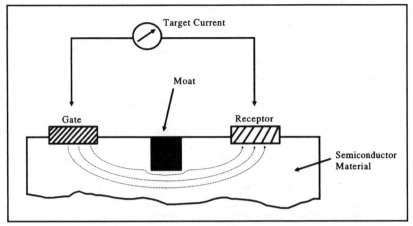

FIGURE 9.8   MOAT ETCH DIAGRAM

This process is usually done in four to six steps, which require etching for a predetermined time. The semiconductor device is received from the previous manufacturing process station with a measured post-alloy current in the range of 130 to 150 milliamps. It is then removed from the etch tank, rinsed, dried, and finally tested by making five current measurements. Design specifications usually call for a required flow of 65 milliamps.

We'll need a few definitions:

- I_{sat} = Current post alloy as received
- I_t = Current after etching for time (t)
- E_{t-out} = Etch time required
- I_{avg} = Average current for each group taken at time (t)

Inputs: The historical process data received from the semiconductor process manufacturing lists the manual testing shown in figure 9.9. Note that time (t) is listed incrementally for six etching procedures. This is the way we receive the historical data sheets.

From these historical data sheets (and we have several hundred of them), we can make the following input data presentation for the training set. Note that now we show time (t) as cumulative. This cumulative time is our desired output, D.

I	137.45	101.3
D	40	

Isat= 137.45ma	t=40 sec	t=20sec	t=38sec	t=17sec	t=9sec	t=2sec
	i=101.4ma	i=88.1ma	i=77.2ma	i=71.4ma	i=69.1ma	i=66.1ma
	i=100.2ma	i=87.9ma	i=76.5ma	i=71.2ma	i=68.9ma	i=65.5ma
	i=102.1ma	i=88.1ma	i=77.2ma	i=72.1ma	i=69.1ma	i=65.3ma
	i=101.4ma	i=86.9ma	i=76.5ma	i=71.8ma	i=68.7ma	i=65.5ma
	i=101.5ma	i=89.2ma	i=77.4ma	i=71.3ma	i=69.2ma	i=65.1ma
	Iavg=101.3ma	Iavg=88ma	Iavg=76.9ma	Iavg=71.5ma	Iavg=69ma	Iavg=65.5ma

FIGURE 9.9   HISTORICAL DATA SHEET FOR ETCH INPUTS

```
I       137.45   88.0
D       60
I       137.45   76.9
D       98
I       137.45   71.5
D       115
I       137.45   69.0
D       124
I       137.45   65.5
D       126
```

The data above represent one curve with five I(t) data points. We use Iavg as representative of all current measurements made for a single I(t). The time of etch is the desired output for each input pair. All that remains is to scale the data between 0 and 1 to allow the utilization of the sigmoid function; we must also add more data sets for a trial run to appraise the network's training. After all inputs are divided by 150 (larger than the largest value in the historical data set), the data presentation to the network appears as follows.

```
I       0.916    0.675
D       0.267
I       0.916    0.586
D       0.400
I       0.916    0.512
D       0.653
I       0.916    0.476
D       0.766
I       0.916    0.460
D       0.827
I       0.916    0.436
D       0.840
```

A Practical Guide to Neural Nets

We continue in this manner, using all but 20 percent of the historical data. The 20 percent is reserved for the test set, which will be used when the network is fully trained, or has converged.

This particular network design is, again, a back propagation paradigm with a cumulative-delta error summing technique. We used two inputs with two hidden layers of eight neurons each and one output. The layers are fully connected. In shorthand, we can write this as follows: Etch Study Net=2x8x8x1, Backpropcum-delta. Specifications are given in figure 9.10.

Training: We trained the network on 25 inputs to determine quickly how accurately the network could be trained. The training time was less than 45 minutes with an unacceptable error of 9 percent mean average. We feel it is worth noting how this particular problem was solved, using techniques to reduce the error after convergence. The next paragraphs detail what we did.

Second Input Training Set for the Same Etch Problem: We first squared Isat, then formed the product (Isat) x (Iavg) and added these two terms to the original data, which now takes the following form:

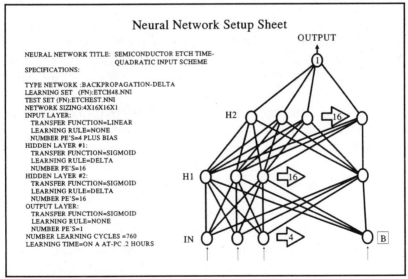

FIGURE 9.10   SPECIFICATIONS FOR ETCH NEURAL NETWORK

I	Isat Iavg Isat^2 (Isat x Iavg)
D	It
I	
D	(Enter the same Isat, followed by same Iavg, followed by
I	Isat squared and finally the product of Isat multiplied
D	by Iavg. Enter the same It for desired output, D.)
I	
D	

Now the data are in a quadratic form. The network now requires four inputs, two hidden layers of 16 neurons each and a single output described as net = 4x16x16x1. Again, enter the 25 sets of data. This network converged in ten minutes and tested out with less than a 3-percent mean average error. We gained a threefold improvement in accuracy and almost a fivefold improvement in required off-line training time.

The final network used for this process involved an additional step of introducing fourth, third, squared, and product terms. This resulted in less than 1-percent error with a five-minute off-line training time.

Using a Neural Network for Statistical Analysis

This problem will illustrate the vast potential that neural networks promise in the field of statistical analysis. Although it is a simple problem, it will still show how we can utilize neural networks in the solution of statistical problems.

Description of the Problem: Factorial studies are ones in which all the factors that we believe might influence the outcome of a process are studied from a statistical viewpoint. The solution of the problem is a list of these factors from the most significant to the least significant. This list is often referred to as a *Pareto Chart*, named after the investigator who first promoted its use in process control studies.

Semiconductor and electronics equipment employs many "thin film" circuits. These unique circuits contain semiconductor devices as well as other discrete electronic components soldered on a thin alumina substrate. These circuits, which represent a considerable investment or value added, sometimes crack and break apart when being installed in their final configuration.

The process engineering people collected statistical data on 17 parameters involved in the fabrication of thin film circuits. The parameters include area, width, length, aspect ratio (width divided by length), thickness of thin-film materials, method of assembling, types of voided areas (cutouts), slots and plated-thru-holes, to mention a few. The challenge was to design a neural network that could produce an accurate Pareto Chart. As it turned out, we not only accomplished this but were also able to use the neural network solution to predict the "ideal values" needed for each parameter to prevent the formation of cracks. This, as far as we know, has not been possible with traditional statistical analysis computer programs.

Constructing the Training Set: Putting the training set together was relatively easy, becasue the data had been collected for some period of time and was contained on a disk. We read the disk into a Lotus® 1-2-3® program that scaled all parameter values to between 0 and 1 so that we might apply sigmoid transfer functions.

Having never dealt with a statistical neural network, we were uncertain how we could verify the integrity of the network. We decided to try training with a smaller number of parameters by disabling selected inputs. This worked well, but we were reminded by our customer that they wanted a relationship that considered *all* the parameters at one time, such that each and every interaction was accounted for.

The method we used to check the network for integrity was purposely to bias the output for selected input vector sets. The logic was simply this: the network would have to select those biased input/output pairs as having the most significant influence on the cracking. This worked very well, and results were as predicted. We were satisfied on the integrity issue. We then fed the network the actual desired outputs as read off the parametric input disk.

Developing a Network: Because we had 17 parameters, or factors, to input and one factor for a desired output, namely the number of cracks, this determined the input and output layers. Keeping with our rule of thumb that we will require a ratio of four hidden units for each input unit, we ended up with the following fully connected back progagation neural network:

```
                     o                          OUTPUT     (1 PE)
o o o o o o o o o o o o o o o o o.....................o   HIDDEN 2  (34 PEs)
o o o o o o o o o o o o o o o o o.....................o   HIDDEN 1  (34 PEs)
     o o o o o o o o o o o o o o o o o             INPUT      (17 PEs)
```

We next selected all sigmoid transfer functions with a delta learning rule. The network was turned on and took less than two hours to stabilize, with minimal error indicated.

Interpreting the Results: We had read that a Pareto list of the input parameters might be obtained by summing the absolute value of all the input weights leaving the hidden layers. We tried it. This took as long as running the neural network, just over two hours. We ended up with a list of rank-ordered parameters, the first being the most significant contributor to cracking and the last being the least significant contributor to cracking. Fortunately, our customer was running the same problem on a traditional statistical analysis program. Our results were exactly the same as his.

Neural Network Inversion: The inversion technique we tried is a unique attribute that neural networks offer. As far as we know, no other statistical analysis simulation software has even proposed doing this. We inverted the network by merely switching the outputs with the inputs as follows:

```
     o o o o o o o o o o o o o o o o o        OUTPUT LAYER  (17 PEs)
o o o o o o o o o o o o o o o o o.............o   SAME HIDDEN  2  (34 PEs)
o o o o o o o o o o o o o o o o o.............o   SAME HIDDEN  1  (34 PEs)
                     o                          INPUT LAYER   (1 PE)
```

Using the same input file, but marking all the previous 17 inputs now as outputs and listing the number of cracks as the sole input, we ran the network. After the network converged in the same time as the original (about two hours), we could easily select the parameters resulting in the most number of cracks. We happily submitted our results as the idealized parameters that should be sought when fabricating thin-film circuits that will result in minimal cracking when assembled.

Comparisons: Neural Networks versus Statistical Methods: We made the following comparisons between traditional computer statistical analysis and neural network statistical analysis:

Analysis Method	Effort (Person Hours)	Computer Runtime (Hours)	Idealized Parameters
Traditional	54	234	None
Neural Net	6	5	Yes

If you assume the accuracy for both methods is equal, then there is little doubt as to the efficient use of resources that may be enjoyed when applying neural networks to statistical analysis. The unique ability of inverting the network such that an ideal set of parameters is produced is an additional reason for employing neural networks in statistical analysis. A final note: the traditional statistical analysis computer program we used in our comparison is considered to be the best such program available.

Semiconductor Curing Furnace Neural Network

This example illustrates an actual industrial application of neural networks to solve problems that involve multiple factors.

In the semiconductor manufacturing process, slices of silicon or other semiconductor material must be cured in a long five-temperature-zone furnace. The curing furnace can be as much as 120 feet long, with five temperature zones of 20 feet each and 10-feet loading and unloading zones at each end. To calibrate or "profile" a curing furnace is a long and tedious operation.

First-pass dynamic profiles are very rare indeed, and a profile operation that produces a dynamic profile on the first pass can still consume 40 to 80 person-hours of effort. To profile a loaded furnace with parts (slices of semiconductor material) seated in boats is a phenomenally complex project involving many factors. Usually the position of the boats on the chain must be altered (see figures 9.11 and 9.12) for optimization of maximum product loading versus the most desired product yield. Chain speeds usually run in the range of .2 to .5 feet per minute, which means one complete test cycle through the furnace could take more than six hours. Temperature settings may have to be altered for one or more zones, and changes in chain speed may also be required. After many hours the yield still may not be acceptable. This profiling process can go on for as long as two or three weeks.

We had to have some mathematical way of representing the boat position on the chain. Because all boats are one width for a

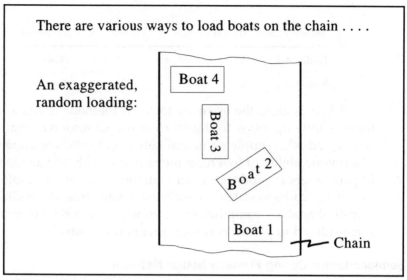

There are various ways to load boats on the chain . . . .

An exaggerated, random loading:

Boat 4

Boat 3

Boat 2

Boat 1

Chain

FIGURE 9.11 BOATS ON CHAIN, RANDOM POSITIONING

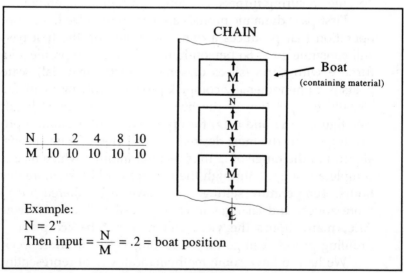

CHAIN

M

Boat
(containing material)

N

M

N

M

N	1	2	4	8	10
M	10	10	10	10	10

Example:
N = 2"
Then input = $\dfrac{N}{M}$ = .2 = boat position

FIGURE 9.12 BOATS ON CHAIN, STANDARD POSITIONING

A Practical Guide to Neural Nets

given furnace, the sides' dimension is not a factor. Standard procedure is to center all boats on the chain. Therefore, we can use the aspect ratio of spacing between the boats.

If we design a neural network to learn from historical data, and there is usually a great deal of such data, we should be able to predict performance on the first pass, providing the data are mostly reliable.

Description of the Problem: To design the neural network we must first describe the problem we wish the neural network to solve. We'll start by defining the following variables:

Variables	Units
Zone identification	Assigned number
Zone temperatures	Degrees F
Chain speed	Feet/min
Boat position on chain	Ratio (see figure 9.12)
Number of slices in boat	Assigned number

Our neural network needs to allow us to try various values for different sets of these variables and then predict the desired output, which in this case is the plate resistance of silicon semiconductor slices. Several additional variables could be considered, such as reduction atmosphere (type gas, pressure), other boat loading considerations, diameter of semiconductor slice, etc. However, we will design our neural network for the variables listed above.

Constructing the Training Set: A first pass at the required training set is given in table 9.3. We can try developing a simpler training set by condensing the data as in table 9.4. Further condensation yields the inputs in table 9.5.

We arrive at the figures in table 9.5 by taking the temperature at the entrance to a zone minus the temperature leaving the zone. For example,

Zone 1 = (90-1250) = -1160.

Table 9.3: Data for Training Set

Zone Number	Temperature Degrees F	Chain Speed Ft/Min	Boat Position Decimal	Number Slices
1	90	.4	.833	6
1	200	.4	.833	6
1	350	.4	.833	6
1	575	.4	.833	6
1	890	.4	.833	6
1	1250	.4	.833	6
2	1500	.4	.833	6
2	1550	.4	.833	6
2	1600	.4	.833	6
3	1642	.4	.833	6
3	1623	.4	.833	6
4	1612	.4	.833	6
4	1590	.4	.833	6
5	1490	.4	.833	6
5	1424	.4	.833	6
5	1400	.4	.833	6
5	800	.4	.833	6
5	450	.4	.833	6
5	220	.4	.833	6
5	90	.4	.833	6
5	80	.4	.833	6

Table 9.4: Simplified Training Set

Zone Number	Temperature Degrees F	Chain Speed Ft/Min	Boat Position Decimal	Number Slices
1	90	.4	.833	6
1	1250	.4	.833	6
2	1500	.4	.833	6
2	1600	.4	.833	6
3	1642	.4	.833	6
3	1623	.4	.833	6
4	1612	.4	.833	6
4	1590	.4	.833	6
5	1490	.4	.833	6
5	80	.4	.833	6

Table 9.5: Further Simplification of Training Set Data

Zone Number	Temperature Degrees F	Chain Speed Ft/Min	Boat Position Decimal	Number Slices
1	−1160	.4	.833	6
2	−100	.4	.833	6
3	+19	.4	.833	6
4	+22	.4	.833	6
5	+1410	.4	.833	6

The next step requires scaling the data to be in the range 0 to 1 where necessary so that we may use the sigmoid transfer function. Because the sigmoid function does not recognize negative numbers, we have used absolute values and will rely on the network to work out the correct relationships. Table 9.6 shows the results of the scaling.

Now we add the historical resistance values, our desired outputs, associated with the scaled inputs, as follows:

Table 9.6: Training Set Data after Scaling

Zone Number	Temperature Degrees F	Chain Speed Ft/Min	Boat Position Decimal	Number Slices
.2	.822	.4	.833	6
.4	.071	.4	.833	6
.6	.013	.4	.833	6
.8	.016	.4	.833	6
1.0	1.000	.4	.833	6

```
I    .2    .82    .4    .833    .6
D    .43
I    .4    .07    .4    .833    .6
D    .38
I    .6    .01    .4    .833    .6
D    .37
I    .8    .02    .4    .833    .6
D    .35
I    1.0   .9     .4    .833    .6
D    .33
```

We continue in this manner until we have a representative training set that we can use for a trial run. At least twenty or thirty sets of data will be required. Inspection of the above training set indicates that we will need a five-element input layer. In our experience, two hidden layers of approximately four to five times the input layer work well. So, we will use 25 neurons for each hidden layer and, of course, one output. Therefore, our back propagation-cumdelta neural network may be written as net=5x25x25x1,BPCUMDELTA. See figure 9.13 for the specifications.

Results: This network converged nicely, fully trained, after 1,000 cycles. The training took three hours. Accuracy was measured at less than 1.5-percent mean average error.

Several other different data representations were formed. The final network can be used to predict total performance with the ability to play "what if" games. We can optimize belt speed,

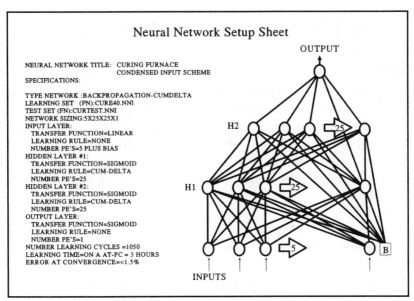

Neural Network Setup Sheet

OUTPUT

NEURAL NETWORK TITLE: CURING FURNACE
                      CONDENSED INPUT SCHEME
SPECIFICATIONS:

TYPE NETWORK :BACKPROPAGATION-CUMDELTA
LEARNING SET (FN):CURE40.NNI
TEST SET (FN):CURTEST.NNI
NETWORK SIZING:5X25X25X1
INPUT LAYER:
    TRANSFER FUNCTION=LINEAR
    LEARNING RULE=NONE
    NUMBER PE'S=5 PLUS BIAS
HIDDEN LAYER #1:
    TRANSFER FUNCTION=SIGMOID
    LEARNING RULE=CUM-DELTA
    NUMBER PE'S=25
HIDDEN LAYER #2:
    TRANSFER FUNCTION=SIGMOID
    LEARNING RULE=CUM-DELTA
    NUMBER PE'S=25
OUTPUT LAYER:
    TRANSFER FUNCTION=SIGMOID
    LEARNING RULE=NONE
    NUMBER PE'S=1
NUMBER LEARNING CYCLES =1050
LEARNING TIME=ON A AT-PC = 3 HOURS
ERROR AT CONVERGENCE=<1.5%

H2

H1

INPUTS

FIGURE 9.13   SPECIFICATIONS FOR FURNACE NEURAL NETWORK

loading, product distribution, or temperature by zones, with product yield. We later improved this network to consider the temperature response for different semiconductor materials, various curing atmospheres, and other new variables not mentioned above.

The bottom line is simply this: an investment of several days' effort can save you in the long term many times that effort. In addition, it can provide you with a powerful tool for solving present curing furnace problems as well as new product design problems.

Comparing Network Applications

The *DARPA Neural Network Study* published in late 1988 has set the standards that most industry and academia are presently using, at least with regard to network size and speed. The DARPA-funded study states that the computational units of neural networks are best understood in terms of interconnects (storage) and interconnects-per-second (speed).[2] We subscribe to this system, because it is obvious as well as simple.

Size

The generally accepted method of measuring size is to add the number of interconnects as well as the total number of processing elements. For example, let's look at the semiconductor etch neural network introduced previously. This network has an input layer of four inputs plus a bias, two hidden layers of 16 processing elements each, and a single processing element in the output layer.

Number PEs	Network	Layers
1	O	Output layer
16	O O O O O O O O O O O O O O O O	Hidden layer 2
16	O O O O O O O O O O O O O O O O	Hidden layer 1
4 + bias	B O O O O	Input layer

We calculate the number of connections as follows. Starting at the input layer, we form the following products:

$$(4 \times 16) + (16 \times 16) + (16 \times 1) = 336.$$

Now add one bias connection from B to each element in hidden layer 1, one connection to PEs in hidden layer 2, and one for the output. We have:

$$16 + 16 + 1 = 33.$$

Summing, we have

$$336 + 33 = 369$$

interconnections. For purposes of computer RAM memory and limitations of various network development programs, you might need to know the number of PEs.

Comparing the size of four of the networks we looked at in this chapter:

A Practical Guide to Neural Nets

Network	Matrix	Product	# Inter-connects
Loan	4 × 16 × 16 × 1	(4 × 16) + (16 × 16) + (16 × 1) + 16 + 16 + 1=	369
Image	28 × 28 × 14 × 10	(28 × 28) + (28 × 14) + (14 × 10) + 28 + 14 + 10=	1370
Etch	4 × 16 × 16 × 1	(4 × 16) + (16 × 16) + (16 × 1) + 16 + 16 + 1=	369
Furnace	5 × 25 × 25 × 1	(5 × 25) + (25 × 25) + (25 × 1) + 25 + 25 + 1=	826

Our size range for the four applications above is 369 to 1,370 interconnects. Within this range, it is relatively easy to achieve off-line training, convergence, and modification. In our industrial environment, this range allows us to prototype a problem rapidly. With rapid prototyping, we can demonstrate satisfactorily to a customer in a matter of hours (never more than two days) that we can solve a given problem. The time required to train a network is directly proportional to the size of the network and the number of training input sets presented to the network. Off-line training time, then, becomes one of the most important elements in initially selling neural network technology.

Speed

Today's computers equipped with neural network development software tools can provide us with simulation capabilities of approximately 10 million interconnects per second. The DARPA-funded study points out that this speed falls far short of the computational capabilities of even modest biological networks. A house fly computes at the rate of around 1 billion interconnects per second. The following chart (adapted) compares the estimated computational capabilities of some biological networks:[3]

Animal	Storage (# Interconnects)	Speed (# Interconnects/Sec)
Leech	9 hundred	30 thousand
Worm	5 thousand	200 thousand
Fly	80 million	1 billion

Cockroach	1 billion	70 billion
Bee	5 billion	500 billion
Man	100 trillion	10 quadrillion

Just think of what a humbling experience we go through when we happily complete a network and then place it on the above chart for comparative size and speed. The largest application presented in this chapter still is only slightly above a leech and way below a worm, and I believe a flatworm at that!

However, hardware technology improvements are in the mill at this writing that will probably provide us with adequate speed and interconnect storage for about the next ten years. For our purposes, we presently have more than adequate technology to design and develop meaningful and cost-effective neural networks.

Training

We generally consider a neural network to be fully trained when several criteria are met. The first and most easily obtained criterion for full training is to test the network with an internal recall of the training set. When the mean average error is acceptable, the network is ready for the most important acceptance test: we recall the network with a test set containing historical data that the network has never seen. Again, when the mean average (or standard deviation, or whatever comparative measures you wish) results in an acceptable range, you may consider the network to be fully trained. A comparison of training cycles, training time, and error for our four applications is shown in the following table:

Network	Training Cycles	Training Time	Mean Avg Error
Loan	17,000	4 hours	0.67%
Image	1,200	1 hour	1.11%
Etch	760	.2 hour	2.78%
Furnace	1,050	3 hours	1.45%

Testing

Several techniques can be used to test our networks. Not only do we test for accuracy in training, but we may wish to test for noise and many other parameters. Testing for accuracy, however, generally accounts for most of the testing efforts.

We construct a test set using some of the historical data from which the training set was made. Customarily we randomly select 20 to 30 percent of the historical data and put it aside prior to constructing the training set. While the network is undergoing training, we can put together a test set from the remaining data. The test set for the loan approval neural network is shown below:

	Salary	Home	Car	Card
I	1.0	.3	.05	.07
I	.3	.2	.1	.3
I	.8	.2	.1	.1
I	.2	.1	.0	.2
I	.7	.3	.0	.3
I	.4	.1	.0	.2
I	.9	.25	.2	.3
I	.75	.31	.2	.2
I	.25	.1	.1	.3

These data are representative of the historical data given to us by several credit unions in the Dallas, Texas area. There is nothing wrong with developing an additional test set using hypothetical data. In fact, there may be much to be gained. The story in the following paragraphs tells of our somewhat surprising encounter with hypothetical data.

When we developed a solder joint image classifier neural network, we trained it on actual data taken directly from the image processing unit on the test equipment. The group for which we were doing the development work brought in a test set on a diskette. We used their diskette, containing 34 sets of data, to test our "trained network."

The results indicated that, of the 34 test images presented, the network correctly classified 32 solder joints. The acceptable solder-joints results were in the output range of 0.999000 to 0.999999. The unacceptable solder joints were in the range of

0.000000 to 0.000010. The two images that were not clearly or easily classified as "accept" or "reject" were in the output range of 0.400000 to 0.600000. Before we discuss the testing and classification of solder joints, let's review the traditional inspection process.

The current method of inspection (see figure 9.14) is for operators to examine briefly an enlarged image of the area of interest as displayed on a TV monitor. The magnification is usually at least thirty times greater than what is normally seen with the naked eye. The operator makes a subjective call resulting in either an "accept" or a "reject" solder joint classification for each image seen. We then have a "qualitative" call with no traceable data supporting that particular call.

Now, compare the neural network classification method (see figure 9.15) and you can see immediately that we can make a "quantitative" measurement from which we can derive a "qualitative" output. More importantly, we retain the quantitative data that allows for post-inspection review or audit. The following tables illustrate this important difference between the current inspection method and the neural network approach.

Typical operator solder joint classification results:

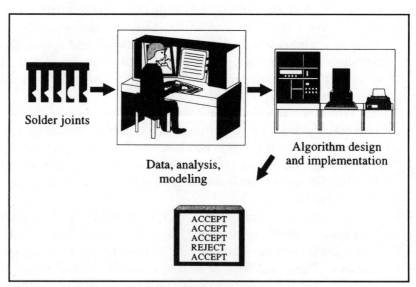

Solder joints

Data, analysis, modeling

Algorithm design and implementation

ACCEPT
ACCEPT
ACCEPT
REJECT
ACCEPT

FIGURE 9.14   INFORMATION PROCESSING—CURRENT TECHNIQUES

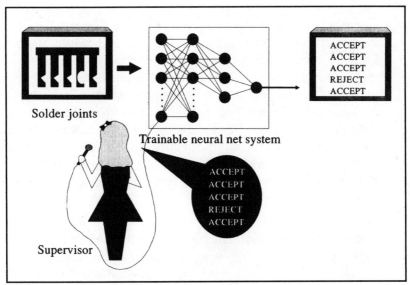

FIGURE 9.15 INFORMATION PROCESSING—NEURAL NETWORK TECHNIQUE

Image Number	Operator A	Operator B
22	Accept	Accept
23	Accept	Accept
24	Reject	Reject
25	Accept	Reject
26	Reject	Accept

Typical neural net solder-joint classification results:

Image Number	Quantitative	Qualitative
22	0.999910	Accept
23	0.999991	Accept
24	0.000011	Reject
25	0.501231	Reject
26	0.510101	Reject

Back to our story. When we were given the 34 test results, the monitoring group listed image numbers 25 and 26 as "Accept."

We were disappointed when we were marked as having correctly classified only 32 solder joints out of the 34. The two we classified incorrectly were images 25 and 26. The test results were taken back to the group's supervisor for review. Unknown to us, he had altered image numbers 25 and 26 prior to presenting the data either to the two operators or to the neural network. He had taken an acceptable image and modified it sufficiently to make it a definite "cliff-hanger," or borderline image. He then placed it in the acceptable classification category. In fact, he was really trying to see if the network could spot an altered image that was not a definite accept, definite reject, borderline accept, or borderline reject.

Subsequent Analysis: The 34 test results showed several close calls by operators that were unquestionably classified by the neural net. That is, the neural net classified the close calls in the range of 0.890000–0.900000 for acceptable images and 0.000100–0.001000 as unacceptable. However, the neural network would not classify or place the "phoney" images in the above borderline ranges. Instead, it placed them squarely in the middle range of 0.400000–0.600000. The scenario that the supervisor was evaluating was simply stated: "Could the neural network spot a phoney image?" The table below illustrates that the neural network was able to make five quantitative classifications in addition to the two qualitative classifications:

Operator A	Operator B	Neural Network
Accept	Accept	0.999910, Accept
Reject	Reject	0.000010, Reject
Accept	Accept	0.895000, Accept (Borderline)
Reject	Reject	0.000101, Reject (Borderline)
Accept	Reject	0.501231, Reject (Phoney)

The conclusion was: Not only could the neural network spot an altered or phoney image, but it refused to classify it as an acceptable solder joint even though its quantitative measurement was greater than 0.500000. Needless to say, we received a final test score of 100 percent as well as a pat on the back.

Recognition-Curve Network Test: The following test will do several things for you. It will immediately indicate noise and predict whether your network will train fully. You will also get a good idea as to how long training will take. Simply input a training set consisting of a well-known curve or familiar pattern. You can easily recognize the curve or pattern as it takes shape. Perhaps an even more important advantage obtained with this technique lies in the knowledge gained by observing the dynamics of the training process. How well the network trains can now be judged instantly without making tedious error calculations.

When utilizing different paradigms and/or different transfer functions, we input different "recognition curves." For example, if we use a sine transfer function in developing our network, or if the training set involves nonlinear data (such as quadratic inputs), then we first test the network by presenting a sine wave as input. This is done prior to inputting the usually unrecognizable pattern or wave-form-type that the input data will eventually exhibit as the training process takes place.

Immediately after inputting a sine wave to your network, you should observe the embryo of a sine wave. As the network training process dynamics continue, you should see the output take the shape of a perfect sine wave. The sine wave will be perfect when the error has been reduced to essentially zero and you have reproduced an acceptable sine wave as your output. Keeping track of the time and reading the cycles as well as doing a comparative analysis of the input file (training set) to the output file (recall set) will tell you the relative accuracy of the neural network.

A sample input set for a simple sine wave test would look like the following (see figure 9.16 for a graph of this data):

I	0.0
D	0
I	0.521
D	0.5
I	1.042
D	0.87
I	1.562
D	1.0
I	2.084
D	0.87
I	2.605
D	0.5
I	3.126
D	0.0

I	3.647
D	-0.5
I	4.168
D	-0.87
I	4.689
D	-1.0
I	5.210
D	-0.87
I	5.731
D	-0.5
I	6.252
D	0.0

Here is a table of suggested test functions for the most commonly used back propagation neural networks:

Transfer Function	Input Test Function
Sigmoid	Saw-tooth or any rectilinear pattern
Linear	y = mx + b or any straight line
Sine	Sine-wave
Tanh	Polynomial

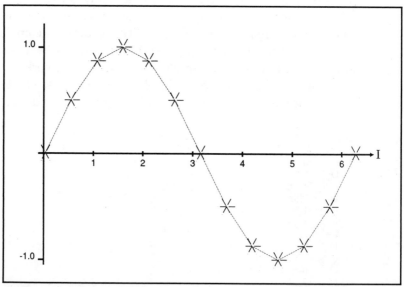

FIGURE 9.16   SINE WAVE TEST INPUTS

A Practical Guide to Neural Nets

When the network design employs various and different transfer functions at each level, a heuristic approach must yield to a trial-and-error method. As you develop neural networks, you will also develop intuitive learning skills on how best to develop, test, and implement them.

Back Propagation Mathematics: How to Compute a Neural Network Manually

The following exercise is presented to show you the actual mechanics of computing a back propagation network. We are not suggesting that you implement these computations when designing a neural network. Rather, we wish to illustrate the methodology and give insight to the internal mechanics required to adjust weights and learn from the training set to produce the desired output.

Figure 9.17 displays the network we will use to do our manual

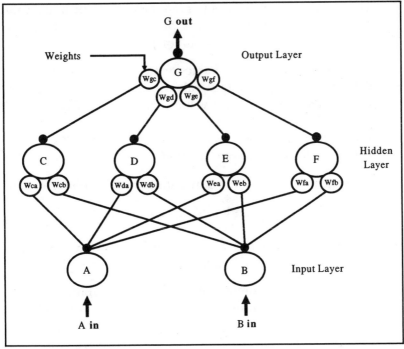

FIGURE 9.17 NETWORK DIAGRAM

computations. Please note that we have drawn our network purposely so as to highlight the weights associated with each respective processing element (PE). This is not quite standard notation, but as we start the computation process, it will be clear why this notation was chosen. For simplicity, we have also omitted the transfer function and its first derivative in order to amplify the weight change process.

The network contains seven PEs, arranged in three layers. The input layer contains PEs labeled A and B. The hidden layer contains four PEs, labeled C, D, E, and F. The output layer has one PE labeled G. Below each PE symbol we have inserted weights for that particular PE. Please note the manner in which the weight is named. We start with the "W" for "weight," and use subscript lower-case letters to identify the connection. For example, Wca would be a weight between processing elements A and C. The letter "c" indicates that the weight is associated with the C PE and, of course, the "a" indicates the connection coming from the A PE.

The following are the data that we may describe as given. The accepted procedure is to randomly select the initial values for the weights. We refer to this procedure as "randomizing" the weights. We need a few definitions here:

- **Ain** refers to an input value for the PE labeled "A."
- **Gout** refers to an output value for the PE labeled "G."
- **Wca** refers to a weight value for the PE labeled "C," coming from the PE labeled "A."
- **Eg** refers to the error value for the PE labeled "G."
- ***** refers to the multiply function.

We start our computations by listing the given information:

GIVEN: Ain   = 0
          Bin   = 1
Desired Gout   = 1 (the output we want from the
                    system)

Next, we randomize the weights with arbitrary values, proceeding from the output layer back to the input layer as follows:

Wgc =   1.2   Wda =   3.6
Wgd =   1.6   Wdb = −4.1

$$Wge = 4.3 \qquad Wea = 2.1$$
$$Wgf = 3.2 \qquad Web = 2.5$$
$$Wca = 1.1 \qquad Wfa = 0.9$$
$$Wcb = -1.4 \qquad Wfb = -1.0$$

To compute the "new" value for the weights (after each cycle), we must know the output at each PE as well as the error at each PE. The formula for computing the processing element outputs is:

Equation 1: (Actual) Gout = [Cout*Wgc] + [Dout*Wgd] +
                                [Eout*Wge] + [Fout*Wgf]

We must compute all the PE outputs connecting to the G processing element before we can compute Gout.

Equation 2: Cout = [Ain*Wca] + [Bin*Wcb] = −1.4
Equation 3: Dout = [Ain*Wda] + [Bin*Wdb] = −4.1
Equation 4: Eout = [Ain*Wea] + [Bin*Web] = 2.5
Equation 5: Fout = [Ain*Wfa] + [Bin*Wfb] = −1.0

We can now compute Gout from Equation 1, resulting in Gout = -.69. Before we can compute the remaining eight weights associated with the hidden layer, we must compute the error for each PE. The error for the network output is equal to the desired output minus the actual output. Therefore, the error (E) for processing element G is:

Equation 6: Eg = DESIRED OUTPUT − Actual Gout = 1.69
Equation 7: Ec = Eg*Wgc = 2.03
Equation 8: Ed = Eg*Wgd = 2.70
Equation 9: Ee = Eg*Wge = 7.27
Equation 10: Ef = Eg*Wgf = 5.41

Now we can compute the "new" values for each of the twelve weights. The general equation for computing new values for the weights is:

NEW WEIGHT = ERROR*OUTPUT + CURRENT WEIGHT.

Equation 11: NEW Wgc = [Eg*Gout] + CURRENT Wgc =   .03
Equation 12: NEW Wgd = [Eg*Gout] + CURRENT Wgd =   .43
Equation 13: NEW Wge = [Eg*Gout] + CURRENT Wge = 3.13
Equation 14: NEW Wgf = [Eg*Gout] + CURRENT Wgf = 2.03

Equation 15: NEW Wca = [Ec*Cout] + CURRENT Wca =   −1.74
Equation 16: NEW Wcb = [Ec*Cout] + CURRENT Wcb =   −4.24
Equation 17: NEW Wda = [Ed*Dout] + CURRENT Wda =   −7.47
Equation 18: NEW Wdb = [Ed*Dout] + CURRENT Wdb = −15.17
Equation 19: NEW Wea = [Ee*Eout] + CURRENT Wea =   20.28
Equation 20: NEW Web = [Ee*Eout] + CURRENT Web =   20.68
Equation 21: NEW Wfa = [Ef*Fout] + CURRENT Wfa =   −4.51
Equation 22: NEW Wfb = [Ef*Fout] + CURRENT Wfb =   −6.41

The following chart compares the weights just computed to the original value resulting from random selection:

PE Name	Weight	Original Value	New Value
C	Wca	1.1	-1.74
C	Wcb	−1.4	−4.24
D	Wda	3.6	−7.47
D	Wdb	−4.1	−15.17
E	Wea	2.1	20.28
E	Web	2.5	20.68
F	Wfa	0.9	-4.51
F	Wfb	−1.0	−6.41
G	Wgc	1.2	.03
G	Wgd	1.6	.43
G	Wge	4.3	3.13
G	Wgf	3.2	2.03

Considering that it may take as many as 20 or 30 thousand cycles to satisfactorily train a network, and that each cycle requires all the calculations shown above, it becomes quite clear that we need computer help.

Implementing Your Network

Computer Simulation

This is where all neural network design, development and implementation begin. We have already illustrated why we need a computer for the design and development phases, but it is not a must that you implement your neural network on a computer. By implementing we mean fielding, or applying, the developed neural network to the solution of the problem for which the network was designed.

The design and development effort generally has the following steps:

1 Derive learning equation, recall equation, and stability-test equation.
2 Derive the input equations.
3 Establish the weights.
4 Code, or program, a computer simulation.
5 Adjust the equation coefficients.
6 Thoroughly test the network.

Implementation efforts can vary, but many will follow one or more of these steps:

1 Construct an electronic breadboard with resistors.
2 Employ an EPROM (Erasable Programmable Read Only Memory).
3 Design or employ a semiconductor integrated circuit.
4 Deliver an executable neural network run-time diskette (not particularly user-friendly).
5 Deliver an executable neural network run-time diskette embedded in an expert system.

Executable Code

In order to field and deliver a neural network after completing the design and development stages, you must remove the neural network from the development tool. This is a tricky operation. There are designer software packages that will assist you in turning your neural network into an executable program on a run-time floppy disk. This is a start in the right direction. However, most neural networks are not user-friendly and require considerable input data preparation and output data interpretation. One solution is to embed your neural network in an expert system. The expert system can do all the mundane operations and still interface with the user in a most friendly manner.

Embedded Neural Networks

A neural network embedded in an expert system has many advantages. Personally, we would not consider delivering a neural network unless it was embedded in an expert system. We have been able to greatly enhance the operation of the neural network and reinforce the solution to the problem using expert systems. The expert system adds traceability to some of the "Why" and "How" questions as well. Figure 9.18 illustrates our methodology for developing a neural network.

Summary and Recommendations

We started this chapter with our experience in moving from theory to applications. Our approach has worked satisfactorily for the problems we have encountered to date. We know from reading the literature that there are many ways to implement a neural network. Figure 9.19 shows current options.

However, we must remind you that, with few exceptions, few fielded neural applications exist. There are many "toys" or simulated problem-solving neural networks. Our recommendations are obviously biased toward the methods that have worked

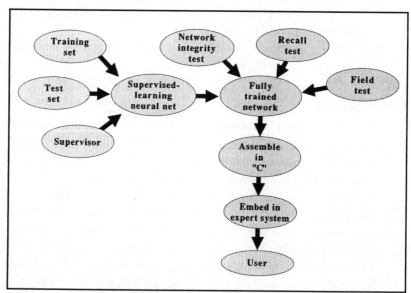

FIGURE 9.18   NETWORK DEVELOPMENT METHODOLOGY

A Practical Guide to Neural Nets

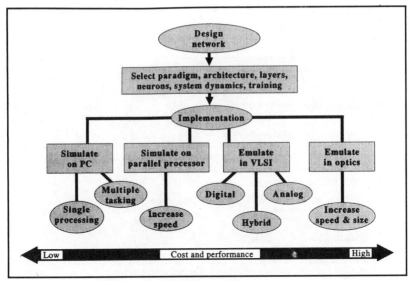

FIGURE 9.19 NEURAL NETWORK IMPLEMENTATION OPTIONS

well for us. When we state that we have fielded a neural network system, we mean that we have delivered a solution to a problem for which no solution was previously present. In the three manufacturing process areas where we have delivered embedded runtime diskettes, traditional software solutions had failed or were judged unsatisfactory. Eventually, as we climb the learning curve and increase the size of our networks, we will be looking at optical and other implementation techniques. For the next year or two, however, we see the embedded run-time system and the application-specific integrated circuit (ASIC) as our implementation methodology (see figure 9.20).

---

1. Anderson and Rosenfeld, editors, *Neurocomputing: Foundations of Research.* Cambridge, MA: MIT Press, 1988.

2. *DARPA Neural Network Study* (Fairfax, VA: AFCEA International Press, November 1988), page 31.

3. Ibid., p. 33.

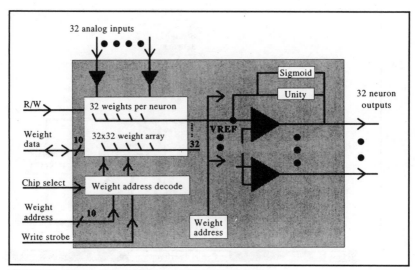

FIGURE 9.20   TYPICAL APPLICATION-SPECIFIC INTEGRATED CIRCUIT

A Practical Guide to Neural Nets

10

How Are Neural Networks Being Implemented?

The Law of Computability applies to neural networks: If at first you don't succeed, transform your data set.

Introduction

> Neurocomputing is neither a technology nor a product. It is a series of products (software, hardware, course ware, consulting applications, etc.) and a number of technologies (electronics, computer science, optoelectronics, etc.).[1]
> —Derek F. Stubbs, M.D.

The earliest neural networks were done with paper and pencil. That is, they were just ideas. But the ideas grew. When computers became more sophisticated it became possible to try these ideas out in a more concrete way. Computer simulations occasioned refinements in both the theory and the models. Software simulations have not only moved this fledgling technology along, they continue to provide an environment that nurtures testing and experimentation.

The goal for many researchers has been (and still is) to find implementations which are fast and yet not too expensive—in other words, practical. Generally, this means implementing in hardware, though some implementations we mention at the end of this chapter are actually biological. Hardware implementations currently come in several species: computer emulations which involve special boards or other special hardware, integrated circuit chips, optical or holographic devices, and other substrates (see figure 10.1).

In chapter 4 we talked briefly about Doug Conner's experiment in implementing a network directly in hardware. In his network a physical component represented each processing element. Using analog circuits, weights were represented as resistors on connection wires. Summation was achieved with weighted summing amplifiers; a diode clamping circuit worked as the threshold limit. It was a way to make the theory operational in terms of components that were well understood.

A considerable amount of the current neural network research effort is being directed to hardware implementation technologies, not all of which are so well understood. However, before we look at specific implementation schemes, we want to introduce a few terms to use in making comparisons.

Terminology

Several descriptors are typically used in evaluating neural network implementations. Of these, the two most important are size and speed. How large a network can you build, and how fast can it

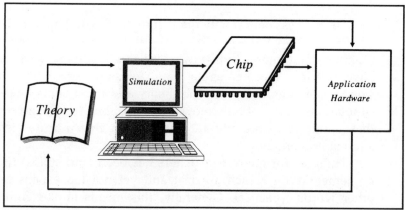

FIGURE 10.1 THEORY TO APPLICATION

A Practical Guide to Neural Nets

perform updates? For digital computers we have measured memory in bytes and speed in instructions per second.

Size

Size for a neural network involves two categories: (1) the number of processing elements and (2) the number of interconnections. The number of interconnects in a neural network is directly proportional to the complexity of the model that can be implemented. If it is possible to implement n processing elements and each has c connections, then the number of possible interconnections will be $n*c$. A fully connected network would have a minimum memory requirement of $n^2 + n$ memory units: at least n^2 units would be needed to hold the interconnection information, because each node is connected to all other nodes; and at least n units would be needed to hold the information on the node itself. Note that we didn't define the size of a "unit"; that dimension depends on how much information needs to be stored for each processing element.

Although there are no standards, several new terms have been suggested in the literature as being representative of the types of categories that could become standard. *AIS* stands for *Activities and Interconnections Stored*. Early implementations cost around 20 cents per AIS. Typical of most electronic products, costs are dropping as parts miniaturization increases. It is likely the cost will drop to 1 cent per AIS or less.

Another size issue has to do with the number of networks that can work together simultaneously. One of the characteristics that defines early neurocomputers (see the section on early neurocomputers later in this chapter) is the number of networks that can be resident on the board simultaneously. Complex applications will require several networks to be linked together. Information may need to be shared. One net may need to see objects and to process information that will become the input to another network for some subsequent action. Or, different nets may need to process data simultaneously to produce a combined result. Sensor fusion applications will require multiple networks. Compare this to when you use several senses at once: the kitchen smells like something good is baking, an empty chocolate chip package is on the counter . . . must be cookies! Processing from several sensors is combined to produce a decision, or output.

Speed

The other primary descriptor besides size is *speed*. Here the critical issue is the number of interconnections that can be processed per second. The learning mode is always slower than the operational mode, because the added work of adjusting the weights is a necessary part of each learning cycle. Consequently, some implementations may list two speeds: learning mode and operational mode.

Suggested terminology for the speed category includes *CUPS* for *Connection Updates Per Second,* and *IPS* for *Interconnections Per Second.* What finally evolves as standard jargon may be entirely different than anything suggested so far.

It's worth remembering the comparisons for human processing. Capacity of the human brain is around 10 billion neurons with more than a thousand times that many interconnections. Although individual neurons compute operations at a rate as slow as that of a single instruction of a digital computer, most cognitive processes take no longer than a few hundred milliseconds. The massive parallelism is responsible for the speed. Current implementations come nowhere near the capacity and flexibility of the human brain, nor are they likely to in the foreseeable future.

Software Simulations

The early neural network implementation efforts were almost exclusively simulations on conventional computers. (The Perceptron is a good counterexample.) Our seminar students were quick to note the inconsistency of using sequential machines to implement parallel processes. Obviously, the speed benefits of massive parallelism cannot be realized with this method, but the ease of making software changes has been a significant advantage. Redesigning chips takes time and money; simulations can help avoid costly mistakes.

Software simulations generally support several different network models and may allow choices in factors such as transfer functions. This enhances the testing of ideas and the learning of how to manipulate the variable parts. The disadvantage of having the ability to tune nearly every feature is that the complexity can quickly become overwhelming, a common trade-off.

Many software packages run on a PC. Some require coprocessor boards. PCs with a neurocomputing coprocessor can perform tasks that would require a minicomputer when algorithmic or AI techniques are used. As an example, robots implemented with coprocessor boards can learn to move in less precisely mapped environments than robots that use a rule-based system.

Also available are neural-network-based turnkey software packages. Excalibur Technologies (Albuquerque, NM) debuted its (soft)wares at the 1989 International Joint Conference on Neural Networks.[2] The Excalibur packages include a variety of pattern-recognition and process-control applications. Powerful parallel data structures in the software eliminate the need for special hardware; the software runs on standard VAX computers attached to Compaq PCs. Excalibur's proprietary neural net learning technology is called Savvy. Solutions to problems are learned by example. A circuit-board inspection system, for example, was trained on boards that were known to be good. After training, the system could then detect solder bridges, bent pins, and other visual defects.

Excalibur has several Savvy systems. The Savvy/TRS text retrieval system can compress the Bible into a 1.5-Mbyte neural net data structure. If you ask for any part of a verse, the system instantly recalls the entire verse. The Savvy/VRS vision recognition system can circle moving images on a TV screen as objects move in real time. Savvy/PixTex combines the retrieval of text with pictures of documents from large databases. Queries can be processed even with errors in both queries and the original text. Savvy systems can do sensor fusion, intelligent message handling, and monitoring of process-control applications.

Emulation within Parallel Architecture

A more efficient method than computer simulations for implementing neural networks is to emulate within parallel architecture. The parallel structure of processing elements and their interconnections is matched one for one with simple processors and communications links. Examples of this are hypercube- and Transputer-based systems, discussed next.

The concept of a hypercube was mentioned previously (chapter 7). It is a more-than-three-dimensional "box" existing in more-than-three-dimensional space. NCube Corporation has capitalized on this concept with their hypercube supercomputer hardware. They can accommodate up to 1,024 (2^{10}) processors within a single enclosure of about 0.5 m^3. Each processor is designed to operate at speeds comparable to a VAX 11/780. You pick the number of processors you need for your application. Late 1989 models featured even more processors and faster speed—27 Gflops, 9 times quicker than the fastest supercomputer from Cray Research.

In 1989, NCube announced an agreement with Oracle Corp.[3] This represents one of the first major business-oriented applications to be ported to a parallel-processing computer. This aspect may be more significant than NCube's recent improvements in speed. After being primarily a research technology, parallel hardware now seems to be making inroads in the commercial market.

Why hasn't parallel hardware made more of an impact commercially? One of the barriers concerning use of massively parallel computers has been the difficulty in developing algorithms and applications that can make effective use of their speed potential. Programmers tend to think sequentially. Operations have dependency constraints. If x and y are to be added, for example, the values of x and y must first be calculated. Some things must be done before others, and this limits how much faster a multiprocessor computer can chug along. The goal of dividing a program into sections that could be executed among separate processors has not achieved the hoped-for speed-ups.

Sandia National Laboratories took a different approach. Instead of partitioning a single task among the many processors of such machines, they scaled up the size of the tasks in proportion to the number of processors available. For instance, one structure problem they estimated would have taken 20 years to run on a single processor was completed in a week. Researchers are finding speed-ups of over 1,000 times in certain classes of problems.[4] An analogy: Instead of dividing up a single recipe among a number of cooks, it's more like giving each cook their own recipe. The result is better than a single dish supposedly made faster; the result is enough dishes to produce a feast.

In another hypercube architecture project, researchers are working on efficient use of the 64 processors on-board mobile intelligent robots dedicated to time-critical missions.[5] Their work currently uses a 64-node (2^6) NCube machine and a methodology for optimizing the computational load for sets of tasks that contain complex interrelationships. Features developed in this effort are applicable to general implementation methods for massively parallel asynchronous neural networks.

The Transputer parallel processing chip, developed and made by Inmos, Ltd., was initially used in powering accelerator boards for PCs. Whereas earlier signal processing systems were locked into dedicated hardware, the software-programmable Transputer offers significantly lower-cost array processing and significantly greater flexibility. The variety of applications enhanced with this technology include sonar, infrared sensors, and image processing. With the growing availability of cross-compilers, the Transputer chip is finding increased support as a tool for parallel processing.[6] Its high-speed interconnection links and relatively high processing speed provide a viable alternative to simulation on large supercomputers.[7]

Neurocomputers

Neurocomputers represent a new class of computers, optimized for running neural networks. Their architecture is quite different from that of parallel machines such as the hypercube. Although a high degree of parallelism is employed, algorithmic programming is still required for computations. In fact, the information-processing mechanisms are designed for implementing the systems of differential equations associated with neural networks. Additionally, the ability of a neurocomputer to self-organize its architecture is a key feature in utilizing parallel architectures to solve particular applications problems.

Neurocomputers can be classified in several ways. Implementation classes include electronic, optical, and optoelectronic. Types could include general-purpose neurocomputers (capable of implementing many architectures), hard-wired (implementing a specific application type), and partially general (a compromise between hard-wired and general-purpose, capable of implementing a particular class of networks, such as Hopfield networks).

Neurocomputers have been implemented on the chip, module, and systems level.

General-Purpose Neurocomputers

Frederico Faggin, vice president for advanced research at Synaptics, affirms the complementary relationship between neurocomputers and traditional von Neumann-type computers. He expects neural systems to become "the eyes and ears of general-purpose computers."[8] The two types of computers compensate for each other's weaknesses. The conventional computers can execute programmed functions very quickly; neurocomputers can "learn" and add to the functionality that can be performed.

NEC Corporation has produced a personal neurocomputer.[9] (We referred to this previously in chapter 2.) It includes neural network software and a special neuro-engine board. The software allows you to define the network structure and performs the calculations and updates. The board uses four of NEC's data-flow microprocessors for high-speed parallel processing. The maximum simulation size is 82,000 processing elements and 246,000 connections. Maximum speed is 196,000 links per second.

The first demonstrated application of the NEC machine was character recognition. Using 220 neurons and 7,000 interconnects in a 3-layer back-propagation structure, researchers confirmed a 99.95-percent recognition rate of 76 characters in 12 different fonts. The training to achieve a recognition speed of 60 characters per second was accomplished in 3 1/2 hours. Compare this with a recognition speed of 4 characters per second in 130 hours' training on a regular PC. Other applications include sound recognition, fault diagnosis, and robot control.

The European effort (Esprit II) is aimed at developing a general-purpose neural computer that will support a variety of network models. Industry and academia from eight European nations have combined in this five-year project expected to cost tens of millions of pounds and involve several hundred worker-years of effort.[10] It's an ambitious task, involving problems such as development of a suitable programming environment and an appropriate high-level language (HLL) for programming. The first couple of years are being spent studying architectures and algorithms for neural processors in an attempt to find the best structure for a general-purpose system. Again, standards are an issue. One

A Practical Guide to Neural Nets

suggested low-level language is called NIL, Neural network Implementation Language.

Special-Purpose Hardware

A few paragraphs back we talked about parallel computers. Several parallel processing companies that have in the past advertised their equipment as general-purpose machines are now retargeting to specific markets.[11] As the application focus for these more general parallel machines seems to be narrowing, other application-specific hardware architectures have incorporated specialized processors from the beginning. These systems include array processors, symbol processors, and other tools. They generally require host systems or powerful front ends that are not needed with the more general parallel hardware.

Some neural network implementations require this special-purpose hardware. Often, these devices are dedicated to one specific model, or network paradigm. The flexibility in models is traded for improved performance.

Hecht-Nielsen Neurocomputer Corporation (HNC) designed the ANZA coprocessor board for IBM PC/ATs and compatibles. The host is a Zenith 386–80, which serves basically as an I/O device for the neurocomputer. A program running on the host serial computer could call the neurocomputer as a subroutine. Up to 30,000 PEs and 480,000 interconnects are possible with a speed of 25,000 updates per second during training.[12] The ANZA can perform real-time signal analysis and has been used by AVCO Financial Services in the application mentioned in chapter 1.

Another example of special hardware is Texas Instruments' multiprocessor Odyssey Board. Neural network simulations can be accelerated substantially using the board's DSP (digital signal processing) modules. Update computations can be distributed to the various modules. For large networks, multiple boards can be used to partition the computations even more. The Odyssey's floating-point software capabilities become valuable if computations are complex.[13] The many tasks of a neural network are divided for improved performance.

Mark III, Mark IV, and Mark V

Several neurocomputers built at TRW use partially parallel hardware to do network simulations. The Mark III has eight physical processors, each of which emulates about 8,000 processing elements. This gives a total of around 65,000 PEs. In tests of an earlier version of this machine, it ran 21 times as fast as a simulation on a VAX superminicomputer.

The Mark IV, used exclusively by DARPA, handles 250,000 PEs and 5 million interconnections. An example of the real-world types of problems it can handle is aircraft identification, which it does with an accuracy of about 95 percent. The input image of an airplane is digitized into pixels and the brightness is color coded. The neural network takes each pixel, does calculations, and enters information on a graph. A mathematical procedure known as a Fourier transform gives a processed image that is independent of the rotation of the airplane in the input image. The processed image is then fed to a second neural network, which has been trained to recognize images and classify them.

In the summer of 1988, TRW released specifications for its Mark V. Built especially for neural network research, this 16-processor (or more) machine will be capable of 10 million virtual interconnects. It can be programmed with a VAX. One projected use is for optical recognition experiments.

Early Neurocomputers

Table 10.1 has been adapted from a chart that originally appeared in the *IEEE Spectrum* in March of 1988. It lists some of the early neurocomputers. The numbers given pertain to individual boards or chips. A "*" designation means the neurocomputer is available commercially as opposed to being purely an internal research machine.

Networks on a Chip

Real-time applications generally require even greater speed than can be achieved with neurocomputers that simulate large numbers of processors. Many researchers are investigating ways to build neural networks directly in integrated circuits. Instead of merely simulating parallelism, it is inherent in the hardware design.

Neural microchips come in a variety of designs. Some are digital simulations, some are analog devices. Neural systems are inherently analog and parallel in nature; electronic systems have been digital. Some designers are trying to match the biological

Table 10.1: Early Neurocomputers

| NEURO-COMPUTER | YEAR | TECHNOLOGY | CAPACITY | | | SPEED CUPS |
			# PEs	# Conn	@ Nets	
PERCEPTRON	1957	ELECTRO-MECH	8	512	1	10^3
*ADALINE/ MADALINE	1960/62	ELECTRONIC	1/8	15/128	1	10^4
ELECTRO-OPTIC CROSS-BAR	1984	ELECTRO-OPT	32	10^3	1	10^5
*MARK III	1985	ELECTRONIC	8×10^3	4×10^5	1	3×10^5
NEURAL EMULATION PROCESSOR	1985	ELECTRONIC	4×10^3	1.6×10^4	1	4.9×10^5
OPTICAL RESONATOR	1985	OPTICAL	6.4×10^3	1.6×10^7	1	1.6×10^5
MARK IV	1986	ELECTRONIC	2.5×10^5	5×10^6	1	5×10^6
*ODYSSEY	1986	ELECTRONIC	8×10^3	2.5×10^5	1	2×10^6
CROSSBAR CHIP	1986	ELECTRONIC	256	6.4×10^4	1	6×10^9
OPTICAL NOVELTY FILTER	1986	OPTICAL	1.6×10^4	2×10^6	1	2×10^7
*ANZA	1987	ELECTRONIC	3×10^4	5×10^5	any	2.5×10^4 (1.4×10^5)
*PARALLON 2	1987	ELECTRONIC	10^4	5.2×10^4	any	1.5×10^4 (3×10^4)
*PARALLON 2X	1987	ELECTRONIC	9.1×10^4	3×10^5	any	1.5×10^4 (3×10^4)
*DELTA FLOATING-POINT PROCESSOR	1987	ELECTRONIC	10^6	10^6	any	2×10^6 (10^7)
*ANZA PLUS	1988	ELECTRONIC	10^6	1.5×10^6	any	1.5×10^6 (6×10^6)

Notes: numbers given pertain to individual boards or chips.
    * = Commercial
    @ = # of networks that can be simultaneously resident on the board
    () = speed without learning

Used with permission of HNC, Inc. and IEEE (c) 1988 IEEE.

architectures. Other models seek to emphasize the computational aspects of memory, thought, and cognitive processes.

VLSI (Very Large Scale Integration) technology has been in process for several years. Caltech's early Hopfield circuit chip had 22 processing elements and 462 interconnections. One CMOS (Complementary Metal Oxide Semiconductor) implementation supported 289 artificial neurons. Resistors are small. It is possible to achieve a density of half a billion interconnections per square centimeter. AT&T built an Electronic Neural Network (ENN) chip that had 256 processing elements etched onto it. Resistors were used for both the nodes and the interconnection synapses. AT&T's application for the ENN chip is to compress data, such as video images, for transmission in real time over telephone lines. It is important to have the design right because this particular chip is not modifiable. A 54-PE programmable chip whose weights can be changed by an external program is also being tested.

Ten new chips were described at the International Joint Conference on Neural Networks (IJCNN) in the summer of 1989, "kicking off a new era in neural microchips."[14] Of these ten, two were already commercially available (Micro Devices' MD1210 and Syntonic Systems' Dendros-1). Additional chips were in fabrication and still others were expected to be available soon. Major semiconductor businesses working on neural microchips include companies like AT&T, Texas Instruments, Motorola, Fujitsu, and Intel. Besides these, a number of new companies have emerged with neural net products; some of these companies are also building neural microchips.

Intel's N64 chip (64 neurons) is an analog model that uses E^2PROM technology to store continuous synaptic weights and handle 100,000 connections per second; a newer analog chip from Intel runs at 2.5 billion connections per second. The Syntonic Systems chip also uses an analog circuitry, based on ART (adaptive resonance theory) to model real neurons even down to their "need for sleep."[15] A sleep-refresh system stores analog memory values as a charge on capacitors, but the architecture itself compensates for any leakage that occurs in the capacitors. Explains Syntonic's founder Carlos Tapang, "After many patterns have been learned, the system needs sleep in order to enhance their contrast."

Nippon Telephone and Telegraph (NTT) showed an array of

65,536 1-bit processors packed into 1,024 digital chips that can run at 18 million connections per second. Hecht-Nielsen Neurocomputer Corporation (HNC) has two high-speed digital simulator chip projects in design.

Fujitsu Ltd., like Intel and Syntonic, has gone with a basically analog model.[16] The company's board incorporates 40 of the chips. Weights are stored off-chip. Learning is accomplished ahead of time in software on a PC and then downloaded to the board. Although Fujitsu's first pilot chip models only a single neuron, it can connect to 1,000 other chips. Future models are predicted to handle 32 neurons on a 10-mm-square chip and run at much faster speeds than the current 70,000 connections per second.

Hitachi has developed a wafer-scale neural network. The 5-inch wafer holds 576 artificial neurons and uses a novel time-division multiplexing method to make 100 physical connections appear to be 10,000 virtual connections.[17] The system is scheduled for delivery around 1993.

Science Applications International (SAIC) is working on a new neural-network microchip that can do on-chip learning.[18] The chip is generic in the sense that it can handle a number of different network models, and modular in that you can put together as many chips as necessary for solving your particular problem. The hardware learning mode is fast (about the same speed as the normal operational mode) and can learn in several different styles for a variety of feedforward and recurrent networks.

The Encephalon Project

Encephalon—literally, "the brain"—represents a rigorous biologically oriented approach to neural network chips. This is the project of Odin Corporation, a new start-up company in Manhattan, Kansas. We telephoned Odin to see what they were doing and talked with Willard Olson. The staff consists of only two: Olson, a neuroscientist formerly with Intel and instrumental in design of that company's neural network chip as well as a consultant to Synaptics, and Yee-Wei Huang, a chemical engineering professor at Kansas State University who has database expertise. They hope to achieve the functionality of the vertebrate brain in a silicon machine.

They began by looking at the lowest-level biological systems. "All have precise, systemic architectures," said Olson. "There are precise areas, areas analogous to the cortex, and also relationships of precise organization among the areas." He noted that it is not the precision of individual connections that is key, because you can lose up to 30 percent of the connections without bad effects. The importance of structures is Odin's foundational assumption. The duplication of the entire brain structure, not simply the cerebral cortex, is the company's goal.

"Systemic neural network modeling,"[19] they call it, questioning other models that seek to duplicate the complexity of the cerebral cortex alone. "If we could duplicate the cortex in silicon tomorrow, would we have anything?" mused Olson. "In searching for parallelism, we tend to forget about sequential activity."

For justification of their approach, Olson and Huang compare human senses of sight and smell to those of other organisms. Bats have superior auditory processing capability, yet their auditory cortex is less complex. The brains of birds are specialized for optical processing. Insects have highly and predictably organized brains, similar in many respects to the brains of higher animals. "Each is a manifestation of exquisite architectural order." The relationship between complexity and organization becomes a key question in trying to simulate the processing of sensory inputs.

Another observation giving support to the importance of structure is what happens in the surgical procedure of prefrontal lobotomies. " . . . the major fiber (association) tract connecting the dominant frontal association cortex to the temporal association cortex of the same hemisphere is severed. No damage whatsoever is done to the cortical structures—the complexity of the brain remains intact—but the functional organization of the brain has been destroyed."

Olson and Huang set out to identify the critical structural elements in sensory processing. They identified 26 synaptic rules, converted these to a C++ program, and began simulation at the lowest level. Encephalon I, the functional simulation, was running by Christmas 1989. Next a team from Motorola, who is backing the whole-brain concept and funding the project, will help implement the design in test hardware. Their target completion date is late 1990.

The Encephalon design uses Hebbian learning, but does not include the popular concept of weights; weights have no basis in biology. Consequently, there is no need for the immense resources needed by other neural network systems in calculating thousands of weights. Encephalon models not just the separate parts of the brain, but the whole brain: cortical column, basal ganglia, reticular formation. Control is decentralized. Each neuron is autonomous. Synchronization is critical.

"We have discovered how to give instant readout of the state of a multidimensional machine with our concept of holographic memory," Olson said.[20] Different views of an object—say, front, side, and rear—are stored in related locations so that the object can be recalled no matter what the viewing angle. There is no distinction between recall and learning, declared Huang: "They are not two separate operations as with other neural networks." Knowledge is added incrementally; new patterns can be associated with other patterns already in memory. Lengthy training, the bane of many other systems, is not required. "Encephalon works like the real brain."

When we first spoke with Olson, it was October of 1989, shortly after the San Francisco earthquake. He talked about watching the TV coverage of the quake—and thinking about how useful his planned chip could be in quickly amassing information from direct analog inputs from seismic monitoring equipment. He talked about his hopes and dreams. Twenty years ago he might have worked on problems such as cancer, or aging. But if he solved *this* problem, and built *this* machine . . . it would fulfill all the dreams.

Silicon Retinas

Another chip designer who believes in the importance of biological structure is Carver Mead (of CalTech), considered by many to be the "guru of representation." Mead attempts to achieve the same kind of representation in silicon as he sees in the biological. He believes that biological structures owe their architectures to the structure of data passed to them. The structures of the ear, for example, are designed to process the particular wave structure of sound. Mead and his coworkers use the term *eclectronics* to describe their approach in creating synthetic biological devices.

The silicon retina developed by Mead and his colleagues is a photodetector fabricated on an analog VLSI chip of 6 × 8 mm. A single chip contains 100,000 transistors and has more than 2,000 photosensitive cells arranged in a square array. Each cell is 100 by

125 microns and has a small circuit built entirely from CMOS. The wiring simulates the cones found in a human retina. The data are preprocessed, as is done by the eye and the ear.

Conventional image processing attempts to discover boundaries of objects and their movement by correlating points from snapshots taken at discrete time intervals. These traditional procedures record absolute intensities and then attempt to reconstruct the information later. Because this is not how biological systems "see," Mead rejected these procedures. He calls the approach "too costly" for nature. Instead, his system models the eye in responding to the rate of change in light intensities.

Mead's silicon retina can register the continuous movement of an object accurately and smoothly without using a computer to do any image processing. If conventional sensors were used to accomplish the same task, they would require the power of a CRAY supercomputer, and even then, the recorded movement would not be as smooth as what his chip can accomplish.

In addition to the retina (which Mead claims can do nearly half of what a human retina can do), Mead has also developed a silicon cochlea. He eventually hopes to build an entire nervous system of silicon and to create artificial neural networks that never stop adapting. His book, *Analog VLSI and Neural Systems* is likely to become a foundational work in the field.[21]

Optical Neural Networks

In most optical neural-network implementations, activity levels of processing elements are represented by the brightness levels of pixels, arrays of LEDs, or other discrete emitters. Light beams can cross paths without interfering with one another. Because high-density electrical signals interfere, optical implementations in which the movement of photons, or light beams, is substituted for electrons, have distinct advantages.[22]

Optical interconnections between electronic chips will ease the bottleneck found in conventional computers. The density of optical interconnections can be much greater than even the most advanced silicon and gallium arsenide processes. Optical approaches also generate less heat and may eventually operate at speeds up to 1,000 times faster than electronic approaches. They offer greater bandwidth and easier integration with front-end sensors.[23]

Dana Anderson (University of Colorado) has built an optical associative memory. If the system is shown part of a pattern, the memories retrieve the entire pattern. If the system is not presented any pattern, it displays a random pattern that Anderson calls "daydreaming." Bell Labs scientists, among others, are also doing considerable research on optical neurocomputers and the practicality of optical switching techniques.

Massive database management may be one area that could be dominated by optical technology. But it will take time. All-optical computers are not yet possible. Before optical interconnections will be practical, optical switches must become affordable. It's hard to compete with the currently more mature and ever-improving technology of electronic computers.[24]

Optoelectronics

Many neural network models that have shown useful promise have to date been too complex to build in hardware. Consequently, they have been run as software simulations, often on supercomputers. An optoelectronics approach, however, would allow design of complex models from neural network ICs. Hardware-implemented neural networks orders of magnitude more complex than was previously possible can now be built with today's technology.[25]

The optoelectronics scheme can support a density of 250,000 interconnections per square inch. As mentioned above, photons don't interfere with each other as electrons do. In addition, the scheme allows the flexibility of reconfiguring the hardware into entirely different mathematical models, or upgrading the current model's performance, without hardware modification.

The photoconductive neural network construction has five layers that resemble a "Dagwood sandwich" (see figure 10.2). A planar light source layer illuminates a photoconductive layer. A layer between these two serves as a mask. This middle layer has a spatial light modulator that acts as a light valve to modulate the illumination. This stores the interconnection weights between arrays of discrete emitters and detectors.

At the top and bottom of the sandwich are opaque layers that allow the structure to be repeated and achieve a higher density

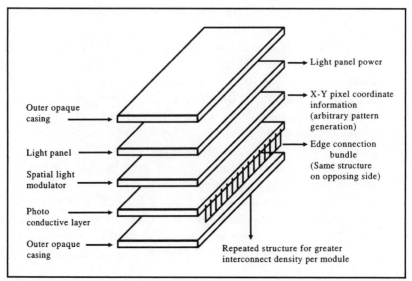

Light panel power

X-Y pixel coordinate
information
(arbitrary pattern
generation)

Outer opaque
casing

Edge connection
bundle
(Same structure
on opposing side)

Light panel

Spatial light
modulator

Photo
conductive layer

Outer opaque
casing

Repeated structure for greater
interconnect density per module

FIGURE 10.2   LAYERS IN AN OPTOELECTRONIC NEURAL NETWORK (REPRINTED WITH PERMISSION FROM *ELECTRONIC DESIGN*, VOL. 37, NO. 12, JUNE 8, 1989. © 1989, RENTON PUBLISHING.)

of interconnects per module. Any arbitrary two-dimensional pattern can be created, and three-dimensional interconnections would be possible if shades of gray are allowed. Different "masks" could switch the pattern of interconnections and accomplish different tasks without having to change the hardware. Such schemes as this will offer the possibility for speed with flexibility and relative ease of use.

Holographic Implementations

One of the most promising devices for implementing neural networks may be holograms. Holograms can be "programmed" to allow a variety of mappings. A conventional lens maps each light ray to a particular point on an image plane. A planar hologram 1 inch square might connect 10,000 sources of light to 10,000 arbitrary destinations. To achieve real density would require a volume hologram, made from a photorefractive crystal.

Although holograms still seem somewhat mysterious to most of the general population, they are becoming more common. The *National Geographic* magazine put a globe hologram on its December 1988 cover, and you may own a hologram on your credit card.

Although a strict description of a holographic neural network is beyond the scope of this book, it may be useful to present some general information and a simplified picture of how the process works.

A hologram is a kind of three-dimensional picture produced by lensless photography. The image can be seen from a variety of angles. Somewhat ghostlike, it appears to be suspended in space. Any piece of the hologram contains the same information as the whole and can reconstruct the entire image. This property is responsible for the hologram becoming a popular metaphor for human memory.

A common hologram is made by projecting light onto a photographic plate from two sources: from the object itself and from a reference beam, the light deflected by a mirror from the object onto the plate. The plate then contains patterns that do not resemble the original object and that appear to be meaningless. A coherent (constant phase difference) light source, such as a laser beam, can be used to reconstitute the image. What you see is a three-dimensional likeness projected into space, at a distance from the plate.

In a neural network holographic implementation, holograms can serve as memory storage.[26] Light from a laser is used to illuminate two objects that are to be associated with each other. The two light beams cross within a holographic substance, such as a photorefractive crystal, and produce an interference pattern that is recorded on the medium. A photorefractive crystal will bend a light beam when it strikes the crystal; lasers can be used to change the amount of bending. This process forms gratings in the crystal, a record of the interference pattern. After the recording has been made, you can turn off the light from one object and reconstruct the light from the other object.

There are many variations, but the basic operating principles are similar. "They all store reference images in either a thin or volume hologram and retrieve them in a coherently illuminated feedback loop. An input image, which may be noisy or incomplete, is applied to the system and is simultaneously correlated optically with all of the stored reference images. These correlations are thresholded and fed back to the input, where the strongest correlation reinforces (and possibly corrects or completes) the input image. The enhanced image goes around the loop repeatedly, approaching the stored image more closely on each pass, until the system stabilizes on the desired image." [27]

To recall an association from distorted data requires using some nonlinear optical devices such as lenses and mirrors. Suppose a number of pairs of objects are associated and recorded on the hologram. For example, one association pair could be dog/bone and another could be cat/mouse. Then suppose you input an image that was a combination of two objects, such as part of a dog and part of a cat. The holographic memory may output a combination of the two associated objects, a combined bone and mouse. Confusing? Yes. Should the output image be a bone or should it be a mouse? If a decision is required, optical circuits can do the decision-making process. A set of mirrors, for example, can take the output beam and propagate the light beam circularly back to the input where it intersects itself in the medium (crystal). With such an iterative loop going, energy reinforcement and possible noise help decide the competition among stored possibilities. The memory will recall an entire image of a single object, not parts of images.

There is an important difference between holograms on photographic plates and holograms on photorefractive substances. The former can be read but cannot be rewritten. Photorefractive media, however, can be used to read and write holograms simultaneously. The recorded grating will evolve over time, producing a dynamic memory. The time scales for change are different for different substances, but objects in holographic memory could be altered, reinforced, or erased, over time. It depends on how closely the input resembles objects already stored or whether it is entirely new input.

The dynamics of such systems are an area of considerable research. The addition of nonlinear optical feedback to holographic memories, for example, has resulted in a new class of nonlinear holographic associative memories (NHAM).[28] These systems perform associations between input patterns and stored patterns as in classical holography. Unlike classical holography, however, external nonlinearities are used to make decisions and select between competing alternatives, perform error corrections, and increase storage capacity. In addition to working on better nonlinear mechanisms, research concerns include better image

A Practical Guide to Neural Nets

quality, larger and permanent storage capacity, and programmability. To achieve practicality, holographic systems will need to be integrated with general-purpose optical neural networks as well as interfaced to conventional electronic host computers.

Biological Computers

Some implementations do more than model the biology; they *are* biological. *Wetware*, it's sometimes called. There are biochips, with actual cells on electrode grids. The cells (fetal mouse tissue, sea slugs, etc.) differentiate into neurons and organize themselves into networks. Their signals are monitored by electrodes and may be passed on to a computer. Researchers hope to develop mathematical models of how neurons interconnect. (Research stories in the next chapter feature this strategy.)

The April 1988 issue of *Lotus* talks about organically grown systems.[29] Speakers at the BioTech Conference in San Francisco in 1987 told about biological computer circuits created by lithographing protein patterns onto silicon chips. They predicted that within five years these biocomputers may be able to do things like the color-sensing of the human eye.

The Japanese government is reported to be funding molecular computers built of proteins and enzymes.[30] Using recombinant DNA, polymer chemistry, and artificial membranes, the computer functions depend on recognizing particular patterns within a protein chain. Signals change the shape of an enzyme, thus affecting its reaction with a protein. The molecular computer has three layers. Inputs could be variables such as light, pressure, temperature. Messenger molecules are released and interact with enzymes in the middle layer. Molecules read the result of the reactions and generate output signals. The definition of *computer* may be in for radical changes.

Synergistic Efforts

With such a diversity of disciplines involved in neural net research, such varied possibilities for implementation, such divergent applications potential, and such wide interests in academia, industry and government, the benefits of coordinating efforts and sharing breakthroughs become obvious. The many conferences and symposia provide much information for researchers as well as the general public. One illustration of a private service is the clearinghouse of Battelle-Columbus Labs (see chapter 2).

The neural net team of MCC (Microelectronics and Computer Technology Corporation, Austin, TX), is trying to bring together groups doing neural network software simulations and those implementing actual neural network hardware. Their goal is to advance both hardware implementation and learning algorithms. By playing middleman and demonstrating short-term, real-world gains, they hope to achieve greater corporate involvement while still focusing on long-term research objectives.

Some of MCC's own projects are noteworthy; its optical computing program is strong. Recent studies of intermittent turbulence within chaotic systems are being applied to process control with considerable success. Using algorithms developed internally, the company's researchers have been able to anticipate random fluctuations in manufacturing lines by predicting turbulence across 50 to 100 variables.[31]

Summary

Most scientists working on neural network systems believe that such systems will have a profound impact on computing and on understanding the brain, but only after a decade or so of hard work. "They will change the way we think about computation," says Carver Mead. "They will give us a lot of things people have already thought about, like artificial speech recognition and vision, but they will also give us a lot of things we never imagined, just as the microprocessor did."[32]

Mead further estimates that analog VLSI ultimately will create neural networks that run at 10 quadrillion operations per second, but only if designers start doing their homework.[33] Engineers must learn neurobiology in order to build useful architectures. There are no shortcuts. Simply scaling up simulations running on digital systems will not address the fuzzy sorts of problems researchers are trying to solve with neural net technology.

Neural networks have gained considerable sophistication in implementations. Awkward simulations on digital computers have given way to special processors and high-powered chips. The inefficiencies of mapping highly parallel, associative, nonlinear analog processes onto single-processor serial computers are being overcome with new implementation schemes and possibilities.

There are fewer limitations in today's implementations. Neural networks can produce very good answers, though not necessarily optimum solutions, in remarkably short times. Despite immature theory and premature hype, researchers are moving ahead. We were persuaded of this in recalling the technological gains of the space race and the number of practical advances made in medicine, in miniaturization, in better understanding of human beings. Involving engineers in research on the understanding of the brain, through neural networks, could have similar impacts.

1. Derek F. Stubbs, editor, *Neurocomputing Newsletter*, vol 3, no. 1 (January 1989): 3, 4.

2. R. Colin Johnson, "Turnkey Neural-Net-Based Packages Appear," *Electronic Engineering Times*, issue 553 (August 28, 1989): 29.

3. Terry Costlow, "NCube Hits 27 Gflops," *Electronic Engineering Times*, issue 543 (June 19, 1989).

4. M. Mitchell Waldrop, "Hypercube Breaks a Programming Barrier," *Science*, vol. 240 (April 1988): 286.

5. Jacob Barhen, N. Toomarian, and V. Protopopescu, "Optimization of the Computational Load of a Hypercube Supercomputer Onboard a Mobile Robot," *Applied Optics*, vol. 26, no. 23 (December 1, 1987): 5007–14.

6. Roger Woolnaugh, "Transputer Uses Touted," *Electronic Engineering Times*, issue 554 (September 4, 1989): 22; "Radar Application Exploits Transputers," *Electronic Engineering Times*, issue 557 (September 25, 1989): 39.

7. D. Suter and X. Deng, "Neural Net Simulation of Transputers," *Proceedings of the 1988 IEEE International Conference on Systems, Man, and Cybernetics*, Aug. 8–12, 1988, pp. 694–97.

8. Richard Dalton, "Ideas & Trends: Future Computers," *Lotus* (April 1988): 19–22.

9. Miyoko Sakurai, "NEC's 'neuro'," *Electronic Engineering Times*, issue 494 (July 11, 1988): 19; "NEC Develops PC Neuro-Computer System," *Comline Computers* (December 1, 1988): 2.

10. Angeli Mehta, "Nations Unite for Electronic Brain," *Computer Weekly*, issue 1148 (January 11, 1988): 1.

11. Terry Costlow, "Parallel Processing: Searching," *Electronic Engineering Times*, issue 554 (September 4, 1989): 1.

12. Lisa Stapleton and Paul E. Schindler, Jr., "New Kids on the Block," *Information Week* (December 14, 1987): 33.

13. Wanda S. Gass, et al., "Multiple Digital Signal Processor Environ-

ment for Intelligent Signal Processing," *Proceedings of the IEEE,* vol. 75, no. 9 (September 1987): 1246–59.

14. R. Colin Johnson, "10 Neural Chips at IJCNN," *Electronic Engineering Times,* issue 546 (July 10, 1989): 39, 42.

15. R. Colin Johnson, "Syntonic's Neural Chips Are Sleepers," *Electronic Engineering Times,* issue 507 (October 10, 1988): 49–50.

16. R. Colin Johnson, "Neural Chip Readied," *Electronic Engineering Times,* issue 552 (August 21, 1989): 29.

17. R. Colin Johnson, "Japan Mounts Neural Push," *Electronic Engineering Times,* issue 572 (January 8, 1990): 20.

18. R. Colin Johnson, "DARPA Neural Awards Stress Practical Use," *Electronic Engineering Times,* issue 558 (October 2, 1989): 22.

19. Willard Olson and Yee-Wei Huang, "Toward Systemic Neural Network Modeling," IEEE/INNS International Joint Conference on Neural Networks (IJCNN), Washington, D.C., June 1989.

20. R. Colin Johnson, "'Whole-Brain' Neural Chips," *Electronic Engineering Times,* issue 561 (October 23, 1989): 33, 36.

21. Bill Bien, "The Promise of Neural Networks," *American Scientist,* vol. 76 (November/December 1988): 561–64

22. Yuri Owechko, "Photonic Hardware Is Used to Implement Neural-Network Models," *Laser Focus World,* vol. 25, no. 1 (January 1989): 166.

23. Bruce D. Nordwall, "Photonics Will Boost Near-term Computer Processing Speeds," *Aviation Week & Space Technology,* vol. 130, no. 16 (April 17, 1989): 57–59.

24. "Optical Computing Looks for Its Niche," *SDI Monitor,* (December 12, 1988): 279, 280.

25. Johna Till, "Optoelectronic Scheme Opens Doors for Neural Nets," *Electronic Design,* vol. 37, no. 12 (June 8, 1989): 27.

26. Dana Z. Anderson, "Optical Systems That Imitate Human Memory," *Computers in Physics,* vol. 3, no. 2 (March/April 1989): 19–25.

27. Philip D. Wasserman, *Neural Computing: Theory and Practice* (New York: Van Nostrand Reinhold, 1989): 159.

28. Yuri Owechko, "Nonlinear Holographic Associative Memories," *IEEE Journal of Quantum Electronics,* vol. 25, no. 3 (March 1989): 619–34.

29. Richard Dalton, "Future Computers: Researchers Focus on Organic and Parallel-processing Models," Ideas and Trends, *Lotus* (April 1988): 21.

30. Peter Judge, "Neurocomputers Are News," *New Electronics* (May 1988): 36, 37.

31. Loring Wirbel, "Neural Funding Sought," *Electronic Engineering Times,* issue 554 (September 4, 1989): 29, 31.

32. Bill Bien, "The Promise of Neural Networks," *American Scientist,* vol. 76 (November/December 1988): 561–64.

33. R. Colin Johnson, "IC Guru Mead Blasts Neuro Hot Shots," *Electronic Engineering Times,* issue 540 (May 29, 1989): 33.

What Is the Current Research?

A new idea is delicate. It can be killed by a sneer or a yawn; it can be stabbed to death by a quip, and worried to death by a frown on the right man's brow.

—*Charlie Brower*

Introduction

A "state-of-the-art" assessment in any technology is a bold attempt. It has to be a combination of areas, it has to be current, and it often sports the flavor of an exotic edge. Usually it includes an attempt to pin down where the field currently is (in relationship to some sort of continuum), recent gains made, barriers yet to be overcome, and foreseeable next steps. There might be some statistical information quoted to show how well things are (or aren't) progressing, and possibly an analysis of emerging directions. Although we do include some of the above information, we are not quite so bold, and will settle for sharing some of the current research. The few statistics we want to quote appear in the next chapter.

In this chapter, we have opted for a topical format. We'll look first at a few of the issues and problems facing the development of artificial neural networks. Unsolved problems provide much of the research agenda. Along the way we'll highlight several specific examples of current research efforts. Detailing the study of specific groups provides a focus for research components and presents a more coherent view of research efforts. This field is being investigated by researchers from such a wide range of disciplines that it's hard to say any particular research is representative of the whole. What we can say is that what we read in the journals and what we hear from researchers is exciting and exhibits guarded optimism. We'll end with a discussion of some of the more obvious directions that seem to be surfacing.

Issues and Problems

Often, amid a variety of problems, some are key. If you can solve them, an avalanche of new possibilities is set in motion. The area of training/learning is one such key for the development of practical neural network applications. Another key issue is the choosing of appropriate neural network architecture and paradigms to match applications. That area has many unclear aspects, and is inspiring research and development of yet new models and better representations. Other problems, such as implementation techniques, scaling, time, practicality, standards, performance, and I/O constraints, all demand attention. The Institute of Electronic and Electrical Engineers (IEEE) has established a task force to consider standardization and other issues relating to the neural networks industry. Research is needed in neural network theory; today's theoretical foundations, although expanding rapidly, are still inadequate to support the more optimistic projections.

Learning/Training

Researchers are continually seeking better learning and training algorithms. Different needs require different types of learning. Learning and training involve a number of aspects beyond the implementation of appropriate learning rules. Knowing how to select the input information, how to choose the training sets, and how to do preprocessing of data are skills in their own right and are not particularly straightforward, either.

At present, training is expensive and often very time-consuming. Delivery versions of systems can be produced much more cheaply once the training has been completed. Research departments may be able to swing the necessary funds for development projects, but costs must be decreased to produce deliverable, practical applications. Better training methods would help in the short term, but having a system that can actually do independent learning is a much longer-range endeavor.

Part of the problem is that learning is so poorly understood.

A Practical Guide to Neural Nets

We understand so little of how the brain works, and perhaps even less of how learning occurs. We may be our own best examples, but it's hard to imitate without a strong basis of understanding. Research in neurobiology is making progress here, but nature's secrets are only slowly being revealed.

Autonomous Learning: There is a difference between learning and recall. It is much easier to regurgitate previously assembled information than to ascertain new relationships and organize original categories and assimilations. If a neural network system is good at recall functions only, then it is necessary to impose constraints and limitations. Inputs must be binary only, or linearly separable, or orthogonal. We would also have to restrict environments. An autonomous land vehicle, for instance, would *not* be autonomous if it could only operate on paved roads.

Autonomous means without outside control: independent. Such systems would have to learn from their mistakes, their observations and experiences of the world. They must be able to generalize from specific to general categories. Such systems would need to organize their knowledge, figuring out what data is significant, reorganizing when necessary. Details that were unimportant previously may now be relevant, and an autonomous system would need to self-adjust. This property is sometimes called *vigilance*. Also, it may be necessary to revise or forget what worked before when a situation changes.

An autonomous system would need to be able to respond rapidly. Twenty-four hours may be adequate in a laboratory, but not on an assembly line. Additionally, the amount of available storage should be adequate for any anticipated (or unanticipated) needs.

Some paradigms have achieved limited success in some areas; others do better in yet other areas. Some networks need to perform only limited functions and can concentrate on specific features to the exclusion of others that are not important for that specific application.

Two network models based on adaptive resonance theory, ART-1 and ART-2, developed by Stephen Grossberg and Gail Carpenter (Boston University) show promise but can process only limited inputs.[1] ART-1 can automatically categorize input patterns, reorganize categories, and recall patterns rapidly. ART-2 is much more complex, but at present lacks robustness. Grossberg and Carpenter's third-generation model, ART-3, extends the architecture to accommodate multilayered hierarchies and adds a chemical transmitter model. It can more closely mirror the complexity of the brain.

None of the current network models discussed in this book incorporates all of the properties needed true for autonomous learning.

Research on Learning: GTE Laboratories is one of the corporations involved in research on how neural networks learn. The company's goal is to develop systems that can learn quickly from limited experience in order to be useful in real-time control applications. One of the unique aspects of the research is the company's work in reinforcement learning. The researchers need a system that can learn from its own failures by trial and error, much as animals learn. When something goes wrong, what caused the failure? What features are important to success? The system should answer these questions without benefit of human intervention.

Pole-balancing experiments (see chapter 7) and simulations are one vehicle for assessing progress. Most previous efforts by others to balance a broom or a pole have used a human or some control mechanism to perform the balancing. The network then attempted to mimic the results. GTE researchers want their network to learn to balance the pole without providing a model of how to do it. When the pole falls to one side or the other, the network must determine on its own which features are important. This development of needed features is very slow, partly because inputs (states) to the network are not under the control of a trainer.

Research at GTE also involves learning representations, a separate issue, that is as important as reinforcement learning in the development of intelligent control systems. The problem of finding good representations is common to all decision-making systems. In connectionist networks, error back propagation is a method often used to improve the representation automatically by learning new features. The disadvantage of conventional gradient descent methods such as back error propagation (see chapter 8), is that they can require much time and experience to discover useful features. GTE researchers are pursuing alternatives. They want representations that can be developed quickly in reinforcement systems.

Achieving the necessary complexity requires use of multilayered networks with nonlinear processing units. The learning paradigm under investigation is a novel combination of back propagation and reinforcement learning. A modified gradient descent method occasionally makes drastic changes in unused processing units to direct the gradient search toward features that help discriminate difficult input patterns from others. In other words, at the stops, the learning method goes into the network, selects units not currently being used, and resets the weights so the units can become useful at detecting features.

Another focus of the research involves consideration of the function used for the output of a processing unit. These functions can have a large impact on the speed of learning. GTE is testing locally tuned Gaussian-shaped output functions as options to the more common sigmoid functions. (Gaussian functions are also known as bell curves; see figure 11.1.) Although both halves of the function are monotonic, or continuously increasing, the curve itself is nonmonotonic, continuous, and continuously differentiable. The peak corresponds to the value of the input at which the

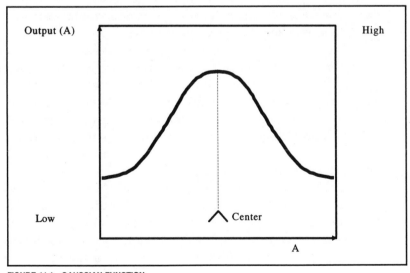

FIGURE 11.1 GAUSSIAN FUNCTION

output is high. This function permits the unit to generalize only to nearby states, because the curve may drop off rather steeply (the width is variable). The processing units are therefore more locally tuned and the result is faster learning of complex functions for which this kind of generalization is appropriate.

Related is the concern for having the network determine the granularity it needs to form: coarse or fine. Some features are meaningful for a wide variety of inputs; others apply only to a narrow spectrum. When is it appropriate to develop broad, general features, and when is it necessary to focus on very specific ones?

Humans have some intuitive idea of how to do this. We usually begin by looking at broad issues to collect more data, and then concentrate on areas that appear to be more productive. Consider for a moment the tasks involved in assessing figure 2.2, the sequential versus gestalt experiment presented in chapter 2. Initially, you might discern the larger category of three different word groupings. A more detailed examination would show the vowels are missing. Finally, noting that the category is "proverbs" might be useful. An autonomous robot would have to perform some similar "judgments." It would have to survey the general environment, then perhaps move to a specific location, and perhaps finally manipulate a specific control mechanism. Having a learning representation accomplish the task of determining how fine the focus should be at the given time would certainly contribute to realizing the preceding goals.

Sometimes the toughest aspect of research is technology transfer. It can be difficult to get a trial, to prove the value of the technology. We were curious about how the research efforts at GTE made the journey from laboratory to application. (GTE's primary neural network application was featured in chapter 1.) GTE's John Doleac told us a story that was unusual, delightful, and exemplified a grass-roots approach, with management support, that ought to be more typical.

The GTE researchers were holding an AI workshop. Because it was just down the road from Doleac's office instead of across the continent, Doleac easily got permission to go. After all, the workshop would deal with CIM (Computer Integrated Manufacturing), and he might pick up some ideas for the manufacturing process.

A Practical Guide to Neural Nets

Among other presentations, the workshop showed films of the pole balancer. The researchers were looking for test beds. The production line at Doleac's plant already had some sensors attached for another project, and flopping a few more sensors on the line seemed to have few disadvantages. Doleac volunteered to try to supply a test bed.

Some said detailed proposals approved by upper management would be needed. Others leaned back, shaking their heads, and said, "Don't worry about proposals." After all, virtually no funding would be needed in this instance. In most corporations, projects generally originate from the top down, as a regular part of management by objectives. This case was an exception. Doleac says that although there is not yet enough data to provide the proof of the research, "if—when—it does come, it will be a big personal payoff" for those involved.

The above paragraphs on learning represent only a part of the larger effort at GTE.[2] (The conceptual diagram from chapter 1 is repeated in figure 11.2 as a reminder of GTE's manufacturing process. NADALINE stands for Normalized ADALINE. The NA-

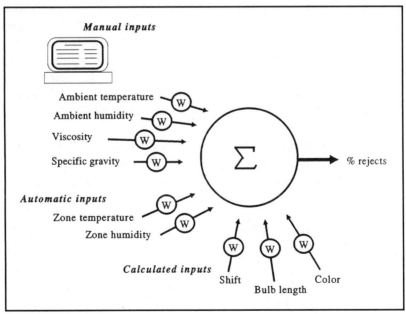

FIGURE 11.2 NADALINE

DALINE algorithm is simply the ADALINE algorithm with input values automatically normalized to have zero mean and unit variance.) Current research efforts will produce application enhancements. Many steps will be required to achieve the longer-range goal of specifically controlling the line. The prediction of all the observable states of the system will involve modeling at a variety of time scales—months, weeks, days, hours, minutes, and even seconds. The hybrid controller will need to be iteratively refined; it will need to learn an internal model of the system rather than learning control laws. Hierarchies of learning must be developed to satisfy a number of differing goals at differing levels. VLSI implementation will be essential to achieve the real-time speed, and a VLSI project is underway. Learning more about nonlinear regression functions and how to apply them, which is rather difficult with conventional methods, will be a continuing research effort.

Improving Computational Models

A significant portion of neural network research centers on the improvement of computational models. In many designs, the learning mode is separate from observation and storage modes. Frequently learning is turned off during recall because it requires more time and resources. That is *not* the way humans process data. Overcoming these and other such limitations provides impetus for the continuing refinement of current paradigms and the development of new neural network models. Research in neurobiology is one source of contributions to the store of knowledge essential for improving computational models.

Neurobiological Research: Artificial neural networks exhibit a number of characteristics that are brainlike in nature: the ability to learn from experience, to make abstractions and generalizations, and even to make mistakes. It is reasonable to assume that better understanding of how the brain works and how biological neurons perform their tasks will aid in the development of computational technology and result in improved artificial neural systems. Likewise, as long as computational models remain true to biological realities, the models can contribute to the understanding of complex biological phenomena. Interaction can be profitable in both directions.

Neurobiological research is quite varied. Much of it is tedious. Some of it is downright fascinating. Researchers are learning more about the molecular mechanisms that control synaptic activity. They are expanding their knowledge of brain circuitry and learning-related physiological changes in the brains of higher mammals. They are even creating computational maps of mammalian brains. There is still much to learn: organization, features, structures, mechanisms, representations, behaviors. Some of the simplest ideas are very powerful. Gains in neurobiological understanding certainly have the potential for being exploited by those modeling in artificial systems.

Neuroscience Network Projects: Scientists are increasingly turning to chemistry and biology to create new designs for neural network computer systems. Much of the current research on biological neural networks involves the study of invertebrate animals, such as sea slugs or starfish. Organisms such as these are useful in the lab because of their simplicity and relatively short growth periods.

At the Center for Network Neuroscience at the University of North Texas, Guenter Gross heads a project to capture simultaneous electrical events in small biological networks. (We first met Dr. Gross at the Fourth Annual Symposium on Networks in Brain and Computer Architecture in Dallas in October of 1988; telephone calls and correspondence have provided updates on his project.)

The goal of the project is to achieve a comprehensive theoretical explanation of the internal dynamics and self-organization of random networks. Mouse spinal cord, olfactory bulb, cortex, or cerebellum tissue is used to form a monolayer network of 100 to 500 neurons. The dissociated tissue is randomly reassembled to grow on photoetched, thin-film multielectrode surfaces. Although the original circuitry has been altered, the cells are not destroyed. The physical and chemical environment can be easily manipulated as well as observed in the living state.

The analysis of network dynamics involves long-term monitoring of 64 electrodes that capture a large proportion of the signal traffic within the networks, which have a diameter of 1 to 2 millimeters. Activities may be spontaneous, may be evoked, or may result from pharmacological alterations (such as the injection of strychnine). Laser cell surgery during recording (even to specific cell and neurite elimination) can test system homogeneity, existence of percolation thresholds, critical mass phenomena, and fault tolerance.

Figure 11.3 is a photograph of a culture on a section of a multimicroelectrode plate. It gives some idea of the cell/electrode arrangement and the random sampling of activity. The gold conductors are 10 micrometers wide and the halos are deinsulation sites produced with single laser shots. Newer electrodes using transparent indium-tin oxide as conductor material have increased the electrode density from 36 to 64 per square millimeter.

Similar studies in the past were based on single cell neurophysiological data. Breakthroughs in intracellular recording technology, both electrical and optical, are opening up more sophisticated experiments. The dynamic modeling of simple, one-layer networks is seen as a logical step toward the future modeling of more complex cellular mechanisms. Although the random biological network was not previously considered representative of

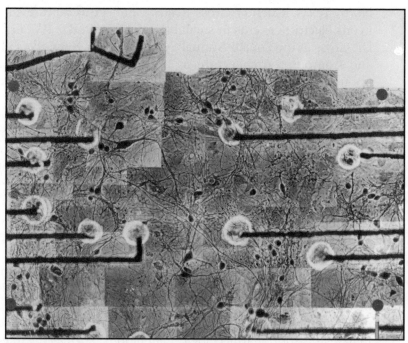

FIGURE 11.3 CULTURE ON SECTION OF MULTIMICROELECTRONIC PLATE (PHOTOGRAPH COURTESY OF DR. GUENTER GROSS, UNIVERSITY OF NORTH TEXAS.)

A Practical Guide to Neural Nets

the intact central nervous system tissue, Dr. Gross believes his approach will provide significant information. " . . . It is now apparent that 'order' in the nervous system must be seen statistically and that structure and function is linked less deterministically and much more probabilistically than had heretofore been assumed."[3]

Computers are modeling the emerging algorithms, and an eventual VLSI implementation is planned. If dissociated neurons in cell culture attempt to reconstruct some of the basic circuitry of the parent tissue (as expected), project results may enhance progress in information processing. Conclusions may indicate how systems exposed to local damage or structural transformation organize themselves dynamically to generate a wide variety of patterns.

Another wetware project is being performed by Mitchell D. Eggers (Lincoln Laboratory) and Professor Ronald McKay (MIT).[4] They are analzying signals between neurons to develop mathematical models of neuronal behavior. They test their models by sending signals back through the electrodes and observing changes in behavior. They try to "teach" cells by using the signals to adjust connection weights (relationships) between them.

Currently, recordings can be made from only a few cells simultaneously. Knowledge obtained is fragmentary. It is difficult to understand the mechanisms of the network as a whole. A modeling approach, such as Fukushima's Neocognitron, helps simulate brain behavior. Discrepancies between the model and the brain lead to changes in the hypotheses and modification of the model. Fukushima describes the relationship between modeling neural networks and neurophysiology as one resembling that between theoretical physics and experimental physics. Modeling takes a synthetic approach; neurophysiology or psychology take an analytical approach.[5]

Experiments such as these will provide basic neuronal design information to extend compatibility between the dynamics of biological and artificial neural networks. Researchers may learn more about synaptic changes involved in learning and memory. They may use resulting algorithms to better understand the brain and duplicate some of its functions.

Matching Architecture and Paradigms to Applications: Work on neural network models is addressing many different problem areas. Some researchers are attempting to discover better ways of clustering, or separating inputs into groups with common features. Clustering applications would include things like character recognition, sonar/radar signal classification, and robotic control.

Other research deals with problems such as rotation, translation, and scaling. Items on a conveyor belt do not always appear at identical angles; it is easy to forget just how much preprocessing our eyes do for us. In a similar fashion, if inputs to neural networks could be preprocessed (even by another neural net), you might significantly improve the ratio of solution space to error space and cut down on the network size required. Neural networks can use all the hints you can provide.

Whereas some networks depend on a reduction of dimensions to discern the essential features (much effort is being applied here), others require an extension of dimensions. Motor control and pattern generation efforts both fall into this category. Kuperstein (see chapter 5) is one of those investigating vision-controlled robots; Eckmiller's work provides an example of research on cyclic (breathing, heartbeat, etc.) and noncyclic pattern generation. A continuing problem is how to coordinate observation and action, and how to exploit the duality between classification (which reduces dimensionality) and prediction (which extends dimensionality).

Hardware design efforts were described in chapter 10. Current research includes work in silicon (Carver Mead of CalTech), VLSI (JPL, AT&T, MIT, University of Arizona, Texas Instruments, others), optical technology (NRL, University of Colorado, University of California at San Diego), superconductivity (Szu and Chu), and thin film (JPL). One of the continuing problems in hardware implementations is being able to change the synaptic weights in real time. Most current implementations "burn in" the weights, often after optimization with a software simulation. This procedure does not allow for adaptability, essential for applications such as process control, which must change as conditions fluctuate.

Learning law developments (see the learning research mentioned earlier in this chapter) encompass another significant arena of study relative to paradigm development. Also previously encountered were the drive reinforcement work of Klopf (chapter 8) and Grossberg's Avalanche (chapter 8). New paradigms are sure to emerge.

Bernard Widrow had developed the MADALINE III as an alternative methodology to the popular back propagation of errors network architecture. This paradigm has the capabilities of back propagation, requires less hardware, is easier to train, and is based on a simpler theory. By mid-1989 Intel was readying a chip to implement the MADALINE III learning rule.

Another new model, for which a patent was applied in 1989, is the Parametric Avalanche, summarized next.

Martingale Research: Bob Dawes of Martingale Research (Allen, TX) presented his Parametric Avalanche (PA) paradigm at the International Joint Conference on Neural Networks in June 1989. This model was developed for spatiotemporal filtering and control of nonlinear systems. Dawes describes his product as implementing "an 'innovations method' approach to the stochastic filtering problem for the state of a nonlinear system in nonGaussian noise."

What does that mean? Most neural network paradigms work with stationary patterns. The Parametric Avalanche, a recurrent network that uses Hebbian learning, is an exception (as are others, such as Grossberg's Avalanche model). It deals with time-varying signals. Recognizing patterns with a temporal context becomes very important for tasks such as speech recognition, motion detection, signature verification, and sensor fusion. Nonlinear wave packets serve as internal carriers of the external system dynamics, accomplishing the filtering of large dimensional signals. According to Dawes, an untrained Parametric Avalanche can balance an inverted pendulum on the first try.

In December of 1989, NASA announced selection of Martingale Research for negotiation of a Phase II SBIR (Small Business Innovative Research) award. The resulting project will develop Martingale's Parametric Avalanche architecture for application as an autopilot for shuttle orbital maneuvers.

Dawes believes the power of neural network methods is wasted on stationary pattern recognition. "We need methods that build operationally predictive models of the observed world, seen as an evolving dynamical system."

Justification and Audit Trail: One of the commonly cited limitations of neural network systems is their inability to justify conclusions or provide any sort of audit trail. Stephen Gallant has been working on "Connectionist Expert Systems,"[6] expert systems that have a neural network as the knowledge base. His two-program package constructs the systems from training examples. The first program uses neural network learning techniques to generate the knowledge base; the second program is a stand-alone inference engine that interprets the knowledge base.

In addition to allowing interactive acquisition of new information, the system can answer both "how" and "why" questions. How was a particular conclusion determined? Why is this piece of information necessary? A combination of both forward chaining (making new inferences from existing data) and backward chaining (finding what values are still needed to determine this conclusion) is used.

Gallant's initial connectionist systems involve several limitations: they are classification systems, involve only feedforward networks, and use integer arithmetic. But the pocket algorithm (a modification of Perceptron learning) works well with nonseparable or even contradictory training examples. Gallant talks about the ease of extending the techniques for dynamic systems with on-line learning and noisy data.

Performance issues are given precedence over the modeling of human decision-making, so the resulting systems are closer to conventional expert systems than to psychological models. Although there may have been some initial hopes for an automated tool that would solve the knowledge acquisition bottleneck in expert system development, this technology is seen as merely a tool, not as a replacement for knowledge engineers.

Hecht-Nielsen Corporation is commercializing Gallant's patented approach. Not only will the company's product allow automatic production of expert systems from neural networks, but resulting systems will have the ability to produce a rule set for an audit trail. Such rule sets could identify problems in diagnostic systems and explain credit-scoring in loan application models. Research on answer justification is also going on elsewhere both in this country and in Europe.

A Practical Guide to Neural Nets

Analyzing Hidden Layers: The above justification of conclusions is not the same problem as having a neural network explain how or why it adjusts weights in its internal layers. After all, these weights are really the key to the encoded knowledge distributed within the network. Better understanding of how this happens would enable researchers to develop better intermediate representations.

Touretzky and Pomerleau of Carnegie Mellon discuss "What's Hidden in the Hidden Layers?"[7] Their research on analysis of these hidden layers is discovering what feature detectors are best for various tasks. Back propagation models develop feature detectors that are underconstrained. Additional training data or constraints are necessary to produce representations that will correctly classify all patterns as well as generalize to new patterns.

ALVINN (Autonomous Land Vehicle In a Neural Network) is a project whose success depends on proper generalizations from input data. ALVINN's goal is to drive the NAVLAB vehicle along a winding road. Sensory inputs come from a video camera mounted on the roof of the vehicle and from a laser range finder. Output is a linear representation of the direction the vehicle needs to travel to keep in the center of the road.

Proper training of the network results in development of a hidden layer between the input and output layers that generalizes correctly to new situations. Visualization tools for analyses of the hidden layer representations have been made practical by microcomputers and personal workstations. Researchers can display weights. They can measure and plot response patterns to various inputs. They are learning more about what's going on in these hidden units. Limiting the number of hidden units forces the use of general-purpose feature detectors that are more likely to be relevant to novel inputs. Reducing the size of the hidden layer can thus improve the network's performance while also increasing the speed of a computer simulation.

How ALVINN accomplishes sensor fusion (see chapter 8) is another research question. Data from both sensors are combined to determine the position of the road more accurately than would be possible with either sensor working alone. There is much to learn from the hidden layers.

Speech Recognition: There are a number of research projects working on speech recognition implementations. Southern Illinois University's EE Department is comparing traditional approaches with artificial neural network systems approaches to speech recognition. The Naval Ocean Systems Center in San Diego is exploring how back propagation networks, trained to learn the significant representations of preprocessed speech, affect novel speech data. An MIT/Lincoln Lab project describes neural network classifiers for speech recognition and compares them with conventional classification algorithms. A new network architecture called a Viterbi net recognizes time-varying input patterns with better than 99-percent accuracy on a large speech database. Using a VLSI device, they have implemented Perceptron and feature maps networks. Long-term goals include the development and implementation of speaker-independent continuous speech recognition systems. Other researchers are pursuing the same goal.

A master's thesis[8] at Wright-Patterson Air Force Base details the combining of Kohonen nets with word recognition algorithms using dynamic time warping. A digitized utterance is sliced and processed to obtain a sequence of vectors, which are compared to template utterances. Success rates are 99 percent for isolated speech and 93 percent for connected speech. Future work will increase the vocabulary and work on speaker-independent recognition.

Johns Hopkins University claims significant progress has been made in estimating the acoustic characteristics of speech from the *visual* speech signals. Input consisted of the raw images of faces, aligned and preprocessed. The performance of networks on a database of vowels was better than that of trained humans. Work in 1989 will extend these results to diphthongs. Such information could be used to supplement acoustic signals in noisy environments, such as cockpits.

HIERtalker,[9] at Los Alamos National Lab, NM, is a project in learning to read English aloud. It uses a new learning algorithm based on a default hierarchy of high-order neural networks to learn phonemes, the building blocks of words. The default hierarchy prevents a combinatoric explosion of rules. Accuracy on trained words is 99 percent and ranges from 76 to 96 percent for sets of new words.

Size and Scaling Issues: The size of network needed to solve a particular problem is a continuing question in neural net research. If the network is too small, training produces no learning. The process of deciding that no learning is occurring is slow. The network must then be increased in size and training repeated. On the other hand, too large a network also slows processing, particularly in digital computer simulations. Sietsma and Dow discuss an approach based on learning with a net larger than the minimum size required to solve the problem and then pruning the solution network.[10] Although the size of a neural network is theoretically almost without limit, today's computer architectures impose severe limitations.

Related to this is the problem of moving from a working laboratory experiment, which may work on only a subset of an application, to a real-world application. What proves feasible on a smaller scale may be impractically lengthy when moved to a full-blown model. One of the criticisms has been that networks have dealt primarily with "toy" problems.

Scaling was one of the key questions in a study done on neural networks for routing communication traffic.[11] The authors used a small network for the study, depicting a communication network with two satellites, five earth stations, and a total of 16 nodes with up to four links from origin to destination. The small network showed reasonable convergence in 250 iterations. A realistic application for traffic routing might have 100 nodes, with each node needing to communicate with 20 other nodes. The number of processing elements and connections required becomes large quickly, though still within the range of proposed neural network computers. The authors' conclusions emphasized the unknowns related to scaling: "Will this neural network routing algorithm converge satisfactorily to a reasonable answer for a larger communication network with 1,000 nodes?" Currently there are no good algorithms for training a network that scale up well to handle complex problems. Guidelines and methods need to be developed for problems of scaling and size.

Emerging Directions

Several specific directions are emerging on the neural network scene. Hardware improvements in speed and storage capabilities are boosting some research projects into candidates for real-world applications. Neural network solutions are increasingly being integrated with other current technology. Expert systems, database techniques, management science, and other applications are being enhanced by the addition of neural network subsystems. Neural networks appear to be good for data intensive problems and for dynamic environments, such as vision, robotics, speech, battle management, and laser radar sensors.

Researchers and developers are creating tools to assist others in developing their own neural networks. Educational opportunities are expanding rapidly. Not only are neural-network-related consulting services increasing, but we are seeing companies whose main thrust is the offering of such services. Next, let's examine some of the particulars of these trends.

Speed and Storage Improvements

Sophisticated software packages, accelerator boards for conventional computers, new chip designs, and new methods are improving both the speed and storage capabilities for neural network applications. Hardware research is leading to the development of computers that are projected to be 6–7 orders of magnitude faster than the current state of the art.[12]

Oxford Computer (Oxford, CT) builds neural network computer chips. The company plans to build a prototype system with a speed of at least 16 billion operations per second.[13] Toshiba announced a fourfold increase in the learning rate of neural recognition technology in late 1988. Its optical character reader based on this technique has a 99.9-percent accuracy rate for handwritten letters. It uses conventional static technology to preprocess the data and then extracts the character using neural network technology.[14] California Scientific Software (CSS) has developed a network accelerator board that supports 3 million connections per second. The board is compatible with an XT and runs CSS's "Brainmaker" software. Because it uses coded integer routines, many of the problems of floating-point arithmetic methods are eliminated and simulations run more quickly.[15]

The growth in processing power will be gradual, driven by market forces. As has been true in the electronics industry, someone will figure out how to pack more elements in a smaller space, multiply speeds, and produce other improvements in neural net hardware and related software technology. In the near term, optical devices may replace electrical connections between chips to increase computer speeds and bandwidths, and offer easier integrations with front-end sensors.[16] The competition in neural network computing will lead to the introduction of technologies and many new and improved products.

Integration with Current Technology

Neural network technology is being integrated with considerable current technology. This results in added value: a process becomes faster, development becomes easier, applications become more robust, and so on. We already mentioned in chapter 6 the integration of neural networks with traditional AI techniques. Neural networks are being combined with vision and speech recognition systems, expert systems, database methods, signal processing, and robotics, to name just a few.

The Carnegie Group announced in April 1989 a research project to explore the possibility of linking neural networks to knowledge-based diagnostic systems. An expert technician distinguishes between the sound of a generator running normally and one about to fail. Neural networks can be used to perform a similar task by examining digitized vibrations of a running generator. The system subsequently could decide when the patterns of signals indicate problems. Carnegie Group already has a product, Testbench™, which is a shell for building knowledge-based diagnostic systems. If neural networks were added to Testbench, information could be provided to assist a technician in troubleshooting, diagnosis, and repair of machines. Hardware systems could be built to perform hazardous tasks without requiring human operators.

Robotics Applications: Chapter 5 contained several examples of the use of neural networks in robots: Martin Marietta's forklift robot, Nakano's robots, and Kuperstein's robot called Infant. The autonomous land vehicle ALVINN was presented earlier in this chapter.

Intelligent robots operating in unstructured and perhaps hostile environments will require enormous onboard computing power and flexibility. Such robots will need to solve many complex mathematical problems repeatedly: sensor fusion to keep track of positions, courses, and identities of all objects and potential threats in a constantly changing world; navigation; dynamics and coordinated control of one or more effectors; and online planning.

The Hostile Environment Robotic Machine Intelligence Experiment Series (HERMIES) is being developed (under government sponsorship) as a testing ground for robot dynamics. HERMIES-IIB was designed to increase the degree of self-contained autonomy. It is propelled by a dual set of independent wheels having a common axle alignment and driven by separate direct-current motors. Sonar scan data are preprocessed onboard for navigation planning. It has a ring of five sensors, each of which is an array of four Polaroid transceivers. The five degrees of freedom in its manipulators are being upgraded to seven degrees of freedom in HERMIES-III. The HERMIES robots are believed to be some of the most computationally powerful mobile robots in existence today.[17]

The ability to learn complicated control functions, and the ability to respond to changing or unexpected environments, expands the usefulness of robots. This technology is being researched for unmanned land and underwater craft, in automated machinery, on assembly lines, and for hazardous tasks such as disposal of radioactive materials. Increasingly sophisticated real-time software, intelligent sensors, and image-processing subsystems will combine with neural networks to enable robots to interact with their environments.

Chemistry and Medicine: Neural network applications in chemistry are beginning to appear.[18] Research involves using neural networks to predict such things as product distributions from chemical reactions, adverse drug reactions, prediction of the physiochemical properties characteristic of a safe drug, and three-dimensional structures of proteins from amino acid sequences. Chapter 6 reported on the use of neural networks in research at Los Alamos National Laboratory on DNA sequences.

Researchers in the United Kingdom are exploring neural computing techniques to aid deaf people. The networks could be used to analyze the sounds of speech in hearing aids, pick out relevant information, and provide important components of speech as a person reads lips.[19]

A Practical Guide to Neural Nets

Bernard Widrow is developing a miniature neural network computer for implantation in amputees.[20] The idea is for the network to receive the nerve signals and transmit them to an artificial limb, translating the nerve signals into mechanical movement. There are no road maps to interpret nerve signals; together the patient and the neural net would have to learn how to use the natural information to make an artificial limb work.

Other Fields: The U.S. Postal Service wants new equipment to deliver 250 billion pieces of mail by the year 2001 (compared with 160 billion in 1989). Technology is already providing optical character readers (OCRs), bar code sorters, and multiline optical character readers and sorters (MLOCRS). Now researchers are interested in machines that incorporate neural networks, robotics, and MLOCRS to apply bar codes.[21]

Fujitsu has developed an analog neural processor (ANP) for highly interconnected neural networks, which works in combination with digital components. Designed to be a general-purpose chip, the ANP can process digital weights and analog signals at speeds that enable 80,000 connections per second.[22]

Consider programming applications. Because many neural net simulations are written in the C language, integration with other software applications is not difficult. If specifications change, it is usually much faster to retrain a network than to reprogram a conventional procedural application.

Development of Tools

Just as the increase in expert systems technology a few years back ushered in the era of expert system shells, so now there are many neural network development tools coming on the market. Many will run on a personal computer. People with application ideas are examining the features and flexibility of these products to get a leg up on their development timeline. If a suitable product exists, they are freed to concentrate on other design details without having to learn all the intricacies of neural network implementation.

Even beyond tools for developing neural networks, there is increasing recognition of a neural network *as a tool*. Again, the analogy to expert systems is appropriate. As expert systems are being billed as "just another tool in the programmer's toolbox," so, too, neural networks themselves will come to be considered simply another tool that is useful at performing a specific task within an application.

Education

Successes with this technology have brought increased interest and subsequent requests for improved educational opportunities. Those who want to know more about almost any aspect of this technology can do so by reading magazines, journals, and books, or by attending seminars and other classes. Such avenues are becoming more and more numerous.

Many magazines are featuring articles on neural networks; some have devoted entire issues to this topic. The offerings don't come solely from technical magazines and journals, either. As we mentioned before, some articles have appeared in such popular publications as the *New York Times* and *Time* magazine. Articles can be written rather quickly on specific issues and can respond to very current events.

Books take a bit longer. The public interest has to have more than just flash-in-the-pan promise before many authors will spend the energy required to prepare a manuscript. Publishers have recognized this educational requirement and are responding. A number of new books on various aspects of neural network technology continue to appear. Some are quite technical and will appeal to only a select, knowledgeable few. Some books are bundled with software packages; sometimes a piece of software will come with the book. As the target audience grows in size, additional books will surface for the interested general population.

Seminars are becoming increasingly abundant. They range from half-day introductory types to a several-days' format for particular audiences such as engineers and the scientific community. Intellimetrics (Bethesda, MD) sponsored a short course called "Problems in Collective Computation" following the June 1989 International Joint Conference on Neural Networks (IJCNN 89), complete with a take-home exam and prizes. Hecht-Nielsen Neurocomputer Corporation offers a one-month hands-on training course. The more detailed the information supplied in the class, the more background is required (such as higher mathematics).

Some seminars are being held within corporations for their

staffs; others are open to anyone with the registration fee. Fees vary considerably. We went to one symposium in late 1988, for example, that was a real bargain at $25 for the day. We got much more than we paid for. Noted researchers presented some of their work, coming either at their own expense or being funded by their companies. Although this style of sharing research was common a few years ago, it is typical for today's educational programs to charge a more substantial amount. Presenters are more proficient, research is more competitive, and now events generally must pay for themselves.

Other neural network educational opportunities are being provided by university courses and continuing education programs. UCLA Extension (Department of Business, Engineering and Management), Boston University, and the George Washington University (School of Engineering and Applied Science), for example, all offer short courses on a regular basis. In late 1989 and early 1990, some of their course titles included "Neural Networks: Translating Theory to Real-World Applications" and "Applied Neural Networks Computing." Lecturers are well-known participants in the field. Additionally, UCLA and others advertise on-site continuing education courses, tailored specifically to a particular organization's needs.

Obvious special groups providing significant educational opportunities include the various neural network conferences, such as the IJCNN (International Joint Conference on Neural Networks). Published conference proceedings are a rich source of papers and are available even after the events themselves have been completed. Also, expect more programs such as the satellite videoconference on neural networks sponsored by the IEEE in September 1989 (see chapter 3). Some areas have local groups, such as MIND (Metroplex Institute for Neural Dynamics) in Dallas, Texas, with monthly educational programs and/or newsletters.

Neural network newsletters (see the end of appendix B) are another excellent resource. There is much variability in articles, level, frequency of publication, and cost. Many newsletters review other publications and provide lists of current writings. If you can find one (or more) newsletters whose content suits your needs, you will have an excellent way to keep up with current neural network events.

Consulting Services

Most of the companies involved with neural network products provide some combination of education, consulting, contract research, and assistance in application development. However, several firms are emerging that specialize in consulting services.

These consulting companies offer a variety of knowledge and skills useful in the development of both internal applications and neural network products for external marketing. They can perform preliminary assessments, such as feasibility and market studies, requirements analyses, functional specifications, and help with preparation of proposals. They can provide consulting for strategic planning. They can assist with system design and development on through the product life-cycle to benchmarking, testing, and evaluation.

The staff members of these consulting organizations are generally well qualified. Many are professionals with extensive experience in the industry. They have been trained in both theory and applications and have hands-on experience with neural network computers. They are knowledgeable about the applicability of neural network technology to today's problems. Some have presented papers at conferences or written articles for periodicals. Some publish their own newsletters.

Examples of such companies include Adaptics (San Diego, CA), Judith Dayhoff Associates (Mountain View, CA), Logical Designs Consulting (San Diego, CA), Neurocomputer Connections (South Hackensack, NJ), and Tom Schwartz Associates (Mountain View, CA). This list is not exhaustive; remember that most companies currently involved with neural network technology also offer consulting as one of their services.

Summary

A single chapter can in no way do justice to the multitude of interesting neural network research projects now in progress at numerous locations in this country and abroad. It would take volumes to adequately describe the work being done, the gains made, the plans for the future. Not only would space be required, but in the time required to detail current efforts, new projects would certainly arise. Where problems exist in neural net technology, researchers are attacking them. Where potential applications are impractical because of current technology limitations, barriers are being pushed back.

The *DARPA Neural Network Study* lists the most promising benefits of this technology:[23] processing speed through massive parallelism, learning as a means of efficient knowledge acquisition, and embedding, robustness with respect to fabrication defects, and compact processors for space- and power-constrained applications. The study points out the current absence of neural network hardware and that what hardware exists is almost all experimental. There are few good demonstrations of the benefits listed above. Although research has been going on for several decades, neural network technology is still in its infancy.

Most current activity is directed toward the understanding of neural networks. Capabilities are being demonstrated through the development of simple applications. Much remains to be done in demonstrating the benefits of hardware implementations. Signal-processing applications are mostly simulations. More powerful machines are needed. Important steps include the development and evaluation of algorithms suitable for hardware (and software). The DARPA study suggests that any government-sponsored program initially should address research and development efforts to advance the general technology rather than focusing on producing any specific large, complex systems. This is appropriate advice.

1. Maureen Caudill, "Neural Networks Primer, Part 8," *AI Expert*, vol. 4, no. 8 (August 1989): 61–67.

2. Franklin, Sutton, Anderson, Selfridge, and Schwartz, "Connectionist Learning Control at GTE Laboratories," *Proceedings of the SPIE 1989 Symposium on Advances in Intelligent Robotics Systems*, Philadelphia, PA, November 1989.

3. Guenter W. Gross, Jacek M. Kowalski, and David Golden, "On the Behavior and Significance of Random Neuronal Networks," Department of Biological Sciences, Department of Physics, and Center for Network Neuroscience University of North Texas, Denton, TX 76203.

4. William J. Cromie, "Neural Networks: What Can They Do?," *The MIT Report* (December/January 1988–89): 15.

5. Kunihiko Fukushima, "A Neural Network for Visual Pattern Recognition," *IEEE Computer*, vol. 21, no. 3, (March 1988): 65–75.

6. Stephen I. Gallant, "Connectionist Expert Systems," *Communications of the ACM*, vol. 31, no. 2 (February 1988): 152–69.

7. Touretzky and Pomerleau, "What's Hidden in the Hidden Layers?," *Byte*, vol. 14, no. 8 (August 1989): 227–33.

8. G. D. Barmore, *Speech Recognition Using Neural Nets and Dynamic Time Warping*, Master's thesis, Wright-Patterson Air Force Base, December 1988.

9. Los Alamos National Lab, "HIERtalker," report no. LA–UR–88–1849, 1988.

10. Sietsma and Dow, "Neural Net Pruning — Why and How," IEEE International Conference on Neural Networks, 1988.

11. Herbert E. Rauch and Theo Winarske, "Neural Networks for Routing Communication Traffic," *IEEE Control Systems Magazine*, vol. 8, no. 3 (April 1988): 26–31.

12. "Market Research: Neural Networks," *EDP Weekly* (May 15, 1989): 5.

13. William D. Marbach, "Giving Brainy Computers Cooler Heads," *Business Week*, Industrial Edition, no. 3094 (March 6, 1989): 103.

14. "Neural Recognition Technology Speeded Up Fourfold," *Office Equipment and Products* (December 1988): 25.

15. R. Colin Johnson, "Neural Acceleration," *Electronic Engineering Times*, issue 526 (February 20, 1989): 37, 45+.

16. Bruce D. Nordwall, "Photonics Will Boost Near-term Computer Processing Speeds," *Aviation Week and Space Technology*, vol. 130, no. 16 (April 17, 1989): 57–59.

17. Jacob Barhen, N. Toomarian, and V. Protopopescu, "Optimization of the Computational Load of a Hypercube Supercomputer Onboard a Mobile Robot," *Applied Optics*, vol. 26, no. 23 (December 1, 1987): 5007–14.

18. S. Borman, "Neural Network Applications in Chemistry Begin to Appear," *Chemical and Engineering News*, vol. 67 (April 25, 1989): 24–28.

19. Pallab Ghosh, "Software 'Mimic' Comes to the Aid of Deaf People," *New Scientist*, vol. 121 (March 18, 1989): 38.

20. "When Nerves Speak, This Chip Listens", *Discover*, vol. 11, no. 6 (June 1990): 12.

21. Abner A. Layne, "The High-Tech Needs of the Postal Service," *High Technology Business*, vol. 9, no. 6 (June 1989): 14–19.

22. "Analog Neural Processor," *Electronic Engineering Times*, issue 528 (March 6, 1989): 41–42.

23. *DARPA Neural Network Study* (Fairfax, VA: AFCEA International Press, November 1988), p. 231.

12 Where Do We Go from Here?

Every sentence I utter must be understood not as an affirmation, but as a question.

—Neils Bohr

Introduction

After all that we've said so far, what remains to be said has something to do with directions, and also with passions. The time has come to consider where we go from here. What are the trends? What are the likelihoods? What are the far out possibilities? The time has also come to talk about how people *feel* about this technology. We want to reflect some of the fervor, positive and negative, that is a part of any radical endeavor and that is certainly apparent in the developing neural network technology.

Some people are very positive about this technology. They have put their lives into neural networks and are staking their futures on it. They have built new companies, are designing new products, and are researching new ideas. Their comments reflect optimism and hope. Others are guarded, even skeptical. Their lives are currently involved in pursuing other directions and other technologies. They are weary of sure bets and a free-lunch mentality. They may have been burned by past promises. Technology's hoped-for wonders have often left a bad taste: witness the overabundance of cheap throwaways and dangerous nondisposables that clutter our planet. Most people take a position somewhere in between. They may be intrigued, but they have a wait-and-see attitude.

Leon Cooper predicts that "just as the 20th Century is famous for its automobiles, airplanes, and computers, the 21st Century will be the century of intelligent machines."[1] He talks about electronic duplications of brain functions that will progress rapidly beyond the initial models and become the inevitable accompaniment of what we today call computers. "We will not only learn to live with these machines," says Cooper, "but someday we will wonder how we ever lived without them."[2] The Age of Intelligent Machines. That phrase brings up an assortment of images. Just what might we mean by machines that are intelligent?

Are Neural Networks Intelligent?

We've said a lot about the potential for neural networks to adapt. The DARPA study's conclusions pointed to this feature, along with the massive parallelism, as being the two arenas of greatest interest. We devoted an entire chapter to learning, to the building of intelligent machines. We talked about autonomous learning. We talked about artificial intelligence and compared neural networks with traditional AI approaches. Are neural networks "intelligent"? Before you can answer that question, you have to first define what you mean by intelligence. That's not as easy as you might think.

What is Intelligence?

Dictionary definitions of intelligence talk about reason, intellect, and comprehension. *Webster's Seventh New Collegiate Dictionary* says "the capacity to apprehend facts and propositions and their relations; the act of understanding." Fischler and Firschein's *Intelligence, the Eye, the Brain, and the Computer* points out that although the word *intelligence* has a dictionary definition, there is no agreed-upon scientific meaning. Moreover, the concepts that do exist are dynamic. As we learn more about human intelligence, our concept of intelligence changes. The more we find out about the human brain, the more intricate and complex we discover it is.

The absence of a scientific definition makes it more difficult to make comparisons between human intelligence and machine intelligence. Bringing in issues of intuition and skill only muddies the waters. Considering the arena of human emotion blackens

A Practical Guide to Neural Nets

the waters altogether. So, we'll only attempt some thoughts on the difficult, as related to the intelligence of pattern matching.

How Do We Measure Intelligence?

Consider some of the traditional ways we have attempted to measure intelligence. Figures 12.1 and 12.2 show examples from the Wechsler Adult Intelligence Scale and the Differential Aptitude Tests (DAT). You probably remember taking such tests at some point in your life. Notice how much these particular examples depend on pattern-recognition skills.

Of course, you had a substantial training period to learn that baby buggies need four wheels or the baby may get a very bumpy ride. You learned things like this early by observing lots of examples. Developing your abstract reasoning probably took a little longer. Here the object is to recognize the patterns and select the correct next step. If you can do this, you will get a better score on the test and be said to have a higher intelligence quotient

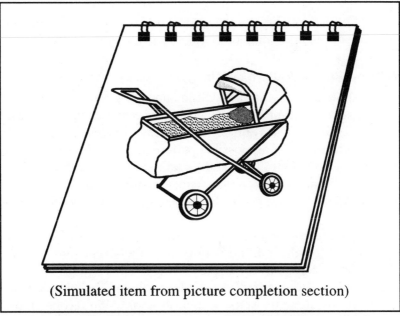

(Simulated item from picture completion section)

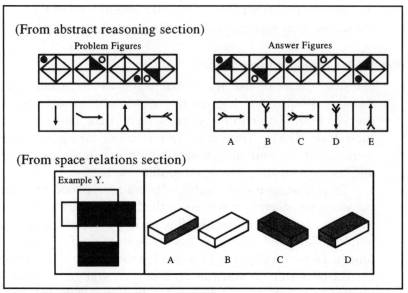

(From abstract reasoning section)

Problem Figures   Answer Figures

A   B   C   D   E

(From space relations section)

Example Y.

A   B   C   D

FIGURE 12.2 DIFFERENTIAL APTITUDE TESTS, FORM S (DIFFERENTIAL APTITUDE TESTS. COPYRIGHT
© 1947, 1948, 1972 BY THE PSYCHOLOGICAL CORPORATION. REPRODUCED BY PERMISSION. ALL
RIGHTS RESERVED.)

(I.Q.). The ability to recognize and match patterns has become one of our measures of intelligence.

Mathematics and Pattern Matching

Mathematics is often called the queen of sciences. A British mathematician/author who helped reshape mathematics education in the U.S. in the 50s and 60s, W. W. Sawyer, described mathematics as "the study of all possible patterns." In his *Prelude to Mathematics,* he says that "Life, and certainly intellectual life, is only possible because there are certain regularities in the world."[3] In a constantly changing world, patterns are the only relatively stable thing.

Nature provides us with countless patterns. Who is not entranced by the infinite variety of snowflakes? Or the variety of birds that appear in our parks and at our feeders? We all understand that the growth of a plant follows the planting of seed. Patterns allow us to make identifications. We recognize our children, even though they grow and change.

Mathematics helps us with abstract reasoning. Algebra takes

A Practical Guide to Neural Nets

the patterns in nature and abstracts them into general formulas. The area of any rectangle, for example, can be found by multiplying the length by the width: A = lw. Science depends on regularities in nature. "Mathematics," said Poincaré, "is the art of giving the same name to different things."

It is a distinct advantage to have general rules that work for all instances of a pattern. The recognition and classification of patterns has a long and respected history as an intelligent endeavor.

Neural Network Implications

Compare the above paragraphs with the way neural networks learn. Could a neural network be trained to score well on the DAT? If it did achieve a high score, would we then call it "intelligent"? What about a network's ability to discern patterns it has never seen before? What about the ability to discern patterns whose existence no one has ever recognized before?

We want to quickly point out, however, that tests like the DAT examine lots and lots of patterns. Most neural networks would be trained to recognize rather specific patterns, and would be optimized to do a good job in a rather limited area of interest. They can, however, display highly complex behaviors and can exhibit intelligence within their domain.

To construct a large enough neural network to even come close to the 10 to 100 billion or so processing elements within the human brain is far beyond current storage capabilities. To achieve the estimated number of interconnections between this many processing elements, 100 trillion or 10^{14}, is a quantum leap beyond that. DARPA's five-year goal is to simulate what some researchers estimate to be the processing power of a honeybee—roughly a billion (10^9) interconnections. It's an ambitious goal.

Why Use Neural Nets?

Why or when should you use neural networks? What images of neural networks should remain branded in your consciousness? We can't answer this for you. It's somewhat like asking where creativity comes from. People look for where they have problems, situations where they say, "It would certainly be nice if. . . ." They start with a problem, extrapolate to the future, and then close the loop. Problems get solved. Creative new things happen. It makes sense to look at your problems first. Neural networks may offer potential new solutions to old problems.

Do neural networks have a future in your company? Consider the types of problems your company encounters. Is it necessary to read handwritten forms or signatures, read zip codes, extract from large databases, deal with many cases? Are there applications that require significant preprocessing, QC inspection, recognizing assembly line parts, optimization of variables, and so on? You know why you decided to read this book and you should make your own list of useful information about neural networks. Remember that you can now have 20 MIPS PC computing on your desk. Almost any institution has access now to supercomputing, and soon any PC owner will have cheap on-line access. Plenty of opportunities exist to try out simulations now. Boards are available to give extra processing power if needed. By the time you decide on the usefulness of an application, more chips will be coming along to make your application productive and cost-effective.

Review of Advantages: We want to recall and summarize here some of the potential advantages of neural networks. Regardless of how you feel about the intelligence questions, neural networks have a number of characteristics that not only make them interesting but also sometimes give them advantages unmatched by other approaches.

Neural networks offer a greater degree of robustness than current digital systems. The way knowledge is distributed throughout the system provides high resistance to hardware failure. The output will *not* be seriously compromised if 5 to 10 percent (arbitrary numbers in this case) of the components quit functioning. Cutting a wire in a conventional computer would be disastrous.

Ask Intel's Mark Holler, architect of the N64 analog neural network chip and manager of their Novel Device Group, about fault tolerance.[4] California Scientific Software's BrainMaker software was being used to load and test Intel's N64 chips. One chip, which initially got only 103 of 124 patterns correct, was later discovered to have a bad row of synapses, amounting to a "dead" neuron. Holler's comment was: "These things really are robust;

all the theory points to that fact, but actually seeing it happen is still an eye-opening experience." If the N64 with the bad row had been a standard E^2PROM (electrically-erasable programmable read-only memory) chip, it would have been junk. Instead, the neural network's distributed memory model simply works around a dead cell.

Both positive and negative aspects of information can be balanced automatically in a neural network. Inputs can excite (or strengthen) connections; or they may inhibit (or weaken) connections. A network can be set up to emphasize either aspect.

Networks can capture patterns in both time and space—auditory signals as well as visual data. Data-intensive problems and dynamic environments (vision, robotics, speech, battlefield management) are good candidate applications areas. Hierarchical data structures can be represented as multiple layers. Data abstraction and generalization are automatic. Systems figure out, without having to be told, which data are relevant and which are not, and what intermediate representations need to be made. This last feature also makes them good nominees for data-compression applications.

Adaptive behavior potential is perhaps the key advantage of neural network technology. A system could improve performance based on current results and experience. Remember, though, that the more adaptive a system is, the harder it is to predict a specific response. The output you get may be quite different from what you expected.

For some problems involving parallel processing, the speed with which a neural network can potentially operate will be the key advantage. Speed, parallelism, and potential ease of implementation are all reasons to consider this technology.

The integrating of neural networks with other technologies may provide the best of all worlds. It makes sense to use the right tools for the various jobs.

New Horizons

There's a lot going on—new companies, new products, and even new technologies. New groups and societies are forming. New newsletters are appearing. There are new solutions to old problems.

The potential for new understandings has been referred to in other contexts, but we want to emphasize it again here. What is learned in neural network research may well have consequences beyond our wildest dreams. Not only will we learn more about machine intelligence, but we may come to better understand our own intelligence as well. The complexities of how we learn may become more clear. We may develop new educational theories, new economic theories, new ways of interacting with one another. There may be new breakthroughs in medicine, in psychology, in sociology and other fields.

Human/Machine Interfaces

Imagine a world in which human beings can naturally interface with and converse with machines—machines that can operate autonomously in the real-world environment and learn from experience. Neurologically based computers could change our ways of operating, of thinking about the world.

Current speech-understanding systems are working on semantic analysis of sentences. As gains are made in this technology, it may well become possible for you to tell your computer the instructions you have in mind, rather than typing in cryptic directions via keyboard commands. Further, your computer might respond by asking you what type of output you prefer: a screen listing, printer output, or voice response, for example. Your neural computer might call upon a conventional computer to do any arithmetic and other serial processing tasks.

Neural networks are capturing human and robotic control patterns. Rather than having to program detailed algorithms for complicated start-up procedures, or all possible positions of a robot arm, it may be possible to demonstrate the patterns and movements for robots in training sessions. In addition, goals may be specified in new ways, such as in the broom-balancing example in chapter 7. In order to keep a pole or a broom balanced, it may be necessary to request the network to keep a point on the end of the broom positioned in the center of the camera field; in other implementations, simply a request for the system to balance the pole may be sufficient.

Predictive neural nets running faster than real-time events could be used to anticipate future states. This is quite a step from simply modeling what the system is doing. A particular pattern could be simulated, then run in "fast-forward" mode. Such a system would allow us to plan for rather than merely respond to events.

New Companies, New Products

A new neurocomputing industry has come into being. In the space of about twelve months in 1986–1987, a dozen or more new companies came into being. As in any new and hot field, some companies will mature and stay and others will disappear.

Concentrations within companies vary: software, hardware, chips, applications development, consulting. Publishers concentrate on books and software. Some companies are interested in developing tools, and others are delivering finished applications.

Only two companies shipped products in 1987: Hecht-Nielsen Neurocomputer Corporation (HNC) and Nestor. Since then, numerous other software packages have appeared. We'll address a sampling of what's available in following paragraphs, but because HNC and Nestor were the first, let's look at these companies and their products first.

Hecht-Nielsen Neurocomputer Corporation designs and develops neurocomputers for business, government, academia, and consumers. They offer both general-purpose and special-purpose neurocomputers, standard netware packages, development tools, consulting, and education. The netware packages are neural network building blocks useful for a variety of applications. HNC's AXON software is a tool for the discovery and implementation of paradigms beyond those supplied with the product. The board-level neurocomputer is fully integrated with a PC-AT host computer running MS-DOS. Neural networks are called as procedures by software running on the host processor and then executed on the neurocomputer coprocessor. Additional netware packages, development tools, and peripherals (audio and video I/O, robot arm, tape units, etc.) are also available.

Nestor was founded in 1975 and owns the Nestor Development System™ (NDS). This self-organizing system (written in standard C) is very flexible and does not require extensive programming efforts. It examines the input patterns and writes its own rules about the real-world data. Nestor has entered several joint-venture agreements with product developers in a variety of application areas which rely on pattern recognition. With the critical recognition function supplied, a number of new products could result.

Software products for demonstrations, tutorials, simulations, prototyping, and applications development are becoming numerous. You can buy PC-based packages for less than a hundred dollars or buy systems with special support boards for up to $25,000, and a variety of ranges in between. Many interesting systems will run on the equipment you may already have sitting on your desk. A good resource guide is available in the August 1989 issue of *Byte* magazine; it includes books and articles as well as products. The November/December 1988 issue of *PC AI* magazine and the August 1988 *AI Expert* also both review available software.

The following represents a smattering of some of the products available. NeuralWare developed the product NeuralWorks Professional II, which we used in our demo disk (see appendix A). The demo will give you an idea of how neural net graphics might look. AI-NET 101 operates in real time and is designed for integration into industrial environments. It looks for patterns in input samples and can be customized for particular applications, which might include concept learning, generalization, or categorization. On the less expensive side is Abbot, Foster & Hauserman's Brain Simulator, which allows you to design neural logic circuits: AND gates, OR gates, flip-flops, counters, etc. It's easy to use and includes some interesting challenges in the exercises in the documentation. Another relatively inexpensive package is California Scientific Software's BrainMaker, whose documentation we liked. It provides easy, informative reading regarding neural networks in general, and the software lab exercises are familiar illustrations that are fun to do. Products for Macintosh computers include MacBrain (with Hypercard options) and Neurosmarts, a combination simulation and expert system tool.

Although software simulations are already on the market, researchers are busy figuring out how to build the hardware implementations. "Neural network technology is a hardware technology, not a software technique," says Lee Gammill of Texas Instruments. He is typical of the researchers who believe that the more useful simulation tools are those that aid in hardware development. The important technology for them is neural networks on silicon or gallium arsenide chips.

A Practical Guide to Neural Nets

The computational requirements of real-time processing in many applications will require special-purpose chips. There is also talk about using smart chips to teach dumb chips. Researchers in universities, established corporations and start-up companies are working on VLSI (Very Large-Scale Integration), analog VLSI, and VHSIC (Very High-Speed Integrated Circuits) implementations that can put neural networks directly into integrated circuits. Carver Mead's models of the retina and cochlea in analog VLSI circuitry (chapter 10) are certainly portents of more to come.

Other new hardware products include coprocessors and accelerators. Boards that provide hardware emulation of neural networks come in several categories. Some use conventional architecture and technology; others involve parallel configuration of chips to achieve superior processing speeds. Some of these boards work in AT-class machines, and others are for high-end machines such as the VAX. The Transputer, the Mark III-V, and NEP from IBM exemplify aspects of these new products.

NCR Corporation developed a Geometric Arithmetic Parallel Processor (GAPP) that enables precise object recognition for automatic inspection and robot vision. Working at real-time TV rates, arrays of data such as pixels in a digitized image can be mapped directly onto a two-dimensional arrangement of 72 microprocessors for parallel computing. This allows easy implementation of algorithms for region processing or neighborhood operations, such as convolution, edge detection, and feature extraction. Two GAPP devices operate at 57 million adds/sec and cost less than $500, a considerable improvement over conventional image processing systems.

Some companies began as a one-person outfit. Neuraltech fits that category; Martingale Research, up to five staff members in June 1989, is an example of a small, but growing, company (see chapter 11's discussion of the Parametric Avalanche paradigm). Industry defense contractors such as Hughes Aerospace (where nine out of ten divisions have neurocomputing groups), Boeing, Rockwell International, General Dynamics, and Martin Marietta are among the companies using neural network technology to work on tasks such as automatic target recognition (ATR), robotics, sensor interpretation, battlefield simulation, and more.[5] Other companies are major players in the Fortune 500 list and neural network technology represents only one aspect of diversification: Texas Instruments, AT&T, IBM, TRW, Motorola, GTE, and others exemplify this category.

New Technologies

Not only are there new ways of working with machines, but entire new technologies are emerging as a result of work on neural nets. The network implementations mentioned in chapter 10 fit into this classification. Other fields have also experienced an impact as a result of research in this area.

As the software gurus are busy putting out new products, new algorithms are emerging that are parallel, adaptive. Software development will undoubtedly produce new innovations, new models, new ways of thinking about programming.

Scan-Graphics is teaming with Oxford Computer to apply neural networks to perform automatic symbol recognition for engineering-drawing applications. "With Oxford Computer's breakthrough technology," claims Scan-Graphics president Andrew Trolio, "we can build compact, economical accelerators that perform tens or hundreds of billions of operations per second, compared with the tens of millions available today."[6]

Longer range, optical processors that can take advantage of the high interconnect capability may become even more important than current electronic processors. Light beams can cross one another without signal interference and without the heat generated by electrical systems. Because most networks require a vast number of synapses, using optical connections would allow a high density of artificial neurons per unit area on a device. Optical technology also offers promise for implementing three-dimensional systems.

Some optical systems combine holography and nonlinear media. The essential feature of a hologram is that each part contains the same information as the whole hologram. Holograms can serve as memory storage while a nonlinearity is used to obtain output decisions. Dana Anderson's writings on his work in this arena (see the bibliography in appendix B) are both poetic and highly technical. He seeks to shake the shoulders of our biases about what computers are, how they operate, and what the future might hold.

Research in artificial neural networks stimulates work in neuroscience and vice versa. Progress in the design and implemen-

A Practical Guide to Neural Nets

tation of intelligent machines and improved understanding of the nature of intelligence are companion objectives. When the problem is too big—and developing a model of the brain is very much a "too-big" problem—you settle for pieces you can solve.

As reported in chapter 11, neuroscientists are studying the electrochemical interactions between biological neurons by cells on electrode plates. One of Gross' projects focuses on spatiotemporal pattern generation in small, random, monolayer networks grown in cell cultures on 64 photoetched electrodes. Previous neural modeling has been based primarily on single-cell neurophysiological data and not on biological network data. The goal of Eggers and McKay is to understand how the brain organizes and builds itself. Projects such as these are expected to provide basic information useful in the design of artificial neural network architectures specializing in rapid complex pattern generation and recognition, dynamic self-organization, and fault tolerance.

Neural networks are providing a new conceptual framework for chaos theory. Chaos theory is a recently emerging body of knowledge sometimes called *self-organizing theory*. It has to do with systems stability and systems change: how systems are organized and how they can and do undergo fundamental changes. Sometimes small changes in input can produce widely divergent outputs, and a seemingly orderly system becomes chaotic. Although the chaos may appear to be totally random and unpredictable, it can be following strict mathematical rules.

Chaos theory represents a serious challenge to the Newtonian notion of a predictable universe, because the prediction of a chaotic system is so sensitive to measurement errors. Douglas Greve (Texas Instruments), speaking at a June 1989 meeting of the Metroplex Institute for Neural Dynamics (MIND) in Richardson, TX, noted that the presence of chaos is quite prolific throughout science. It has been found in the study of astronomy, biology, biophysics, chemistry, engineering, geology, and social sciences. Further, he said that although entirely deterministic, chaos is statistically equivalent to white noise. Many cause relationships are being found in systems that were heretofore only thought to be noisy, such as fibrillation in the heart.

Many chaotic systems that people wish to investigate are difficult to set up, and the study of them can become quite complicated. The use of neural networks to represent such systems offers interesting new possibilities. Examples could include weather patterns, some neurological and cardiac activity, and even long-term cultural patterns.

Geneticist Barbara McClintock won a Nobel Prize in 1983 for her work focusing on human society as a living system in which we all play a part. Feminist scholarship is also drawing on biological images and chaos theory in advocating a holistic approach to social dynamics and possible future patterns of relating. Chaos theory and neural network implementations may become useful for analyzing and presenting results.

Neural networks may signal a departure for Western science, which has been, for the past several thousand years, highly hierarchical, mechanistic, objective, and overcompartmentalized. It's about time.

Concerns

A number of people we talked to, or whose papers and articles we read, have expressed concerns regarding neural networks. We have our own concerns. The extensive list of comments comes from supporters as well as critics. Further, we encountered individuals who are both supporters and critics. We had been told by our editor, for example, that Douglas Lenat, AI author and researcher, was "fairly negative" about neural nets. (Lenat's latest book is *Building Large Knowledge-Based Systems*, Addison-Wesley, 1990.) So we made a point of interviewing Lenat. His opinions expressed many considerations of which we already were aware, and more. Some of his views are very representative of a number of people in the field. We also found in him an appreciation for the potential of neural networks.

Concerns are numerous: over-emphasis, misuse of the potential, failure to keep an open mind and an open climate for experimentation, the biological assumptions and attendant misunderstandings, the name of the technology itself. We'll start there.

AI suffered because of its name. Neural network technology may be setting itself up for a similar disaster. "People become excited for the wrong reasons," claims Lenat, who calls neural networks "the technology du jour." "Neural networks are not a panacea. As with AI, HDTV (high definition TV), chaos theory, and other technologies, people lurch, looking for a free lunch. . . . A frightening number of people in the world, especially decision makers, are not aware of the limitations of these technologies."

One of the concerns voiced many times and mentioned throughout the book is a misunderstanding of the relationship of artificial neural nets to the biological models. Lenat points out that there is merely suggestive evidence of any correlation with human processing. "Neuron firing, which is easily measured, could be a second-order process or even a side effect of the real processes." Others express similar cautions. Current neural network models are full of assumptions—of necessity. There is so much we don't know.

At the same time, there is a lot we do know. Some observers have expressed concern that people will depart from and forget the biological basis, and consequently miss out on real advances in learning more about the brain and how biological networks truly function. "Knowledge of how the brain works must be gained in order to make these promising computers completely practical. The benefit to us will come not just in having better computers. That is just the icing on the cake. The neural network field promises to expand our knowledge of the biological brain to carry into the fields of pharmaceuticals, medicine, and psychiatry."[7]

Often industry has settled for short-range productivity, finding it necessary to turn a profit for stockholders. American companies have recently been hard-pressed to maintain some capital-intensive industries. There has been concern about losing the technological edge in making components that go into computers, for instance. Longer-range efforts require financing and faith. It's not an easy balance to keep.

The volume of neural network experimentation provides apprehension for some people, including Lenat. "If everyone looked for a cancer cure, we wouldn't find one any faster. Similarly, in neural network research, only some 50 to 60 experiments are profitable, and these are being done." Other people have an opposite concern. Jim Huffman is distressed to think that the climate of experimentation may become too closed. (Huffman is engineering department manager in the Microprocessor Products Group at Motorola, Austin, TX, and one who is backing Odin

Corporation on the Encephalon chip reviewed in chapter 10.) He wants the greatest possible openness and freedom to experiment. If people try new ideas and publish their results, then other researchers can criticize their work, and all can learn. The worst mistake, he feels, would be to cut off experimentation too soon.

Premature closure is related to impatience. If results do not come as quickly as promised, enthusiasm may slacken. Carver Mead is one researcher who emphasizes that there's a lot of homework to do.

Another issue is the misuse of the potential relative to AI as well as neural networks. Lenat suggested that if you looked at thousands of expert systems and really dug in, you would find that the person who built the system decided early which algorithms should be used. The resulting expert system simply used the shell as a programming language to encode the algorithms previously developed. Our own experience in AI bears this out. In fact, several AI product vendors are currently highlighting the productivity gains possible by using exactly this approach. Although there is certainly commercial validity here (it's much faster to use already written, pretested code for generic portions of an application), the original spirit of expert systems technology emphasized more of an incremental approach to achieving confidence in a task, where the rules would "evolve."

The neural network equivalent of misuse might be in using the technology for problems so simple that anything would have worked. Lenat calls this "superficially appearing to use the technology, but missing the point relative to the function of the technology."

Even amid such concerns, useful processing can be done with neural networks. At MCC (Microelectronics and Computer Technology Corporation, Austin, TX), Lenat and others are working on the CYC project. The name, which sounds like "psych," was chosen as a joke. The project, however, is quite serious. It involves a hybrid, synergistic approach, including both standard symbolic AI and neural network technologies. Researchers are attempting to put down 100 million of the most fundamental facts and heuristics people share. MCC's pragmatic approach is: where the neural network technologies are useful, use them. Neural networks can, for example, look for reasonable analogies between concepts and perform some training on hunches. The more symbolic rules are used to flesh out the analogies. According to Lenat, there is less of this cooperative architecture around than you might expect. People tend to look at a very narrow slice of their own technology. That's another concern.

Beware the Hype

Media stories on neural networks have been uneven. It isn't easy, especially for on-lookers who are not involved in serious research, to distinguish the realistic from the visionary. Everyone comes with biases. Distortions may be subtle rather than obvious. Predictions may be given too much credence. Hyperbole comes under a number of different guises.

Distortions: There is still a tendency to portray neural networks as magical, a sort of black box that does amazing things. Glossing over the detailed mathematics involved and emphasizing the neurobiological underpinnings only aggravates this tendency. Distortions such as these create misunderstandings and false expectations. You might think the scientific community learned their lesson with AI, but excitement with new toys sometimes has led to exaggerations and unfounded claims.

Another distortion to watch out for is equating a research prototype with an application system. Bernard Widrow has commented that even when a system works well in the laboratory, it takes ten years to get it into the marketplace.[8]

Media stories and spokespersons also sometimes confuse what has been done with what might be possible in the future. Even if an application looks promising or possible, there is still a giant leap from dream to accomplishment. Scaling is a case in point here for neural networks. Again, the difference between toy projects and practical applications was one of the big problems AI suffered. People got turned off when AI couldn't deliver in what seemed a reasonable period of time. Most people in the fledgling neural network industry are concerned about not repeating this bit of history.

Some stories focus on hardware as the main hurdle. You might begin to believe that when researchers finally figure out how to do the hardware, we're "home free." Not so. Anderson and Rosenfeld, the editors of *Neurocomputing: Foundations of Research*, point out in their afterword that the software for neural networks will be "by far the most difficult, important, and painful aspect of practical applications." The software won't look anything like what programmers have been used to coding.

The public is accustomed to standards of accuracy and precision in traditional computers. The limitations of neural networks in this area have not been emphasized adequately. Neural network tools can be very low-level; they can also be very high-level, but they don't give exact answers. It has been too easy to see the "good news" without really considering the implications of the "bad news."

Predictions: Predictions can lead to another form of hyperbole. People make statements about events they think might happen. Not that this is bad; predictions have their place. How can we plan unless we somehow envision or anticipate the future? Some people may try to influence the direction of the future with their predictions. Look for anyone who has a vested interest in the outcomes, and evaluate their views carefully. Others just like to say, "Remember, you heard it here first!" Unfortunately, sometimes readers (and writers) aren't careful in separating the likely from the accomplished fact.

Bearing these warnings in mind, we're going to risk restating some of the predictions we've read in the past few years. We found it fun. Remember that we're quoting out of context. Remember also that what was said in the past might not necessarily be what the same people would say today. You can make your own judgments, and be certain that history will judge. Some predictions will be borne out; others will not. Also note that in addition to these "predictions," we later have sections on "Probabilities" and "Possibilities", our three "P"s. Admittedly, deciding where to position what stories was rather arbitrary on our part. Here goes.

Pentti Kanerva (Research Institute for Advanced Computer Science, Mountain View, CA) predicted in a 1987 *New York Times* article that neural networks ". . . will be the next large-scale computer revolution."[9] That's a little milder than an earlier *Electronic Engineering Times* article[10] that noted that IBM ". . . has mounted an effort toward building artificial neural networks that might eventually replace computers. . . ."

Contrast this with a more recent article (*New Scientist*, Vol.

118, No. 1616, June 9, 1988, p. 36) in which IBM Chairman John Akers says of neural computers: "We do virtually no research in that area, because we feel that for the forseeable future it will have little impact." Nevertheless, the same article emphasizes that IBM backs its scientists (some of whom are doing neural computing research—the simulated annealing methodology, for example, was invented by IBM's Scott Kirkpatrick).

Neurocomputers (July 1987), a newsletter edited by Derek Stubbs, predicted that the first Nobel Prize in the area would go to Stephen Grossberg, "not for his work in neural networks, but for his work in showing that combinations of neural networks explain the visuomotor system." This comes right after Stubbs predicts the "first commercially explosive neurocomputer will be a combination of several neural networks. . . ."

Jasper Lupo, DARPA's deputy director of the Tactical Technology Office, made the much-quoted statement that ". . . the technology we are about to embark upon is more important than the atom bomb."[11] Another headline, "Fujitsu Breeding Neural-Computer-Driven Robot,"[12] makes for a catchy title (and we approve of that), but the analogy risks being misunderstood.

Robert Hecht-Nielsen predicted in 1987 that optical neurocomputers would be on the market in ten years, and that most computers would have attached neurocomputers by then. AT&T calls the VLSI approach to neurocomputing "more promising." Several sources predict big bucks. Tom Schwartz of Schwartz Associates, a neural network consultant, estimated in a September 1988 Reuters newswire that "sales of neural network modeling tools, the building blocks for applications, will grow 50 percent a year for the next five years, to $150 million by 1992."

"We believe it's possible to build systems that are smarter than people," says Simon Heifitz, vice chairman of Nestor.[13] A news feature on Ford Aerospace quotes Ford Executive Vice President John A. Betti: "Probably the most exciting team effort presently under way is in neural network computers that can be made to imitate the functions of the human brain."[14]

Predictions are fun, but it's important to keep your perspective. We'll end this with a quote from John Denker, technical staff member at AT&T Bell Labs, in which he reminds us about neural network technology: "Just because it's for sale doesn't mean it exists."[15]

Summary and Opinions

What does all of this mean and where are we headed? We'll try to pull together some of our observations and conclusions. Remember, though, that we are excited about neural networks. Although we are trying to present a balanced assessment, we are not unbiased. We're writing this book to share our excitement about what appears to be a very promising technology.

Some summary information is matter-of-fact in nature and expands on trends already in motion. Some tends to be visionary and extrapolates from current hints of what might be. Jim Huffman terms the categories "probabilities and possibilities," and he's always careful to distinguish which one he's speaking about. We'll start with the more practical probabilities and save the more esoteric possibilities for the finale. It's like talking about hopes and dreams, things you know could happen, "if. . . ."

Probabilities

Though neural network technology is still in its youth, it has experienced significant growth since the days of the Perceptron. Carver Mead believes neural networks will revolutionize computing in its present form and declares himself humbled by the prospect. "It is a profound technology, not a shallow technology. There is no question it is going to be dynamite."[16]

John Dvorak (*PC Computing* columnist) includes neural networks in his ten predictions for 1990, declaring that some of the developments he's seen in this area are stunning and that the idea is solid. His "counterpart," Jim Seymour (another *PC Computing* columnist) claims Dvorak is about a decade early. Seymour names the year 2000 as the time for neural networks to take off, while agreeing that the idea of neural networks makes sense.[17]

Researchers are getting serious. We talked with Bob Dawes of Martingale Research to hear his observations in mid-1989. It seemed to be a time of contemplation, with perhaps fewer articles apparent than in 1988, when several magazines devoted whole issues to neural nets. "The easy paradigms have been worked to death," he commented. "Now is a time of back-pedaling and retraining for scientists to come back up to speed." He paraphrased physicist E. T. Jaynes' comment that it was "easier to sit down and write a program than to think about a problem." In

A Practical Guide to Neural Nets

the past few years it may have been easier to write an article than to think about neural network problems. Now, though, researchers are looking for significant improvements, not just incremental gains.

A down-to-earth assessment comes from Richard P. Lippman of MIT Lincoln Laboratory. He calls neural networks an interesting field that is immature and changing rapidly. Lippman emphasizes that, although practical applications are still to come, preliminary results have demonstrated the potential. "The greatest potential of neural nets remains in the high-speed processing that could be provided through massively parallel VLSI implementations."[18]

One of the general conclusions made by the DARPA-funded study notes that there has been an impressive variety of applications (vision, speech, signal processing, robotics, etc.), but, because of limited funding for research, such applications are not being done on a large scale. Even with few practical examples today, the results are encouraging. Researchers expect to improve with experience.

As funding resources increase, the gap between modest prototypes and commercially viable systems will decrease. The current boundaries of simulation are expanding. Storage and speed capabilities are increasing, and costs are projected to come down. As an illustration, software costs will be reduced; systems engineering costs will be reduced as a result of the self-training of neural networks. Neural networks will result in higher-performance automated systems; autonomous operation will be possible over larger performance envelopes. New technologies are being developed that will affect both simulation capabilities and hardware implementations. DARPA's program will provide money for such areas as new architectures, training procedures, and scaling. Research in a variety of disciplines is moving to meet the needs for practical applications of neural network technology. This is critical for continued development.

Speech recognition is the cornerstone of projects currently being researched in Japan and other places. It is not difficult to imagine speech recognition in inexpensive household products, such as televisions, telephones, and voice typewriters. Speech synthesis is not as close but is a good probability. We have already seen videotapes of AI machines that read to the blind.

Consideration of the areas in which biological systems are

currently superior to conventional processors will guide selection of potential applications. Where traditional digital computers clearly do better than biological systems there is currently little advantage in pursuing neural network implementations. We will no doubt see more comparative performance measurements between neural networks and other techniques.

Neural networks have the potential for crafting unique approaches to long-standing problems. Some existing systems could be combined with a neural net system, resulting in significant value added. Ford Motor Company, for example, forecasts neural-network-based on-board diagnostics for vehicles. They would be transparent to the user, but could maintain near optimum performance as parts, such as spark plugs, age.

The potential also exists for dramatic improvements in current prototypes. By moving from simulations to hardware implementations, we will move from slow mimicry to useful, real-time solutions. At the same time, we will be gaining a better understanding of neurobiology.

Neural network technology will become another tool in the toolbox for hardware and software engineers.

Possibilities

". . . It may thus come to pass that we are now living at the boundary between two great epochs of human existence. . . . If ANS [artificial neural systems] can contribute the final ingredients for making this transition, we will be the founders of a new age."[19] Robert Hecht-Nielsen forecasts a profound impact on human society. He envisions a world of dramatically altered economics in which robots will do the mundane tasks and humankind will be freed to pursue nobler pursuits.

Leon Cooper asks us to imagine that the problem of how the brain functions and organizes information has been solved. He then spins on possible consequences: "There would clearly be medical applications, possible means for treatment and amelioration of various physiological and psychological disorders."[20]

Jim Huffman thinks along the same lines as Hecht-Nielsen and Cooper. He mused about the links between mental and physical health, the power of visualization and positive thinking. "We need practical knowledge about how our minds affect our health,"

A Practical Guide to Neural Nets

he insists. Neural networks could be made to be sick, for example. You could inject problems, simulate illness. You could play with the simulation and fabricate psychosis and manic depression in neural networks. Scientists could study classic symptoms without having to worry about healing the patient and thus eliminating the potential resource for analyzing the source of the problem and improving understanding. Neural networks could also be used for research instead of live animals.

"We are at the dawn of a new age of thought," says Huffman. "The importance of neural networks goes way beyond whether we build a computer or not—that's secondary—the fundamental challenge is learning how the brain works." Our brains have immense capacity and yet we use only about ten percent of the potential. (The rest is overhead for the operating system.) With more knowledge about our biological neural networks, humankind can come up with incredible theories that could change the whole of society's viewpoint. Philosophers could postulate new theories, economists new economic systems, based on new sociological theories. The direction of humanity over the next 20 to 30 years is at stake, says Huffman. "There are two or three isomorphisms to take us into new ways of looking at things." (Huffman named neural networks, chaos theory, and the unification theory of physics.) We could change our understanding of things like religion, philosophy, science. Things like people's everyday lives. Things like prevention/cure of cancer and other diseases, of aging. Things like how we think about ourselves.

As an example, take Huffman's ideas on predisposition. The brain, he affirms, is predisposed to understand information in particular ways. You are predisposed to believe things you already believe. You are wide open to accept things as long as they come from the narrow set of sources you are predisposed to accept. As an illustration, we know from experience how hard it is to test your own software—you know exactly what it is supposed to do. It's difficult to imagine all of the things someone else might try to do.

Predisposition has implications not only for individuals, but also for society. "How does a society reflect the collective beliefs of its people when these beliefs are narrowly focused between the long term memory and the brain stem, instead of in combination with the short-term, sensory based inputs from the universe outside the human and the human's vast collective experiences?"[21]

Some people have a predisposition for music. They could learn other concepts, such as mathematics, through their understanding of music. Instead of coming at mathematics directly, you could teach it through musical concepts: harmonics and vibrations, time signatures, notes as fractions of a beat, and so on. Once you have tapped in to the appropriate predisposition, all sorts of useful indirections are possible. You play to the anticipations and open people up to more. Concepts such as this could change the way we educate our children.

More and more knowledge. The ability of neural networks to "mine" databases may help us keep on top of the proliferation of knowledge, even neural network knowledge itself. We can all relate to Charles-A. Rovira's comments, initially made about AI, but certainly applicable to the intelligence capabilities of neural network technology as well: "Most of us will never see more than a fraction of the books now in print. And in the information revolution, there is something unpalatable about having incomplete knowledge. . . . The need to digest and comprehend ever increasing amounts of data is the heart of AI."[22]

One Last Comparison

The transistor was invented in 1947. It quickly replaced the hot, bulky, breakable vacuum tube. Electronics became simpler, faster, more reliable. But there was a hitch in the process: engineers didn't have a good way to interconnect all the parts. This meant that sophistication and reliability were inversely proportional. In 1958, in a Texas Instruments laboratory, Jack Kilby invented the microchip—the monolithic integrated circuit.[23] A few years later, Kilby demonstrated the value of the microchip to the average person by inventing the hand-held calculator. The electronics industry took off. Society has not been the same since.

The National Academy of Engineering in 1989 awarded the first international Draper Prize to Jack Kilby and Robert Noyce, independent coinventors of the semiconductor microchip. Each received a gold medal at White House ceremonies in February of 1990 and shared the $350,000 award, the largest given exclusively for engineering achievement. (The Draper Prize has been set up to be a type of Nobel Prize for engineering.) Announcing the award, Robert White, president of the Academy, stated, "The development of the integrated circuit was the single most important event that helped usher in the Information Age. Like the invention of the telephone, the light bulb, or the automobile, the creation of the integrated circuit has fundamentally changed our lives."[24]

Some people have suggested that the impact of neural network technology may be comparable to the changes brought about by the invention of the transistor. It could happen.

Step by step the longest march can be won, can be won.
Many stones can build an arch, singly none, singly none.
And together what we will can be accomplished still.
Drops of water turn a mill, singly none, singly none.

—Anonymous

Many processing elements working together in a neural network—many disciplines working together to research neural networks—many technologies combined in applications. There are many new ways of thinking about things. The dawn of a new age? It could happen.

1. Leon N. Cooper, "Brain Research: Theory and Experiment," *Computers in Physics*, Vol. 2, No. 6 November/December 1988): 38.

2. Leon N. Cooper, "First Word," *Omni*, vol. 11, no. 6 (March 1989): 6.

3. W. W. Sawyer, *Prelude to Mathematics* (Penguin Books, Baltimore, Maryland 1955), 12.

4. R. Colin Johnson, "Intel Goes Soft with Neural Nets," *Electronic Engineering Times*, 590 (May 14, 1990): 35, 38.

5. Edward Rosenfeld, *Intelligence: The Future of Computing*, June 1989. (See bibliography for information on this newsletter.)

6. R. Colin Johnson, "Neural Nets for Symbol Recognition," *Electronic Engineering Times*, 567 (December 4, 1989): 35.

7. Jim Huffman, "Neural Networks: Heralding the New Computer-Based Science," (paper courtesy of the author), 1989.

8. June Kinoshita and Nicholas G. Palevsky "Computing With Neural Networks," *High Technology* (May 1987): 31.

9. Andrew Pollack, "More Human Than Ever, Computer is Learning to Learn," *New York Times*, Sept. 15, 1987, section C, p. 1.

10. Tom J. Schwartz, "IBM Research Yields Artificial Neural Net Workstation," *Electronic Engineering Times*, issue 397 (September 1, 1986): 67.

11. R. Colin Johnson and Tom J. Schwartz, "DARPA Backs Neural Nets," *Electronic Engineering Times,* issue 498 (August 8, 1988): 1.

12. Miyoko Sakurai, "Fujitsu Breeding Neural-Computer-Driven Robot," *Electronic Engineering Times,* issue 472 (February 8, 1988): 33.

13. Ann Sussman "AI-based Neural Networks Play Role in Mortgage Process," *PC Week* (July 18, 1988): 18.

14. Ford Aerospace, Online PR Newswire, April 25, 1989.

15. Loring Wirbel, "Neurals 'No Panacea,'" *Electronic Engineering Times,* issue 523 (January 30, 1989): 54.

16. Jeff Ubois, "Mead Foresees Work Ahead on Neural Nets," *Federal Computer Week,* vol. 3, no. 43 (October 23, 1989): 42.

17. John C. Dvorak and Jim Seymour, "Dvorak versus Seymour," *PC Computing,* vol. 3, no. 1 (January 1990): 23, 24.

18. Richard P. Lippman, "An Introduction to Computing with Neural Nets," *IEEE ASSP Magazine,* vol. 4, no. 2 (April 1987): 20.

19. Robert Hecht-Nielsen, "Performance Limits of Optical, Electro-Optical, and Electronic Neurocomputers," *SPIE,* vol. 634, Optical and Hybrid Computing (1986): 277–306.

20. Leon N. Cooper, "Brain Research: Theory and Experiment," *Computers in Physics,* vol. 2, no. 6 (November/December 1988): 38.

21. Jim Huffman, "Neural Networks: Heralding the New Computer-Based Science," (paper courtesy of the author) 1989.

22. Charles-A. Rovira, "Exante AI: Coming Attractions," *AI Expert,* vol. 5, no. 1 (January 1990): 24.

23. Gayle Golden, "High Profile: Jack Kilby," *Dallas Morning News* (June 15, 1989), section E, p. 1.

24. "Kilby and Noyce Receive Top Engineering Award," *IEEE Computer,* vol. 22, no. 11 (November 1989): 77.

Afterword

Toto, I've a feeling we're not in Kansas anymore.
 —*Dorothy (The Wizard of Oz)*

We have made a good team in this endeavor; the synergy of our approaches provided a balance we could use to advantage. Coming by different routes, we found a common inspiration in the promise of neural networks. We have read about some exciting applications and prototypes; we believe in the potential of neural nets because we have seen them work. Old problems are being solved in new ways, efficiently and effectively.

Our past experiences not only give insight into our own fascination with intelligent machines and learning, they also reveal some of the capabilities we value most in this new technology.

Illingworth:

Retrospect convinces me that I have always been interested in neural networks; I just didn't know it at the time. My initial interest was in designing intelligent assembly machines.

Early in my engineering career, I started as a mechanical design engineer responsible for machine design in support of what we then called mechanization of manufacturing lines. Ironically, the first assembly machines that we mechanized were to manufacture the world's first germanium transistors. However, we did not employ these devices in our machine-control logic. We applied relays and air devices to perform the machine control logic required for our relatively large machines to assemble and test very small transistors.

I was concerned and many times frustrated for two reasons. First, after designing a sometimes very complex machine, we mechanical designers then turned it over to the electrical control design engineers, who rarely consulted us on how the machine was to operate. Secondly, when we were given our electrical control design package (six or seven months later), the control housing cabinets for relays, solenoids, transformers, capacitors, and cables equaled the size of the assembly machine. In most cases, it required more floor space than the assembly machine. In all cases, the integration effort was horrendous—usually it took a year of twelve-hour days, six days a week before we had a satis-factorily operating assembly machine.

Several of my fellow machine designers and I decided to do something about this situation. We needed to take over complete control of our designed assembly machines as well as our own destiny. We then turned to our transistors and designed a con-troller that could replace eight relays and occupy less than a tenth of the total system. The design was unique for the late 1950s.

After our initial success we added many functions to our machine controller, including a memory. Our assembly machines started to become intelligent. At least, we thought so at the time. We were able to prevent the biggest problem on all assembly machines, namely "jamming," by simple commands to the con-troller. We did not realize it then, but we had designed a simple microcomputer.

I became so enticed with the controller, and especially the potential of adding intelligence to machines, that I turned away from machine design and entered the field of what was then known as *cybernetics,* now unfortunately referred to as *artificial intelligence.* I went the usual route, including programming and implementing robots on manufacturing lines, employing machine vision for inspecting manufactured products.

We were building expert systems in the 1970s, except that we did not know they were expert systems. I was still frustrated in my attempts to bring intelligence to manufacturing machines. Although the automation systems that flourished in the 1970s

A Practical Guide to Neural Nets

were orders of magnitude better than our early mechanization systems, they could not be trained, and by no means could they ever "learn."

It wasn't until I ran across several papers on neural networks in the early 1980s that I became convinced that we now have the potential, at least, of reaching my 30-years-plus goal of building truly intelligent machines. Neural networks is the only technology that has the promise to meet the challenge of the Japanese "sixth-generation" computers.

These new machines will be fault-tolerant, contrasted with present systems that reject a program for an infinitesimal error in one instruction. These machines will be intelligent and self-programming. They will be considerably smaller, requiring as little as 2 – 10-percent of the power required by today's machines.

Nelson:

All my life I have been interested in helping people find new ways of looking at things, of going beyond what they knew.

Even in junior high school, I understood that our society valued logical, analytical, scientific skills. Further, I then thought that the competitive—the real—challenge was to succeed in what were traditionally male-dominated endeavors. I became a mathematician (and later a software engineer). Because I took as electives the courses required for a teaching certificate, I also became a teacher.

My goal was to enjoy and challenge my students; their "ah-ha!s" were my reward.

In the middle 1970s I spent six years with a non-profit group involved in demonstration villages around the globe. Where people were in poverty and despair, our goal was to give them new ways of thinking about themselves, of thinking about the future. We often used small "miracles," such as lining the main village street with whitewashed rocks. People did not believe that life could be different until they experienced it differently.

At Geophysical Services, the historical parent company and a former division of Texas Instruments, I found myself again in the business of providing people the opportunity for more intelligent responses to their situations.

Our seismic vessels needed information on the position of a

two-to-three-mile-long cable towed behind the boat; it was not unusual to have an eight-million-dollar loss on cables during a year. The crews also needed to be able to assess the quality of their work before they left the area. My task was to write the programs to track the position of the streamer and to provide good images on the underground coverage of the seismic activities.

The boat crews, my customers, would say, "It would really be nice if we could . . . ," and I'd keep a file. More intelligence was needed; more information on the equipment, the environment, the tasks. We were trying to make the machines smarter so the crews could work smarter.

After six years I came back to education, this time in AI at Texas Instruments. So much to learn. Expert systems are removing routine work so people can look at the more interesting aspects of a problem. Robots are being used as aids for paraplegics and the elderly; prototype machines are reading to the blind. My students learned about expert systems by building their own prototypes, often related to their work projects. The more power you can give to the students for their own learning, the more they will learn. Knowledge is like a new toy: "I wonder what would happen if . . . ."

Early in 1988, I began to be aware of more and more neural network articles. It was a fascinating bringing together of my own left and right brain approaches. We can now add new kinds of intelligence to machines, and we have the possibility of learning more about learning. Our options, our horizons, and our imaginations are being stretched.

A Practical Guide to Neural Nets

Appendices

Appendix A: Your Interactive Neural Network Disk[1]

Introduction

We struggled with several different options for the material for this diskette. Some ideas we considered utilized neural networks to good advantage but did not present much in the way of graphics. It was hard to "see" anything. Other ideas provided good pictorial illustrations of neural networks but were fairly cut and dried; they offered little opportunity for interaction. We settled for an idea that combined the best of the qualities we wanted: some graphics, some interaction, and understandable inputs and outputs. The applications we chose are familiar ones: applying for a loan and buying a new car. Simple, familiar applications, we figured, would allow you to focus on the neural network features, which are what we want to emphasize as we go along.

The Diskette Design

Neural network input and output files are not noted for being user-friendly. Indeed, just the opposite is generally true. The use of sigmoid functions further compounds this problem, because they require data to be normalized or scaled. A neat method of getting around this unfriendly, cumbersome, neural network input/output problem is to embed the neural network in an expert system. This is exactly what we have done with your interactive diskette, using the expert system shell, Personal Consultant℗ Plus, from Texas Instruments.

The neural network demonstration diskette is referred to as "interactive" because you will be able to provide inputs to and operate two neural networks. The expert system not only presents a user-friendly format, but does all the housekeeping chores as well. These tedious behind-the-scenes operations include the normalizing of input data and then the later reversal of the normalization operations to present the output in the desired format and interpret the neural network output results.

The expert system run-time delivery diskette provides us with a unique delivery system that expands the overall capabilities to more than just having a neural network. We take immediate advantage of the inference heuristics inherent in an expert system. An example is the interpretation of the output of a neural network.

In the Loan Advisor we set up rules that simply interpret any output values of less than .50000 as "Loan Not Approved." Likewise, any output value equal to or greater than .50000 is considered "Loan Approved." We could write rules that might approve only those output values greater than .80000 for "Loan Approved" conclusions. That would decrease the lending association's risk. On the other hand, we could write rules for what might be considered fuzzy areas, say outputs of .45000 to .55000. In this situation, we could look at the requestor's gross monthly income. If it is greater than $6,500 per month, for example, we could approve the loan. Or perhaps we could just ask the requestor for additional information. The possibilities are now limitless.

In fact, we have found that in some technical neural networks, the user, who in many cases is an expert in the domain of the neural net problem, will add many rules to the embedded system. The final system, when embedded, is an order of magnitude more flexible and useful than if just a stand-alone neural network had been delivered.

Installing the Demonstration Diskette

First things first: you must have an IBM-AT-compatible computer with at least 640K RAM. A high-density floppy drive is also required. (If your drive is low density, see the note that follows the high-density drive installation instructions.) Also, be sure you do not already have a directory named BKDEMO.

To install the neural network demo diskette, insert the diskette in your A: drive and go to the root directory on your C: drive. The information you must type in is the underlined portion following; the portion to the left represents the usual format you would see for your prompt.

```
C:\>A:INSTALL
```

A Practical Guide to Neural Nets

Allow a few moments for installation. Then type in the following:

```
C:\>CD\BKDEMO (to change to the correct directory)
C:\BKDEMO>DEMO (to call up the demo program)
```

Note: If your PC supports low-density drives only, you will need to use a machine with a high-density drive to make copies. First, install the program on the high-density machine as detailed above. Then copy the BKDEMO files to diskettes that have been formatted for low-density drives, using the BACKUP command (four diskettes will be required):

```
C:\BKDEMO>BACKUP C: A:
```

Once you have copied these files, you can delete the files from the high-density drive, if desired, with C:\BKDEMO>DEL *.* and remove the BKDEMO directory using the commands

```
C:\BKDEMO>CD\
C:\>RD BKDEMO.
```

On your machine, make a directory called BKDEMO and copy all files to this directory, using the following commands:

```
C:\>MD BKDEMO
C:\>CD BKDEMO
C:\BKDEMO>COPY A:*.*
```

Copy each of the four diskettes. Then, finally, bring the demo up with

```
C:\BKDEMO>DEMO.
```

What to Look for

Now that you have your demo installed, it's appropriate to say a few words about what you should look for. Because the neural network is embedded in an expert system shell, it is easy to become sidetracked by the window dressing. It is easy, too, to tell yourself that you could just as well perform all the same work with IF-THEN statements. Maybe so, but it won't be as easy as what we have done, nor as able to deal with fuzzy situations, nor as flexible. Remember that the point here is to see how the neural network fits in.

Notice particularly the four introductory screens in the development guide, available only with the "Auto Selector" path.

These screens lay the groundwork for the neural net and talk about how the network structure was developed. It is our recommendation that you keep the illustrations from chapter 9 in mind as you go through the demo. Chapter 9 goes through some of the nitty-gritty required as well as some of the theory behind what you see in this interactive demo, and it details several aspects of the Loan Evaluator.

The highlight of the demo is the graphics screens, which depict the network during training. When you get to this portion, compare what you see on the screen with figures A.2 and A.3. This screen is actually a series of screens, condensed from six hours of continuous training to a time-lapse picture of the network during the training session.

(Ignore the arrows you see on the screens; these merely represent the mouse cursor during screen capture and are not a part of the network graphics. Also ignore the slight pause/flash you may see between some of the screens when the control leaves the expert system shell to perform a DOS-CALL or other external function and then returns to the shell.)

Walking along the Paths

Use figure A.1 to reference the paths you may select when using the interactive demonstration diskette. The first screen you will see is our "Welcome Screen." After reading it and pressing <EN-TER>, you will arrive at the "Development Guide" question. Select YES. Selections are made by highlighting the desired choice and then pressing <ENTER>. You may either move the cursor or type the first letter of your choice to highlight it.

Whatever your answer here, the next screen brings you to choices of "Auto Selector," "Loan Evaluator," or "Both." In order to walk through the development guide and see the dynamic graphical representation of the auto selector neural network as it is learning, you must select "Auto Selector." We have included the development guide and graphics display **only** in this path. (It is shown with a bold line in the flow chart in figure A.1.)

The development guide consists of four introductory screens, the multiscreen graphics display, and one final screen.

The first screen in this set is called "Defining the Task." Here the four auto-selection factors to be used are highlighted: cost,

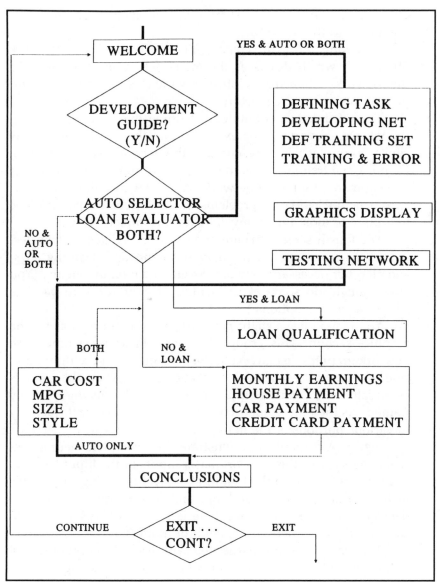

FIGURE A.1 INTERACTIVE DISKETTE PATHS

miles per gallon, size, and style of the automobile. These will be the inputs to the network.

Following this is a screen entitled "Developing a Network Structure," which discusses the methodology used in planning the network architecture. Notice how the inputs and desired outputs influence the architecture.

The third screen is entitled "Defining the Training Set." Although we show only one example from the training set, many similar examples were presented to the network (see figure A.4). Defining the training set is the single most important task in the development of a neural network. When we encounter problems with a neural network, problems in the inputs are perhaps the first place to look: typos, invalid data, incomplete data, etc.

The fourth screen, "Training and Error," relates to the selection of the summation method, transfer function, learning laws, and all other necessary network development requirements. (You may want to do some experimenting if your software package supports various options.)

You may notice a slight pause as the system prepares for the graphics section. This group of screens illustrates a time-lapse network graphics display. Note the instruments at the right-hand side of figure A.2 labeled OUTPUT and ERROR. When the error is essentially zero, or close to a straight line, the network is fully trained. As the time sequence progresses, you can see the activity in various portions of the network.

Figure A.2 graphically illustrates the complete neural network. As shown, this network has 4 inputs in the input layer (2, 3, 4, and 5), 12 PEs in the first hidden layer (6 through 17), 2 PEs in hidden layer two (18 and 19), and finally one single output (labeled 30). Please note that there is always a bias term, which assumes the label here (unmarked) of number 1.

The size of the box associated with each PE is proportional to the value of the previous summation cycle. For example, in the iteration in figure A.2, PE number 6 in hidden layer one is larger than PE number 10. On another iteration, the relative proportions might change. (The network graphics on the computer screen appear in color, allowing an assignment of different colors to a specific range for each interconnection. Unfortunately, our black-and-white illustrations do not differentiate the interconnection strengths.)

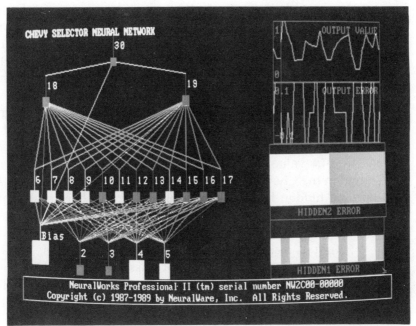

FIGURE A.2 (GRAPHICS ARE COMPLIMENTS OF NEURALWARE, INC.)

Color is a useful tool when developing neural networks. For example, if red is selected for the range of o to −10, and after a reasonable number of cycles we see no change from the negative interconnection values, then we suspect an anomaly exists. Anomalies are usually caused by flawed data, or an input error if the data was keyed in. There are several other trails that can be checked as well. The important point is that humans learn as well as networks, and they soon adapt themselves to the various flags that instantly convey specific knowledge to the network supervisor.

We selected four instruments to observe the performance of the Chevy Neural Network. In almost all network training, it is imperative to observe the learning procedure with at least two instruments, namely an output value and an output error instrument. Because we are using desired outputs in the sigmoid range of o to 1, we must label our output value instrument accordingly. We arbitrarily selected -0.1 to +0.1 for our error output instrument. In this case, we also built two additional instruments to look at each hidden layer output in bar graph format.

As we cycle the network through its learning process, these instruments play an important role for the person (supervisor) training the network. The instrumentation takes on a dynamic nature, and a trained supervisor can tell within minutes whether the network will converge successfully by observing these dynamics.

Comparing figure A.2 to figure A.3, we can easily recognize that the network as shown in the latter figure has successfully converged. The error is essentially zero on the chosen scale and the output value instrument indicates the desired outputs as shown in the Chevy Selector input training set in figure A.4. Note the final hidden layer error values on the two bar-graph instruments in figure A.3: they have stabilized and indicate no change in error at the hidden layer outputs.

Permit us a slight divergence here for comparisons. We want to return briefly to the solder joint classification neural network presented in chapter 9. The solder joint graphic (figure A.5) illustrates how we construct the instrumentation employing output value and output error only. This is a picture of the learning

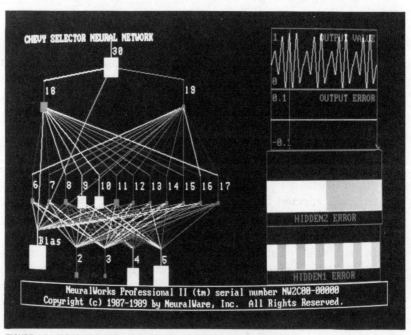

FIGURE A.3 (GRAPHICS ARE COMPLIMENTS OF NEURALWARE, INC.)

A Practical Guide to Neural Nets

```
i = inputs:
* Cost is real cost/50000
* MPG is real MPG/50
*Size is luxury = .99, Midsize = .5, Compact = .01
*Style is sporty = .99, 2Door = .66, 4Door = .33, Wagon = .01
d = Car Model, E.G., 7 = Cavalier


* COST  MPG  SIZE  STYLE
i   .6   .42   .50    .01
d  5
i   .4   .4    .99    .66
d  6
i   .4   .4    .5     .99
d  7
i   .45  .38   .99    .99
d  8
i   .65  .4    .01    .66
d  5
i   .65  .38   .5     .01
d  5
i   .45  .4    .99    .66
d  6
. . . . (continues for a minimum of 25 data sets)
```

FIGURE A.4   TRAINING INPUT DATA FOR CHEVY SELECTOR

process for the solder joint image classification network. This particular graphic utilizes only two instruments, labeled "output" and "error." The instruments were built wide to accommodate 80 desired outputs in the output instrument with a corresponding error output instrument. In this study the network input layer is so large (500 PEs plus a bias) that we block out part of the network purposely so that we can have the desirable larger instrumentation.

With reference to the instruments, we can see that the first 50 outputs appear to have converged to either 1 or 0. This is confirmed by essentially zero error for that range. Note that the error increases at position 48 on out to 80 (end) with a corresponding indeterminate output curve. We originally trained the network

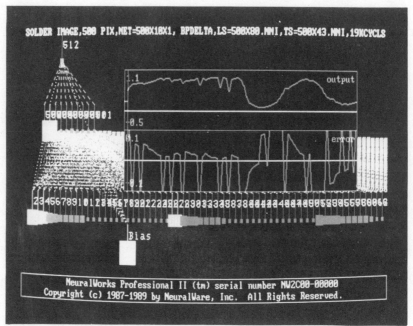

SOLDER IMAGE,500 PIX,NET=500X10X1, BPDELTA,LS=500X80.NNI,TS=500X43.NNI,19KCYCLS

NeuralWorks Professional II (tm) serial number NW2C00-00000
Copyright (c) 1987-1989 by NeuralWare, Inc. All Rights Reserved.

FIGURE A.5 (GRAPHICS ARE COMPLIMENTS OF NEURALWARE, INC.)

with 50 sets of data. After the network converged, we deduced from testing the network that we had not shown the network all types of solder joints in the range we expected it to classify. We then added 30 more data sets with new solder joint categories that it had not previously seen. The network struggled initially in mapping this new training input set. Upon completing an additional twenty minutes of training, the network converged, as illustrated in figure A.6.

(*Note:* If you want to come back later to execute just the training portion of the Chevy Selector demo, you may do so from the DOS prompt. Entering C:\BKDEMO>PRESENTS will bring up a program called "Presents." From the first screen, a menu, follow this sequence: <L>oad, Fl, <ENTER>, <ENTER>, <D>isplay, Y, <ENTER>. This will put you in a continuously looping display of the network training. The <E>dit options will allow you to change the speed of updates to the processing elements. You can slow the sequence down by entering the interval as 3 (or more) instead of 1. <ESC>ape then returns you to the main menu. To terminate, simply enter <ESC>ape, then e<X>it. You will be re-

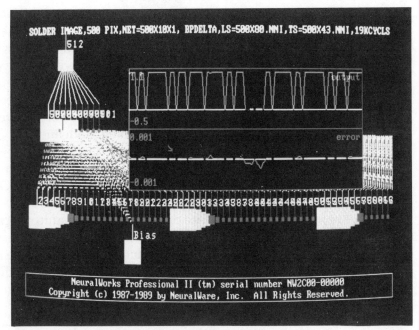

FIGURE A.6 (GRAPHICS ARE COMPLIMENTS OF NEURALWARE, INC.)

turned to the DOS prompt. This is admittedly sketchy, but more detail would go beyond the limits of our primary concern here, the neural network training.)

Upon completion of the graphics, the final screen of this group merely serves as a transition from the training sequence to the upcoming input session for the auto selector neural network.

Now comes your first real opportunity to interface with the diskette program. The system asks you to enter the cost you would like to pay for your new car. The subsequent three screens will request information for desired miles per gallon, size of car, and lastly, preferred style. The final screen on this path will display the conclusion of the auto selector neural network, based on your inputs. Whereas a rule set would have to handle every possible combination of inputs (or have some standard default value for unaddressed cases), the neural network comes up with a good answer no matter what the input combinations.

If you wish to explore the rest of the diskette, select CONTINUE, which returns you to the welcome screen. After pressing <ENTER> select YES to the development guide inquiry and this time select

"Loan Evaluation," which will bring up the loan qualification information screen. After pressing <ENTER>, you will be requested to supply the Loan Evaluation Neural Network's first input, which is monthly gross income. The next three screens will ask for your inputs of monthly mortgage or rent payment, monthly car payment, and your average monthly credit card payment. The conclusion states whether your request for a loan has been approved or denied (based on Dallas-area credit union guidelines).

Selecting CONTINUE will bring you back to the development guide, where you can select the last option to accompany a YES response to the development guide option. Now select BOTH, which will bring up the four auto selection prompt screens. This time there will be no immediate conclusion as to an auto selection. The next four screens will be the prompt screens for the loan qualification neural network. The conclusion will tell you the auto you selected followed by either "approved" or "not approved" for a loan. The BOTH path is not unlike being in a car showroom.

Selecting "NO" to Development Guide Path

The final paths are obvious by now. Selecting NO to the development guide will take you directly to "auto selector," "loan evaluator," or "both," skipping the development guide and graphics section. These routes assume you have seen the development screens and the training graphics. Now it is just a matter of playing with different inputs to see what output results.

How to Ask Questions of Your Expert System

Throughout the consultation, the expert system shell offers you several options for exploring what is going on behind the scenes relative to the shell logistics. The available commands you may use are listed when you press the F2 function key. (The ESCape key will remove the command menu.) There are three different groups of commands. One set of commands is listed when you press F2 while on the first screen, the "Welcome" screen. A second set is available during the consultation, but only prior to the conclusion. At the conclusions screen, the expert system lists the third group of commands without your having to press F2. We'll start with the third group.

At the conclusion of a sequence you will see a menu that lists the following options:

```
CONTINUE
HOW
PRINT CONCLUSIONS
REVIEW
SAVE PLAYBACK FILE
NEW START
EXIT
```

What do these options let you do? CONTINUE simply proceeds to the next screen in the planned sequence. HOW gives you the opportunity to request information about the rules used in the expert system. For example, suppose you select HOW. The next screen presents a submenu of items about which you may inquire. Now suppose you select SIZE. (Select by moving the cursor one column to the right so that the YES column opposite the SIZE item is highlighted; then press <ENTER>. You may select as many items as you wish.) The system will show you the rule that determined a value for the item(s) of interest. (There are not many IF–THEN rules because the output conclusions were determined by the neural network.) PRINT CONCLUSIONS prints the results of the current session to the printer, the screen, or a file. All such files have an extension of .REC (for RECommendation).

REVIEW gives you the opportunity to rerun the current session, changing one or more answers and letting the system remember the inputs you do not wish to change. Selection is done as per the HOW sequence above. This may not seem to be an impressive capability in this small system, because there are only four inputs each for auto and loan, but in a larger system with many inputs, it can be a very important feature. It is an excellent aid in comprehensively testing a large number of paths.

SAVE PLAYBACK FILE lets you save in a file the answers to all of the prompts from the current session (or some of them, if this option is selected prior to the conclusion). These answers then could be retrieved from the file for use in subsequent consultations. The other half of this command is GET PLAYBACK FILE, which is available only at the "Welcome" screen. Pressing F2 at the

"Welcome" screen brings up a menu with this option. The software then presents you with a menu of all the files in the current directory with the appropriate file extension of .PBK, and you may select the entry you want.

NEW START takes you back to the beginning and removes the current choices from system memory. EXIT returns you to DOS. You may EXIT from the expert system software at any time you wish during the consultation.

The only other command not yet explained is the WHY option, available at any question screen prior to the conclusion. This option is like asking the system, WHY are you asking me this question? The system will respond with the rule it is currently trying to examine, and you will see that the value of the current question is needed to determine whether that particular rule is true or false.

The F1 key would provide help if we had felt any "help" were necessary. Instead, we chose to include relevant information with the prompts, a good alternative here as you get the information automatically without having to press another key.

Sometimes you may see more behind-the-scenes information than makes sense to you. This is particularly possible with the HOW and WHY commands. Because our focus is neural nets and not expert systems, we elected not to go into any more detail than what you read here.

Summary

What you have on your diskette is a simple example of a neural network. It has been embedded in an expert system shell for convenience and extended capability. The development screens detail the factors relating to the structure of the network, the inputs, the training set, and the output. The graphics sequence depicts the network during a training session and should give you a visual impression of how the parts fit together.

The expert system aspects of the demo are there for you to examine. Although they simplify the user interface, they do not illuminate the neural network activities. To better understand the network, we encourage you to use this demo in conjunction with the rest of the information in the book, especially the loan evaluation example in chapter 9. There you will find significantly expanded detail on aspects such as scaling of inputs, functions used, training methods, etc. Reading this information provides what we feel is the necessary background for understanding the workings of this demo diskette.

1. Personal Consultant℠ Plus "Material extracted in whole or in part from Personal Consultant℠ Plus. Copyright © 1987, Texas Instruments Incorporated, with permission from the publisher."

Neural networks graphics screens created using NeuralWorks Professional II; compliments of Neural Ware.

Graphics developed and presented using Dr. Halo III Software; courtesy of Media Cybernetics, Inc.

Appendix B:
Bibliography
and
Reading List

Books

Allman, William F. *Apprentices of Wonder: Inside the Neural Network Revolution.* New York: Bantam Books, 1989. (We just bought this gem as our own book goes to press . . . a behind-the-scenes look at the neural network drama and those creating it.)

Anderson, James A. *What Neural Nets Can Do.* Video Companion Manual. Hillsdale, NJ: Lawrence Erlbaum Associates, 1988. (A good introduction to neural networks and Anderson's BSB model. Some interesting application examples from medicine.)

Anderson and Rosenfeld, editors, *Neurocomputing: Foundations of Research.* Cambridge, MA: MIT Press, 1988. (A collection of key papers, each with a short introduction—weaves a good historical picture of events from 1890 to the present.)

Coughlin, James P., and Robert H. Baran. *Problems in Collective Computation.* Bethesda, MD: Intellimetric Publishing Group, 1989. (The authors describe this text as "a preview of statistical mechanics by way of neural networks"; for undergraduate study.)

DARPA Neural Network Study. Fairfax, VA: AFCEA International Press, 1988. (This study compiles the work of many current scientists in the field; it includes theory and application. The purpose of the study was to identify potential DoD applications, assess the current base of technology, identify technology requirements, and identify a DoD five-year program plan.)

Fischler and Firschein, *Intelligence: The Eye, the Brain, and the Computer.* Reading, MA: Addison-Wesley, 1987. (A view of both human and machine intelligence, the nature of cognitive and perceptual skills of people and computers. Appendix 2-1 shows nerve cell and nervous system organization.)

Johnson, R. Colin, and Chappell Brown. *Cognizers (Neural Networks and Machines that Think)*. New York: John Wiley & Sons, 1988.

Johnson, R. Colin. *Neural Network Almanac 1989–1990*. Portland, OR: Cognizer Company, 1990. (Billed as containing reviews of 1989 events, features, and an alphabetical guide to companies, products, reports, periodicals, books, and video tapes. We haven't seen it yet, but we do like Johnson's articles, which appear regularly in *Electronic Engineering Times*, and we would expect this to be very useful, though expensive at $475.)

Klimasauskas, C. C. *An Introduction to Neural Computing* and *Teaching Your Computer to Learn: Applications of Neural Computing*. Sewickly, PA: NeuralWare, 1988. (Contains history, definitions, applications examples, network models, etc., along with product information. Well-written and very complete introduction.)

McClelland, James L., and David E. Rumelhart. *Explorations in Parallel Distributed Processing*. Cambridge, MA: MIT Press, 1988. (This is a handbook of models, programs, and exercises. The IBM-PC-compatible software comes with it.)

Mead, Carver. *Analog VLSI and Neural Systems*. Reading, MA: Addison-Wesley, 1988.

The Metroplex Study Group on Computational Neuroscience. *Computational Neuroscience*. Prepared under the sponsorship of the North Texas Commission Regional Technology Program, 1988. (A strategy study on regional resources, economic potential, and timeliness of setting up a Center of Excellence in Computational Neuroscience.)

Pao, Yoh-Han. *Adaptive Pattern Recognition and Neural Networks*. Reading, MA: Addison-Wesley, 1989. (Introduces and relates the basic concepts of pattern recognition and neural networks. Fairly technical; examines various neural network architectures and implementations for adaptive pattern recognition.)

Simpson, P. K., *A Review of Artificial Neural Systems II*, MZ 7202-K, General Dynamics Electronics Division, P.O. Box 85310, San Diego, CA 92138, July 1988. (Part two of a two-part review; 176 pages submitted to CRC Critical Reviews in Artificial Intelligence. Technical study of 26 neural network paradigms. Considers attributes, encoding, decoding and convergence, strengths and limitations, applications and implementations of each paradigm.)

Stanley, Jeannette. *Introduction to Neural Networks*. Sierra Madre, CA: California Scientific Software, 1988, 1989. (This book comes packaged with the BrainMaker software. The 255-page introduction was easy to read and use. It includes a glossary and some math in the appendixes. We liked it a lot.)

Wasserman, Philip D. *Neural Computing: Theory and Practice*. New York: Van Nostrand Reinhold, 1989. (A primer on better-known neural network computing architectures, including their strengths and limitations. One chapter on each paradigm. Clear technical descriptions, well written. Deals more with theory than with practice.)

Articles

Aarts, Emile H. L., and Jan H. M. Korst. "Computations in Massively Parallel Networks Based on the Boltzmann Machine: A Review." *Parallel Computing*, vol. 9 (January 1989): 129–45. (From the Netherlands. Discusses some of the achievements in research relative to Boltzmann machines and two fields of applications: (1) solving combinatorial optimization problems, (2) carrying out learning tasks. A lot to wade through; read it only if you are interested in Boltzmann machines.)

AI Expert, vol. 3, no. 8 (August 1988). (The whole issue is on neural networks.)

Anderson, Dana Z. "Optical Systems That Imitate Human Memory." *Computers in Physics*, vol. 3, no. 2 (March/April 1989): 19–25. (Clear illustrations on holographic images, nice style.)

Anderson, James A. "Use of the BSB Neural Network for Radar Data Classification," Paper. Providence, RI: Brown University, Dec. 18, 1986. (Examples of using vectors for input and pattern matching.)

Barhen, Jacob, N. Toomarian, and V. Protopopescu. "Optimization of the Computational Load of a Hypercube Supercomputer Onboard a Mobile Robot." *Applied Optics*, vol. 26, no. 23 (Dec. 1, 1987): 5007–14. (Includes math and implementation information that was quite technical. The applications sections were interesting, with a description of HERMIES [Hostile Environment Robotic Machine Intelligence Experiment Series.])

A Practical Guide to Neural Nets

Bien, Bill. "The Promise of Neural Networks." *American Scientist*, vol. 76 (November/December 1988): 561–64. (Overview of possibilities; some good quotes; nicely balanced.)

Brown, Robert Jay. "An Artificial Neural Network Experiment." *Dr. Dobb's Journal*, vol. 12, no. 4 (April 1987): 16+. (This article has general information as well as hardware schematics and some C language source code listings.)

Caudill, Maureen. "Neural Networks Primer.", Parts 1–8, *AI Expert*. Selected issues December 1987 through August 1989. (A series of articles designed to educate AI engineers. Tutorial style with some easy-to-follow examples; includes basic terminology and explanation of major network models. Note: this set is now available as a book, *Neural Network Primer*, [Gilroy, CA: Miller Freeman Publications, 1989]. Cost is $7.95.)

—— "Using Neural Nets: Representing Knowledge, Part I." *AI Expert*, vol. 4, no. 12 (December 1989): 34–41. (Compares AI knowledge representation with that of neural nets, generalizing from a back propagation model. Good tutorial style. Starting new series.)

Churchland, Patricia S., and Terrence J. Sejnowski. "Perspectives on Cognitive Neuroscience." *Research*. (November 1988): 741–45. (Churchland is from the department of philosophy at the University of California at San Diego [UCSD]. Sejnowski is at the Salk Institute and the department of biology at UCSD. They describe three levels of research: analysis, organization, and processing. Presents a case study on color vision. Stresses need for interaction among research domains.)

Churchland, Paul M., and Patricia Smith Churchland, "Could a Machine Think?" *Scientific American*, vol. 262, no. 1 (January 1990): 32–37. (One of two articles in this issue debating artificial intelligence machines; John Searle's article is the counterpoint. The Churchlands conclude that classical AI is the wrong architecture for the job of thinking, but that neural networks are a "compelling . . . prospect.")

Conner, Doug. "Data Transformation Explains the Basics of Neural Networks." *EDN Magazine*, vol. 33 (May 12, 1988): 138–44. (Description of experiment in building simple hardware net; we wrote it up in chapter 4. Good illustrations and diagrams.)

Cooper, Leon N. "Brain Research: Theory and Experiment." *Computers in Physics*, vol. 2, no. 6 (November/December 1988):29–38. (This article is based on a lecture by Cooper at a symposium at the Office of Naval Research, which supported Cooper's research on changes that take place in the visual cortex when learning occurs and memory is stored. Very technical.)

———— "First Word." *OMNI*, vol. 11, no. 6 (March 1989): 6. (A one-page factual, yet imaginative, assessment of neural network possibilities.)

Crick, Francis, "The Recent Excitement About Neural Networks", *Nature*, Vol. 337, No. 6203 (January 12, 1989) :129—132. (Crick, of the Salk Institute, summarizes the what and why of neural nets, topics such as memory and the back propagation of errors method, and discusses the differences between engineering—making nets do useful things—and science—understanding the brain.)

Cromie, William J. "Neural Networks: What Can They Do?" *The MIT Report* (December/January 1988–89): 4–5, 14–15. (Insight into MIT's approach and research plus some good general information.)

Dalton, M. C. "Coming of Age—Neural Networks." *Information Executive*, vol. 2, no. 1 (Winter 1989): 48–50. (DPMA slant in featuring business applications; includes a good picture of Kuperstein's robot.)

Dalton, Richard. "Future Computers." Ideas and Trends column in *Lotus* (April 1988): 19–22. (Examines current research. He comments that concepts sound like they belong on Star Trek rather than a desktop. Easy reading.)

Feldman, Jerome A., Mark A. Fanty, Nigel H. Goddard, and Kenton J. Lynne. "Computing with Structured Connectionist Networks." *Communications of the ACM*, vol. 31, no. 2 (February 1988): 170–187. (Technical presentation on massively parallel computational models. Designing a connectionist network: sample construction program, graphics interface, parallel implementation using the Butterfly computer. Example recognition problems include disambiguation, the Necker Cube, and Tinker Toys. The merging of neural nets and AI approaches is predicted to have considerable scientific and practical consequences.)

Franklin, Judy A., Richard S. Sutton, Charles W. Anderson, Oliver G. Selfridge, and Daniel B. Schwartz. "Connectionist Learning Control at GTE Laboratories." *Proceedings of the SPIE 1989 Symposium on Advances in Intelligent Robotics Systems*. November 1989, Philadelphia, PA. (We drew on this paper, as well as phone interviews with Anderson, for material in the text. See references to GTE.)

Freundlich, Naomi J. "Brain-Style Computers." *Popular Science,* vol. 234, no. 2 (February 1989): 68+. (Excellent review of growth of neural networks with people and events; includes drawing to show basic structure of network and a character-recognition application.)

Fukushima, Kunihiko. "A Neural Network for Visual Pattern Recognition." *IEEE Computer,* vol. 21, no. 3 (March 1988): 65–75. (The best paper we've found on Neocognitron.)

Gallant, Stephen I. "Connectionist Expert Systems." *Communications of the ACM,* vol. 31, no. 2 (February 1988): 152–168. (The article is long, but with our background in expert systems we found it quite interesting. HNC is patenting the approach.)

Gass, Wanda S., Richard T. Tarrant, B. I. Pawate, Michele Gammel, P. K. Rajasekaran, Richard H. Wiggins, and C. David Covington. "Multiple Digital Signal Processor Environment for Intelligent Signal Processing." *Proceedings of the IEEE,* vol. 75, no. 9 (September 1987): 1246–59. (Describes Texas Instruments' Odyssey Board.)

Gerald, Park S. "Getting Started with Neural Networks: NeuralWare's Explorer and NeuralWorks Professional II." *PC AI,* vol. 2, no. 4 (November/December 1988): 55–57. (See the whole issue—it's all neural network stories.)

Glatzer, Hal. "Neural Networks: Software on the Brain." *Software News*. International edition (November 1987): 66. (Good examples of applications areas, diagrams for character-recognition demo; predictions for future.)

Gorman, Christine. "Putting Brainpower in a Box." *Time*. Overseas edition (August 15, 1988): 32. (One-page overview; excellent illustration of learning.)

Graf, Hans P., Lawrence D. Jackel, and Wayne E. Hubbard. "VLSI Implementation of a Neural Network Model." *IEEE Computer,* vol. 21, no. 3 (March 1988): 41–49. (Technical; from AT&T Bell

Laboratories. Includes circuit schematics, math, considerations in programming a chip, and applications examples.)

Grant, Peter, David Wallace, and David Bounds. "Following Nature's Example." *IEEE Review,* vol. 34 (March 1988): 117–19. (Summary of key net features, factors' relation to current interest, U.K. work, graphics examples of nets learning to recognize numbers and text.)

Gross, Guenter W., Jacek M. Kowalski, and David Golden. "On the Behavior and Significance of Random Neuronal Networks." Paper. Denton, TX: University of North Texas. (We used information from this paper in chapter 11.)

Harmon, Paul. "Neural Networks and NeuralWorks Professional." *Expert Systems Strategies,* vol. 3, no. 12, pp. 6–12. (Relationship of neural nets to AI and short historical review, left brain versus right brain analogy, review of NETtalk, Nestor, and NeuralWorks products.)

Hecht-Nielsen, Robert. "Neurocomputing: Picking the Human Brain." *IEEE Spectrum,* vol. 25, no. 3 (March 1988): 36–41. (Tutorial style. Chart of thirteen best-known neural networks, chart of neurocomputers built to date, applications areas. Easy to read.)

Hopfield, John J., and David W. Tank. "Computing with Neural Circuits: A Model." *Science,* vol. 233 (August 8, 1986): 625–32; and *Science,* vol. 235 (March 6, 1987): 1226–29. (Technical article. Neural circuits: relationship to biology, types of problems solved, math and diagrams, research results.)

Howard, Richard E., Lawrence D. Jackel, and Hans P. Graf. "Electronic Neural Networks." *AT&T Technical Journal,* vol. 67, issue 1 (January/February 1988): 58–64. (Biological basis for artificial neural networks, pattern-matching illustrations, on down to CMOS implementation. Good progression of ideas; easy to read.)

Huffman, Jim, and John Scoggins. "Architectural Isomorphisms in Neural Network Applications." Austin, TX: Motorola, Microprocessor Products Group, 1989. (The search for neural network architectures that are functionally more biologically authentic. The application featured is the Luscher Color Test.)

Huffman, Jim. "Human Behavior Paradigms From Ancient Mythology for Artificial Neural Network Research." A paper courtesy of the author, 1990. (This unusual paper has been accepted by INNS-90, Paris, July 9-13. The paper explores ancient writings which contain specific information as to individual human behavior. Huffman suggests these "world scriptures" represent the largest body of experiential behavioral information available to neural network researchers, and although specific inaccuracies exist, the writings can provide an important basis for current research.)

Huffman, Jim. "Neural Networks: Heralding the New Computer-Based Science." A paper courtesy of the author, 1989. (Many ideas for chapter 12 came from discussions with the author.)

IEEE Computer, vol. 21, no. 3 (March 1988). (The whole issue is on neural nets.)

Inglesby, Tom. "No Clowning Around, Neural Networks Can Help Manufacturing." *Manufacturing Systems* (October 1988): 26–31. (Features the broom-balancing experiment and applies concepts to process control systems.)

Johnson, George. "Artificial Brain Again Seen as a Guide to the Mind." *New York Times* (August 16, 1988): Section C, pp. 1, 11. (Popular press treatment with quotes from Churchland, Minsky, Anderson, Sejnowski. Section on NETTalk.)

Johnson, R. Colin. *Electronic Engineering Times*. (See the notes at the end of each chapter for a sampling of specific articles.) (Johnson writes articles on neural networks on a regular basis; we can find something on neural networks in nearly every issue, and we have a whole file of articles. Features technology, new products, events, etc. A good way to keep current if you already have this publication.)

Jones, William P., and Josiah Hoskins. "Back-Propagation." *Byte*, vol. 12, no. 11 (October 1987): 155–62. (A highly readable discussion of back propagation, how it works, limitations, applications. Fun use of Little Red Riding Hood detecting features of the wolf.)

Jorgensen, Chuck, and Chris Matheus. "Catching Knowledge in Neural Nets." *AI Expert*, vol. 1, no. 4 (December 1986): 30–41. (Recent history, advantages of neural nets, terminology, Hopfield and Boltzmann models, future possibilities.)

Josin, Gary. "Integrating Neural Networks with Robots." *AI Expert*, vol. 3, no. 8 (August 1988): 50–58. (Presents supporting statistics from a project that uses a neural network to train a robot arm—

pointing to possibilities of increased functionality in future machines.)

Josin, Gary. "Neural-Network Heuristics: Three Heuristic Algorithms that Learn from Experience." *Byte,* vol. 12, no. 11 (October 1987): 183–92. (Based on the need for a new approach to software design, producing software that can learn from experience. Explores three algorithms developed for testing the validity of network heuristics: associative memory, optimization, and self-organization models. Includes charts of patterns, math, potential applications.)

Judge, Peter. "Neurocomputers Are News." *New Electronics,* vol. 21, no. 5 (May 1988): 36–37. (A summary of neural network use and characteristics; some attention to net hardware pioneers and selected commercial systems.)

Kemske, Floyd. "A New Breed of Expert." *Data Training* (May 1989): 36–37. (Comparisons with expert systems, applications areas, general information. Includes graphic comparing neutron cell and neural network processing element.)

Kepuska, Veton Z., and John N. Gowdy. "The Kohonen Net for Speaker Dependent Isolated Word Recognition." *Proceedings of the IEEE Southeastern Symposium on System Theory* (1988), session 18, paper 5. (Technical, lots of math. Evaluates the effectiveness of a model for a speech-recognition system. Explores the effects of varying network architecture parameters.)

King, Todd. "Using Neural Networks for Pattern Recognition." *Dr. Dobb's Journal,* vol. 14, no. 1 (January 1989): 14+. (King, a programmer/analyst, discusses an executive board simulator, logic gates, and an optical character recognition system.)

Kinoshita, June, and Nicholas G. Palevsky. "Computing with Neural Networks." *High Technology* (May 1987): 24–31. (Covers corporations and new companies, capabilities, biological metaphor, applications, hardware, etc.—a good general article on the state of neural nets.)

Klimasauskas, Casey. "Neural Nets and Noise Filtering." *Dr. Dobb's Journal,* vol. 14, no. 1 (January 1989): 32–48. (Applications of back propagation to noise filtering, or, conversely, identifying fundamental underlying signals. Includes pictures of Neural-Ware screens.)

Kosko, Bart. "Constructing an Associative Memory." *Byte,* vol. 12, no. 10, (September 1987) : 137–144. (A good walkthrough of Kosko's bidirectional associative memory, or BAM, model. Discusses associative memory and includes information on demonstrations available on disk in BASIC, Pascal, and C.)

Kuperstein, Michael. "An Adaptive Neural Model for Mapping Invariant Target Position." *Behavioral Neuroscience,* vol. 102, no. 1 (1988): 148–62. (Technical. Derives and simulates a neural network model that learns precise sensory motor calibrations starting with only loosely defined relations. The model is adaptive to physical changes of the eye and muscles as well as internal system parameters.)

Kurita, Shohei. "Expanding Neural Marketplace Challenges Japanese Engineers." *Electronic Business* (Asia/Pacific Business section) (September 18, 1989): 79–80. (Reviews Japanese manufacturers' interests and achievements.)

Lerner, Eric J. "Computers that Learn." *Aerospace America* (American Institute of Aeronautics and Astronautics). vol. 26 (June 1988): 32–34, 40. (Introductory level material which emphasizes neural net interests of aerospace.)

Levine, Daniel S. "The Third Wave in Neural Networks." *AI Expert,* vol. 4, no. 12 (December 1989): 27–30. (Looks at the reasons for the current interest in neural nets. The First Wave was in the 40s and 50s, the "cybernetic" revolution; the 60s and 70s and the split with AI comprised the Second Wave. The discovery of general principles and types of subnets used in nature has enabled a transformation Levine calls the Third Wave.)

Libet, Benjamin. "Neural Destiny." *The Sciences* (March/April 1989): 32–35. (Philosophical rather than technical; looking at free choice of man by examining electrochemical activity in the brain.)

Lippmann, Richard P. "An Introduction to Computing with Neural Nets." *IEEE ASSP Magazine,* vol. 4, no. 2 (April 1987): 4–22. (Reviews six neural net models used for pattern classification: Hopfield, Hamming, Carpenter/Grossberg, Single Layer Perceptron, Multilayer Perceptron, Kohonen. Includes diagrams, algorithms, and a healthy list of references.)

Mehta, Angeli. "Nations Unite for Electronic Brain." *Computer Weekly,* issue 1148 (January 11, 1988): (Short article on the plan of eight

European nations to build a neural computer with its own programming language.)

Miller, Richard K. "Neural Networks: Implementing Associative Memory Models in Neurocomputers," volume 1. Madison, GA: SEAI Technical Publications, 1987. (A fine introduction to neural networks, detailed biological metaphors, neurocomputer applications, and pioneers in commercialization. Many references to neural network software and hardware status.)

Morton, Steven G. "Smart Memories Beat Bottleneck Blues." *ESD: The Electronic System Design Magazine*, vol. 18, no. 7 (July 1988): 70–73. (States the case for intelligent analog chips. Shows matrix multiplication, Hopfield networks implementation schematics. Discusses limitations and alternatives.)

"Neural Networks for Defense." Program handbook from this conference in Washington, D.C., June 17, 1989. (Some copies of overhead transparencies.)

"Neural Networks: Theory and Practice." *Byte*, vol. 14, no. 8 (August 1989): 244–45. (A good survey of books and articles as well as hardware and software products.)

Obermeier, Klaus K., and Janet J.Barron. "Time to Get Fired Up." *Byte*, vol. 14, no. 8 (August 1989): 217–224. (Survey article on biological inspiration, training techniques, PC and workstation implementations, current applications and events, research problems. Good article. Includes short glossary.)

O'Reilly, Brian. "Computers That Think Like People." *Fortune*, vol. 119, no. 5 (February 27, 1989): 90–93. (Some short, good stories on applications with pictures and a graphic.)

Owechko, Yuri. "Nonlinear Holographic Associative Memories." *IEEE Journal of Quantum Electronics*, vol. 25, no. 3 (March 1989): 619–633. (Lots of math; reviews recent progress in field. Shows how nonlinearities are used to make decisions. Very technical.)

Palmer, Douglas A. "Neural Networks: Computers That Never Need Programming." *I&CS*, vol. 61 (April 1988): 75–77. (Palmer is a staff scientist at Hecht-Nielsen. Tutorial style, very readable overview with some good illustrations, comparisons with von Neumann computers.)

Parker, David B. "Artificial Neural Networks: An Overview." *Andrew Seybold's Outlook on Professional Computing*, vol. 6, no. 10 (May

27, 1988): 23–25. (What it says: reviews concepts, algorithms, implementations, and research.)

PC AI, vol. 2, no. 4 (November/December 1988). (The whole issue is on neural nets.)

Pollack, Andrew. "More Human Than Ever, Computer Is Learning to Learn." *New York Times* (September 15, 1987): section C, p. 1. (Comparing computers/neural networks to brain; characteristics and limitations of neural nets; character recognition example.)

Rauch, Herbert E., and Theo Winarske. "Neural Networks for Routing Communication Traffic." *IEEE Control Systems Magazine*, vol. 8 (April 1988): 26–31. (Information on optimizing traffic routing in communications networks; compares conventional approach with neural networks.)

Reggia, James A., and Granger G. Sutton. "Self-Processing Networks and Their Biomedical Implications." *Proceedings of the IEEE*, vol. 76, no. 6 (June 1988): 680–692. (*Self-processing* means that no external program operates on the underlying network; it literally processes itself. Looks at such networks as cognitive models and as adaptive systems. Considers various representations. Technical.)

Roberts, Leslie. "Are Neural Nets Like the Human Brain?" *Science*, vol. 243 (January 27, 1989): 481–482. (Based on an interview with Francis Crick; discusses NETtalk and goals in learning to understand more about the brain.)

Roberts, Markus. "Twelve Neural Network Clichés." *AI Expert*, vol. 3, no. 8 (August 1988): 40–46. (Fun combination of facetiousness and astute getting-to-the-heart-of-the-matter in current neural network writings.)

Sakurai, Miyoko. "Fujitsu Breeding Neural-Computer-Driven Robot." *Electronic Engineering Times*, issue 472 (February 8, 1988): 33, 34. (Fujitsu simulates first with software, then incorporates neural chip to control mobile robot that learns.)

Schwartz, Tom J. "Eight Parables of Neural Networks." *AI Expert*, vol. 4, no. 12 (December 1989): 54–59. (Hilarious. A quiz on how to convince your skeptical manager to use neural nets.)

———. "Twelve-Product Wrap-Up: Neural Networks." *AI Expert*, vol. 3, no. 8 (August 1988): 73–85.

————. "Using Neural Networks on PCs." *Programmer's Update* (September 1989): 58–63. (Overview of types of applications, the learning process, PC products categories.)

Searle, John R. "Is the Brain's Mind a Computer Program?" *Scientific American*, vol. 262, no. 1 (January 1990): 26–31. (Refutes strong AI; uses Chinese room Turing test and other arguments to refute psychological significance of parallel processing and neural networks approaches; simulation does not equal duplication. See also counter article by Churchlands.)

Sompolinsky, Haim. "Statistical Mechanics of Neural Networks." *Physics Today*, vol. 41 (December 1988): 70–80. (Technical article. Lists historical contributions, discusses relationship of nets to spin glasses, net dynamics and architectures, associative memory. Comparisons of Hopfield and Willshaw models, theory and biology.)

Stapleton, Lisa, and Paul E. Schindler. "New Kids on the Block." *Information WEEK* (December 14, 1987): 33+. (Surveys neural net issues and trends, highlights HNC and Synaptics.)

Stubbs, Derek F. "Neurocomputers." *M.D. Computing*, vol. 5, no. 3 (1988): 14–24. (Stubbs is an M.D.; he also edits a newsletter on neurocomputers. Article contains definitions, overview, medical applications, comparisons with conventional computers.)

Tank, David W., and John J. Hopfield. "Collective Computation in Neuronlike Circuits." *Scientific American*, vol. 257, no. 6 (December 1987): 104–14. (Technical yet readable treatment of computational behavior in neuronlike circuits; collective properties, systems of interacting parts. Illustrates the process with flip-flop circuits and associative memory.)

Touretzky, David S., and Dean A. Pomerleau. "What's Hidden in the Hidden Layers?" *Byte*, vol. 14, no. 8 (August 1989): 227–33. (Good illustrations, insights on hidden layer activity, nice write-up of the ALVINN [Autonomous Land Vehicle In a Neural Network.])

Trelease, Robert B. "Connectionism, Cybernetics, and the Cerebellum." *AI Expert*, vol. 3, no. 8 (August 1988): 30–36. (Trelease is a neuroscientist and software developer. More on the biological networks than we wanted to know, but a lengthy list of references for those interested.)

Trowbridge, David, and Tony Materna. "Hecht-Nielsen Neurocomputer Corporation," an editorial backgrounder; and "Neurocomputers in Banking," a white paper. KPR, Granada Hills, CA: July 1987 (General neural network technology and background on Hecht-Nielsen; nice write-up on financial potential.)

Ubois, Jeff. "Neural Networks." *Federal Computer Week*, vol. 3, no. 43 (October 23, 1989): 34–35, 38–39, 42. (Includes a primer, along with federal government neural network information and forecasts.)

Vowler, Julia. "Making Machines Work Like Brains." *Computer Weekly* (February 25, 1988): 20–21. (A bit of history, some definitions, best-known models, relationship of AI to neural nets.)

Wasserman and Schwartz, and Lance B. Eliot, editor. "Focus." *IEEE Expert*, vol. 2, no. 4 (Winter 1987): 10–13; and vol. 3, no. 1 (Spring 1988): 10–15. (*IEEE Expert* regularly has information on neural network events and new developments.)

Waibel, Alex, and John Hampshire. "Building Blocks for Speech." *Byte*, vol. 14, no. 8 (August 1989): 235–42. (Examines modular neural networks for speech recognition, pointing out that automatic learning and parallel representation of knowledge for rapid evaluation could overcome current deficiencies. Discusses problems of time and scaling. Evaluates the Time-Delay Neural Network, TDNN, with figures of the implementation; and a modular design.)

White, Halbert. "Neural-Network Learning and Statistics." *AI Expert*, vol. 4, no. 12 (December 1989): 48–52. (Nice comparison of networks and traditional statistical methods, such as least squares regression. Each discipline can benefit from sharing ideas.)

Williamson, Mickey. "Neural Networks." *Digital News* (January 9, 1989): 30–34. (Surveys current events in the field, corporations, concepts, products, announced applications. Williamson is a technical journalist, so it's no surprise that the article is well-written and informative.)

Wilson, Andrew. "Cranium Computing: Demystifying Neural Nets" (pp. 38–41), and "Do DARPA's Androids Dream of Electric Sheep?" (pp. 29–30). *ESD: The Electronic System Design Magazine*, vol. 18, no. 7 (July 1988). (The first article has some good examples, such as an ink blob obscuring letters in a word, a pattern associator, and competitive learning architecture; figures courtesy of Rumelhart and McClelland. The second article compares representative neural networks. *Note:* we read in *Marketing Computers* (January 1990, p. 49) that ESD folded on November 30, 1989.)

Xenakis, John J. "Neural Networks." *BCS (Boston Computer Society) Update* (June 1989): 14–17. (Good survey article. Illustration uses Santa Claus for feature recognition. Looks at current applications, software and hardware. Author likes BrainMaker software—so did we.)

Zeidenberg, Matthew. "Modeling the Brain." *Byte*, vol. 12, no. 14 (December 1987): 237–46. (Compares traditional AI with neural networks, discusses examples of parallel computation, such as The Connection Machine, the Boltzmann machine, and related concepts. Includes the Perceptron controversy between Rosenblatt and Minsky and Papert. Concludes that neural networks are good for natural-language processing tasks. Not overly technical.)

Newsletters and Journals

AN^3: Another Neural Networks Newsletter. Intellimetric Publishing Group, P.O. Box 30171, Bethesda, MD 20814. (Published intermittently; the November/December 1989 issue we saw contained articles relating to Defense, DoD's Small Business Innovation Research (SBIR), and use of neural nets in establishing a drug-free workplace. Currently no cost.)

Intelligence: The Future of Computing. Ed Rosenfeld, ed. P.O. Box 20006, New York, NY 10025–1510. (Call 1–800-NEURALS.) (Covers the business side of neural networks: sales estimates, venture capital funding, government grants, military spending, patents, the foreign markets, etc. $295/year.)

International Journal of Neural Networks: Research and Applications. Kamal N. Karna, ed. Quarterly, Learned Information, Inc., 143 Old Marlton Pike, Medford, NJ 08055. (Price is $95/yr.)

Journal of Neural Network Computing. Harold Szu and Judith Dayhoff, eds. Published quarterly by Auerbach Publishers, One Penn

Plaza, New York, NY 10019. (New; will cover tested architectures and designs. Having met Harold Szu, we would expect it to be good. $145/year.)

Neural Computation. Terrence Sejnowski, ed. Quarterly, MIT Press Journals, 55 Hayward Street, Cambridge, MA 02142. ($90 for institutions, $45 for individuals.)

Neural Network News. David A. Blanchard, ed. Monthly, AI Week Inc., 255 Cumberland Parkway, Suite 299, Atlanta, GA 30339. (Articles on applications, international news briefs, product and book reviews, calendar. $249/yr.)

Neural Network Review. Craig Will, ed. Quarterly. Started by the Washington Neural Network Society and now published by Lawrence Erlbaum Associates, 365 Broadway, Hillsdale, NJ 07642. (Goals: critical analysis of published work in research and application of neural networks, publicize news and events. Reviewers point out extremes in positions, make objective comparisons. We particularly enjoy the writing of Craig Will. Fun, and relatively inexpensive at $36/year.)

Neural Networks, The Official Journal of the International Neural Network Society. Amari, Grossberg and Kohonen, eds. Bimonthly. Pergamon Press, Fairview Park, Elmsford, NY 10523. (Along with editors Amari, Grossberg, and Kohonen, the newsletter has a huge editorial board of neural net notaries. Articles tend to be fairly technical—after all, this publication is for those involved in active research. Includes book reviews and information on current events. Free with society membership; otherwise $125/year or $49/year personal rate.)

Neurocomputers. Derek F. Stubbs, ed. Bimonthly. Gallifrey Publishing, P.O. Box 155, Vicksburg, MI 49097. (Call 616–649–3772.) (A highly personal approach with a technical slant. Includes reports on conferences, product reviews, benchmarking neurocomputers, very current book reviews, news, meeting notices, etc. A bargain at the price of $32/year.)

Release 1.0. Monthly. EDventure Holdings, 375 Park Avenue, New York, NY 10152. (Conference reports, current companies reviewed. Clever, readable style. Includes more than just neural networks: PCs, S/W, CASE, AI, etc. fairly expensive at $495/year U.S., $575/year overseas.)

Conferences

Fourth Annual Symposium on Networks in Brain and Computer Architecture. Sponsored by The North Texas Commission, University of Texas at Dallas, University of Texas at Arlington, Metroplex Institute for NeuroDynamics, Rockwell Trust. Hosted by The University of Texas at Dallas, October 27, 1988.

IJCNN-90-WASH-DC, International Joint Conference on Neural Networks, co-sponsored by the International Neural Network Society and the Institute of Electrical and Electronics Engineers, January 15–19, 1990, Washington, D.C.

Neural Networks for Defense. Sponsored by: *AI Expert, The Intelligence Newsletter.* Washington, D.C., June, 1989.

VC31 Neural Networks: Capabilities and Applications — For Today and the Future. IEEE videoconference. Produced by IEEE and The Learning Channel. September 27, 1989.

Appendix C: Selected Mathematics Examples

Symbols for Equations

w_{ij} = Symmetric connection strength from ith to the jth $F_A PE$

F_A = Layer

W = Memory matrix

PE = Processing element

$S()$ = Sigmoid function

α = Positive constant controlling passive decay or LTM (Long Term Memory)

β = Positive constant controlling Hebbian learning term

Symbols for Activation (Transfer) Equations

a_i, a_j = Activation values of ith and jth $F_A PE$;

I_i = Input value

μ = Positive constant controlling activation decay

δ = Positive constant controlling intralayer feedback

t = Time t

or

β = Positive constant controlling excitatory input and recurrent feedback

μ = Positive constant controlling inhibitory input and lateral feedback

R_i = Positive constant controlling decay resistance

X_i $\qquad$ = Is the ith $F_A PE$'s Preactivation value

$\beta_i()$ $\qquad$ = An Arbitrary bounded function

Θ_j $\qquad$ = jth $F_B PE$'s Threshold value

Selected Paradigms

ABAM **Adaptive Bidirectional Associative Memory**

Summation: $\qquad \dot{w}_{ij} = \alpha\,[-w_{ij} + S(a_i{}^k)\,S(b_j{}^k)\,]$

Activation: $\qquad \dot{a}_i = -\alpha_i\,(a_i)\,[\,\beta_i(a_i) - \sum_{j=1}^{p} w_{ij}\,S_j\,(b_j)\,]$

Stability: $\qquad \alpha_i\,(x_i)\,=\,\beta_j\,(y_j)\,=\,1$

Adaline **Adaline/Madaline**

Summation: $\qquad b_j = \sum_{i=1}^{n} w_{ij}\,a_i + \Theta_j$

Activation: $\qquad b_j = f\left(\sum_{i=1}^{n} w_{ij}\,a_i + \Theta_j\right)$

AG **Additive Grossberg**

Summation: $\qquad \dot{w}_{ij} = -\alpha\,w_{ij} + \beta S\,(a_i{}^k)\,S\,(a_j{}^k)$

Activation: $\qquad \dot{a}_i = -\mu a_i + \delta\sum_{j=1}^{n} S\,(a_j)\,w_{ji} + I_i$

Stability: $\qquad \alpha_i\,(x_i)\,=\,1$

ART1 **Binary Adaptive Resonance Theory**

Summation: $\qquad \dot{w}_{ij} = \alpha\,_1 f(b_j)\,[\,-\beta_1\,w_{ji} + S\,(a_i{}^k)\,]$

$$\dot{w}_{ij} = \alpha_2 f(b_j)) [-\beta_2 w_{ij} + S(a_i{}^k)]$$

Activation: $$\dot{a}_i = -a_i + (1 - \mu_1 a_i) [\gamma_1 \sum_{j=1}^{m} f(b_j) w_{ji} + I_i] - (\delta_1 + \epsilon_1 a_i) \sum_{j=1}^{m} f(b_j)$$

BAM **Discrete Bidirectional Associative Memory**

Summation: $$w_{ij} = \sum_{k=1}^{m} a_i{}^k b_j{}^k$$

Activation: $$y_j = \sum_{i=1}^{n} a_i(t) w_{ij}$$

$$x_i = \sum_{j=1}^{p} b_j(t) w_{ji}$$

Stability: $$\frac{\Delta L(A,B)}{\Delta B} = -AW\Delta B^T = -\sum_{j=1}^{p} \Delta b_j \sum_{i=1}^{n} a_i w_{ij} \ 0$$

BM **Boltzman Machine**

Summation: $$R_{ij} = \frac{1}{m} \left[\sum_{k=1}^{m} \Phi(c_j{}^k \cdot d_i{}^k) \right]$$

Activation: $$b_i = f \left(\sum_{h=1}^{n} v_{hi} a_h \right)$$

$$c_j = f \left(\sum_{i=1}^{p} w_{ij} b_i \right)$$

BP **Back Propagation**

Summation: $$b_i = S \left(\sum_{h=1}^{n} a_h v_{hi} + \Theta_j \right)$$

$$c_j = S \left(\sum_{h=1}^{n} b_i w_{ij} + \Gamma_i \right)$$

Activation: Same as encoding

BSB   Brain-State-in-a-Box

Summation:
$$d_j = a_j{}^k - \sum_{i=1}^{n} w_{ij} a_i$$

Activation:
$$a_i(t+1) = f\left\{ (a_i(t) + \beta \sum_{j=1}^{n} w_{ij} a_j(t)) \right\}$$

Stability:
$$\dot{a}_i = -a_i + f\left(\sum_{j=1}^{n} v_{ij} a_j \right)$$

CABAM   Competitive Adaptive Bidirectional Associative Memory

Summation:
$$\dot{w}_{ij} = -w_{ij} + S(a_i{}^k) S(b_j{}^k)$$

Activation:
$$\dot{a}_i = -\alpha_i(a_i)\left[\beta_i(a_i) - \sum_{j=1}^{p} w_{ij} S_j(b_j) - \sum_{h=1}^{n} S(a_h) u_{hi} \right]$$

$$\dot{b}_j = -\alpha_j(b_j)\left[\beta_j(b_j) - \sum_{i=1}^{n} w_{ij} S_i(a_i) - \sum_{h=1}^{p} S(b_h) v_{hj} \right]$$

CH   Continuous Hopfield

Summation:
$$w_{ij} = \frac{\alpha}{R_{ij}}$$

Activation:
$$c_i \dot{a}_i = \sum_{i=1}^{n} S(a_i) w_{ji} - \frac{a_i}{R_i} + I_i$$

Stability:
$$S_j(x_j) = S(a_j)$$

CM   Cauchy Machine

Summation/Activation:

$$P_i = \frac{T(t)}{T(t) + (\Delta E_i)^2}$$

CPN **Counterpropagation**

Summation:
$$b_g = \sum_{h=1}^{n} v_{hg}\, a_h^{\ k}$$

Activation:
$$b_i = \sum_{h=1}^{n} v_{hi}\, a_h$$

DH **Discrete Hopfield**

Summation:
$$w_{ij} = \sum_{k=1}^{m} (2a_i^{\ k} - 1)\,(2a_j^{\ k} - 1)$$

Activation:
$$a_i\,(t+1) = f\!\left(\sum_{j=1}^{n} w_{ij}\, a_j\,(t) + I_i\right)$$

Stability:
$$L(A) = -\ \tfrac{1}{2} \sum_{\substack{i=1 \\ i \neq j}}^{n} \sum_{j=1}^{n} a_i\, a_j\, w_{ij} - \sum_{j=1}^{n} a_i\,(I_i - f(a_i))$$

DR **Drive-Reinforcement**

Summation:
$$\Delta w_{ij}\,(t) = \Delta b_j^{\ k}(t) \sum_{h=1}^{\tau} \alpha(t) \left| w_{ij}\,(t-h) \right| \Delta a_i^{\ k}\,(t-h)$$

Activation:
$$b_j\,(t) = \sum_{i=1}^{n} w_{ij}\,(t)\, a_i\,(t) - \Theta_j$$

FAM **Fuzzy Associative Memory**

Summation:
$$w_{ij} = MIN\left(M_A(a_i^{\ k}),\, M_B\,(b_i^{\ k})\right)$$

Activation:
$$a_i = \overset{\rho}{\underset{j=1}{MAX}}\,[MIN\,(b_j,\, w_{ji})]$$

$$b_j = \overset{n}{\underset{i=1}{MAX}}\,[MIN\,(a_i,\, w_{ij})]$$

Where fuzzy set $A_K = M_A\,(a_i^{\ k})$

and A_K is ith value.

FCM   **Fuzzy Cognitive Map**

Summation: $\dot{w}_{ij} = -w_{ij} + S(a_i{}^k) S(\dot{a}_j{}^k)$

Activation: $\dot{a}_i = -a_i + \sum_{j=1}^{n} S(a_j) w_{ji} + I_i$

LAM   **Linear Associative Memory**

Summation: $W = \sum_{k=1}^{m} A_k{}^T B_k$

Activation: $B_h = A_h W = \sum_{\substack{k=1 \\ k \neq h}}^{n} A_h A_k{}^T B_k + A_h A_h{}^T B_h$

OLAM   **Optimal Linear Associative Memory**

Summation: $W = \sum_{k=1}^{m} \alpha_k{}^T \beta_k = AB^T$

Activation: $\alpha' = \alpha V$

P   **Perceptron**

Summation: $b_j = f\left(\sum_{i=1}^{n} w_{ij} a_i - \Theta_j \right)$

Activation: $b_j = f\left(\sum_{i=1}^{n} w_{ij} a_i + \sum_{h=1}^{n} \sum_{i=1}^{n} v_{hij} a_h a_i - \Theta_j \right)$

SG   **Shunting Grossberg**

Summation: $\dot{w}_{ij} = S(a_i{}^k) [-\alpha w_{ij} + \beta S(a_j{}^k)]$

A Practical Guide to Neural Nets

$$\text{Activation:} \quad \dot{a}_i = -\alpha\, a_i + (\beta - a_i)\,[S(a_i) + I_i] - (a_i + \mu)\left[\sum_{j=1}^{n} S(a_j)\, w_{ij} + J_i\right]$$

$$\text{Stability:} \quad S_j(x_j) = S(a_j - \mu)$$

TAM   Temporal Associative Memory

$$\text{Summation:} \quad W = A_m^{\ T} A_1 + \sum_{k=1}^{m-1} A_k^{\ T} A_{k+1}$$

$$\text{Activation:} \quad x_j = \sum_{i=1}^{n} a_i^{\ k}(t)\, w_{ij}$$

$$\text{Stability:} \quad \frac{\Delta L(A_1, ..., A_m)}{\Delta A_h} = -\sum_{i=1}^{n} \Delta a_i^{\ h} \sum_{j=1}^{n} a_j^{\ h-1}\, w_{ij} - \sum_{i=1}^{n} \Delta a_i^{\ h} \sum_{j=1}^{n} a_j^{\ h+1}\, w_{ij}$$

References

Anderson, J. "A Theory for the Recognition of Items from Short Memorized Lists." *Psychological Review,* 1973.

Barto, A. "Simulation Experiments with Goal-seeking Adaptive Elements," AFWAL-TR-84.

Gold, B. "Hopfield Model Applied to Vowel and Consonant Discrimination." *AIP Conference Proceedings,* Neural Networks for Computing, ed. J. Denkor, American Institute of Physics, New York, 1986.

Grossberg, S. "Neural Pattern Discrimination." *Journal of Theoretical Biology,* 1970.

Hanson, S. "Knowledge Representation in Connectionist Networks," *Bell Communications Research Technical Report,* 1987.

Sejnowski, T. "Higher-order Boltzmann Machines." *AIP Conference Proceedings.* ed. J. Denkor, American Institute of Physics, New York, 1986.

Appendix D: Simulation of a Processing Element on Lotus 1-2-3

The following instructions will allow you to simulate a simple processing element on Lotus 1-2-3. (We used release 2.2 of Lotus; any similar spreadsheet software could be used.) This simulation was designed for a single, basic processing element to allow you to visualize easily the mathematical mechanics that take place in a typical artificial neuron.

We explain the construction of the worksheet first and then follow with suggestions on how to use it. We recommend that you read this entire appendix prior to setting up your own worksheet. It may also be useful to review the section from chapter 9 called "Back Propagation Mathematics: How to Compute a Neural Network Manually." That section details the calculations required for a back propagation network composed of two input nodes, four hidden nodes, and a single output node. The basic formulas for a back propagation network are the ones used in this simulation.

The parameters and formulas for our Lotus 1-2-3 processing element are illustrated in figure D.1, a representation of a typical worksheet. (Notes for inexperienced Lotus users: Lotus 1-2-3 decides with the first character of entered data whether the entry is text or numeric data. The text on line 4 will be interpreted by 1-2-3 as a formula unless you begin the entry with a single quote (') to indicate that the data is text. The cell addresses and formulas (that begin with a left parenthesis) will be incorrectly interpreted as text; both may be preceded with a plus sign (+) to indicate

```
|                                                                                      |
|   A         B        C          D            E          F         G                  |
| 1 Title:    Simulation of a Simple Artificial Neuron                                 |
| 2                                                                                    |
| 3                                                                                    |
| 4 @100 Cycles>> (C106)        (D106)       (E106)      (F106)    (G106)               |
| 5                                                                                    |
| 6  In       Dout     Wbias      Weight      SUM(I*W)    Yout      dError              |
| 7 (any)     (any)    (any)      (any)       (A7*D7)+C7  @SIN(E7)  (B7-F7)             |
| 8  A7       B7       (G7*F7)+C7 (G7*F7)+D7  (A8*D8)+C8  @SIN(E8)  (B8-F8)             |
| 9  A8       B8       (G8*F8)+C8 (G8*F8)+D8  (A9*D9)+C9  @SIN(E9)  (B9-F9)             |
| 10 A9       B9       (G9*F9)+C9 (G9*F9)+D9  (A10*D10)+C10 @SIN(E10) (B10-F10)         |
|  . .         .         .          .           .          .          .                |
|  . .         .         .          .           .          .          .                |
|  . .         .         .          .           .          .          .                |
| 106 .        .         .          .           .          .          .                |
|                                                                                      |
```

FIGURE D.1 WORKSHEET REPRESENTATION

that the data for that cell is numeric or a formula. Use the command range-format-fixed (/REF5, for example) to achieve relevant precision for cells A7..G106. You may wish to set column widths beyond the default of 9 characters: the command column-set-width-12 (/CS12) would set the column in which your cursor is located to a width of 12.)

Constructing Your Worksheet

Here are the instructions for constructing your "artificial neuron" worksheet:

Description	Cell	Formula	Column Extension
Input Value	A7	Any value	
(update)	A8	A7	Copy from A8 to A9 . . A106
Desired Output	B7	Any value	
(update)	B8	B7	Copy from B8 to B9 . . B106
Bias Weight	C7	Any value	
(update)	C8	(G7 ⋆ F7) + C7	Copy from C8 to C9 . . C106
Input Weight	D7	Any value	
(update)	D8	(G7 ⋆ F7) + D7	Copy from D8 to D9 . . D106
Sum (Input ⋆ Weight)	E7	(A7 ⋆ D7) + C7	Copy from E7 to E8 . . E106

Output Value	F7	@SIN(E7)	Copy from F7 to F8 . . F106
Delta Error	G7	(B7−F7)	Copy from G7 to G8 . . G106

The Inputs

The value for input cell A7 may be any value between 0 and 1; the desired output, cell B7, should similarly be between 0 and 1. Later you may wish to experiment with other values, but we suggest you begin with values in the 0 to 1 range. (Remember that the sine function only results in values between -1 and 1. In addition, the simulation works better if you restrict input to the first quadrant.)

Including a bias input produces an effect that is similar to adjusting the threshold of the node and permits more rapid convergence of the training process. The bias input is always 1, but the bias weight is trainable in the same way as other weights. Input any value you wish for the bias weight, cell C7, as well as the initial weight for the neuron input, cell D7.

The Formulas

Cell E7 stores the sum of the inputs multiplied by their respective weights. In this case, the input value (A7) is multiplied by the associated weight of the input element (D7), added to the bias input (1) multiplied by the associated weight of the bias (C7). Because we have assumed the bias input is always 1, this calculation results in (A7*D7)+C7.

The contents of cell F7 represent the output value of our node, Yout. This is calculated by taking the summed inputs (cell E7) and applying the transfer function, which in our example, is the sine function.

The error is stored in cell G7. Here we have used a simplification, taking simply the difference between the desired output (B7) and the actual output (F7). Therefore, we call cell G7 "delta error," or dError. To be absolutely correct in back propagation networks, you should multiply the delta error by the first derivative of the transfer function. The function you select as a transfer function in such networks, consequently, must be differentiable. In this example, multiplying the delta error by the first derivative of the transfer function is not too difficult: cell G7 would require the Lotus expression (B7-F7)*@COS(E7).

For the update values on the weight we use a standard back propagation learning rule: multiply the error (G7) by the results of applying the transfer equation (F7) and add this value to the current weight (C7). The same update rule is used to update the bias weight (D7). These new weights are used for the next series of calculations on line 8.

This autonomous new weight generation is the initiating factor for the training of a neural network. When these weights become stable at a very low and acceptable error, the network is trained. Although we observe this here only on a primitive level employing our single simple neuron, we can see the results of each iterative update—the dynamic pattern of learning is evident.

Comments on the Neuron Simulator

We have redisplayed the last row of calculated data (row 106) at the top of our worksheet in row 4. This design allows us to see the results of changing our input values (including the use of different transfer functions) without having to move to the bottom of the page—a nice convenience.

Constructing a worksheet for this rather trivial set of calculations represents considerable effort. You may question whether it is worth the trouble. Keep in mind that even the simplest of networks will have many processing elements and numerous inputs, and the attempt to understand the mechanics is not trivial. By observing a simple processing element you will have a greater understanding of the total network dynamics. Noting the new weight generation, observing the decreasing error, and finally seeing the weights reach stability is, we feel, worth the effort.

Our simulator will have 100 cycles of input data presented. This input data presentation is repeated over and over because we have only one input coupled with one desired output. The transfer function (or activation formula) chosen here is a simple sine function, that, as we pointed out, limits the output to values of -1 through 1. We chose to start with a simple, uncomplicated function; however, you could substitute other functions.

We encourage you to try different transfer functions, such as the sigmoid function, $(1 + e\hat{\ }-x)\hat{\ }-1$, where $x = Sum(I*W)$ (sometimes also called "Isum") and the caret symbol $(\hat{\ })$ represents exponentiation. You could differentiate the above formula, but it is simpler (and not unreasonable in this experiment) to use the equation as it is. In our next example, however, we do use the derivative of this sigmoid function.

Testing the Simulator

Prior to entering the data, instruct the worksheet to calculate manually. This will delay calculation until you press the F9 key. We do this in Lotus by selecting /WGRM, which is "command-worksheet-global-recalculate-manual."

Enter the data. You should execute a "range format command" to establish four or five decimal places of accuracy. Test the simulator by entering zeros for all four initial input parameters as follows:

Input value (cell A7)	0
Desired Output (cell B7)	0
Bias Weight (cell C7)	0
Input Weight (cell D7)	0

Be sure to enter zeros only as indicated above, and enter in the remaining cells the formulas indicated previously. (If you mistakenly enter data in the wrong cell and wipe out a formula, you will need to recopy or re-enter the correct formula.) When your data is correctly entered, press F9 to calculate. Your results for all values for the 100 cycles should be zeros. You may wish to save your worksheet at this point if you have not already done so.

Additional Tests

Now try several more tests as follows:
Test 1:

				Outputs @100 cycles	
In	Dout	Wbias	Weight	Yout	dError
1	1	(any)	(any)	.9998	.0002

Note: Begin with simple values such as .1, .2, etc., and keep initial weight values random and between .1 and .8 (positive or negative). Later you can experiment with any number. The output value after 100 cycles will vary from our examples depending on the initial values chosen for the weights.

A Practical Guide to Neural Nets

Test 2:

In	Dout	Wbias	Weight	Yout	dError
	Inputs			Outputs @100 cycles	
1	.5	(any)	(any)	.5000	.0000

Test 3:

In	Dout	Wbias	Weight	Yout	dError
	Inputs			Outputs @100 cycles	
0	.5	(any)	(any)	.5000	.0000

Test 4:

In	Dout	Wbias	Weight	Yout	dError
	Inputs			Outputs @100 cycles	
.5	.5	(any)	(any)	.5000	.0000

Test 5:

In	Dout	Wbias	Weight	Yout	dError
	Inputs			Outputs @100 cycles	
.1	1	(any)	(any)	1.000	.0002

Running the Simulator

Now enter your own data and experiment, observe, and appreciate the complexity of a network which consists of thousands of processing elements, and a single element may have 50 to 100 inputs. In imaging or pattern recognition applications there may be as many as 2,000 to 3,000 inputs for each node in the hidden layer.

Table D.1 illustrates the Lotus simulation run where the input value and the desired output are both 1, the initial bias weight is .1000, and the initial input value weight is .4000.

There are a number of extensions you might wish to try. The resultant weight values after 100 cycles can be entered as the initial weight values, then recalculate and see if convergence oc-

Table D.1   Sample Run of Lotus Simulator

A Simulation of a Single Artificial Neuron						
@100 Cycles		0.6305	0.9305	1.5611	1.0000	0.0000
Input Value	Desired Output	Wbias	Weight	SumI*W	Yout	dError
1	1	0.1000	0.4000	0.50000	0.00000	1.00000
1	1	0.1000	0.4000	0.50000	0.47943	0.52057
1	1	0.3496	0.6496	0.99915	0.84101	0.15899
1	1	0.4833	0.7833	1.26657	0.95408	0.04592
1	1	0.5271	0.8271	1.35420	0.97663	0.02337
1	1	0.5499	0.8499	1.39984	0.98542	0.01458
1	1	0.5643	0.8643	1.42857	0.98990	0.01010
1	1	0.5743	0.8743	1.44856	0.99254	0.00746
1	1	0.5817	0.8817	1.46337	0.99424	0.00576
1	1	0.5874	0.8874	1.47483	0.99540	0.00460
1	1	0.5920	0.8920	1.48399	0.99623	0.00377
1	1	0.5957	0.8957	1.49149	0.99686	0.00314
1	1	0.5989	0.8989	1.49776	0.99733	0.00267
1	1	0.6015	0.9015	1.50308	0.99771	0.00229
1	1	0.6038	0.9038	1.50765	0.99801	0.00199
1	1	0.6058	0.9058	1.51163	0.99825	0.00175
1	1	0.6076	0.9076	1.51512	0.99845	0.00155
1	1	0.6091	0.9091	1.51822	0.99862	0.00138
1	1	0.6105	0.9105	1.52098	0.99876	0.00124
1	1	0.6117	0.9117	1.52346	0.99888	0.00112
1	1	0.6128	0.9128	1.52569	0.99898	0.00102
1	1	0.6139	0.9139	1.52773	0.99907	0.00093
1	1	0.6148	0.9148	1.52958	0.99915	0.00085
1	1	0.6156	0.9156	1.53128	0.99922	0.00078
1	1	0.6164	0.9164	1.53284	0.99928	0.00072

Table D.1 *(Continued)*

A Simulation of a Single Artificial Neuron

@100 Cycles		0.6305	0.9305	1.5611	1.0000	0.0000
Input Value	Desired Output	Wbias	Weight	SumI*W	Yout	dError
1	1	0.6171	0.9171	1.53428	0.99933	0.00067
1	1	0.6178	0.9178	1.53561	0.99938	0.00062
1	1	0.6184	0.9184	1.53685	0.99942	0.00058
1	1	0.6190	0.9190	1.53800	0.99946	0.00054
1	1	0.6195	0.9195	1.53907	0.99950	0.00050
1	1	0.6200	0.9200	1.54008	0.99953	0.00047
1	1	0.6205	0.9205	1.54102	0.99956	0.00044
1	1	0.6210	0.9210	1.54191	0.99958	0.00042
1	1	0.6214	0.9214	1.54274	0.99961	0.00039
1	1	0.6218	0.9218	1.54353	0.99963	0.00037
1	1	0.6221	0.9221	1.54427	0.99965	0.00035
1	1	0.6225	0.9225	1.54498	0.99967	0.00033
1	1	0.6228	0.9228	1.54564	0.99968	0.00032
1	1	0.6231	0.9231	1.54627	0.99970	0.00030
1	1	0.6234	0.9234	1.54688	0.99971	0.00029
1	1	0.6237	0.9237	1.54745	0.99973	0.00027
1	1	0.6240	0.9240	1.54799	0.99974	0.00026
1	1	0.6243	0.9243	1.54851	0.99975	0.00025
1	1	0.6245	0.9245	1.54901	0.99976	0.00024
1	1	0.6247	0.9247	1.54948	0.99977	0.00023
1	1	0.6250	0.9250	1.54994	0.99978	0.00022
1	1	0.6252	0.9252	1.55037	0.99979	0.00021
1	1	0.6254	0.9254	1.55079	0.99980	0.00020
1	1	0.6256	0.9256	1.55119	0.99981	0.00019
1	1	0.6258	0.9258	1.55157	0.99982	0.00018

Table D.1 *(Continued)*

A Simulation of a Single Artificial Neuron

Input Value	Desired Output	@100 Cycles 0.6305 Wbias	0.9305 Weight	1.5611 SumI*W	1.0000 Yout	0.0000 dError
1	1	0.6260	0.9260	1.55194	0.99982	0.00018
1	1	0.6261	0.9261	1.55230	0.99983	0.00017
1	1	0.6263	0.9263	1.55264	0.99984	0.00016
1	1	0.6265	0.9265	1.55297	0.99984	0.00016
1	1	0.6266	0.9266	1.55329	0.99985	0.00015
1	1	0.6268	0.9268	1.55359	0.99985	0.00015
1	1	0.6269	0.9269	1.55389	0.99986	0.00014
1	1	0.6271	0.9271	1.55418	0.99986	0.00014
1	1	0.6272	0.9272	1.55445	0.99987	0.00013
1	1	0.6274	0.9274	1.55472	0.99987	0.00013
1	1	0.6275	0.9275	1.55498	0.99987	0.00013
1	1	0.6276	0.9276	1.55523	0.99988	0.00012
1	1	0.6277	0.9277	1.55547	0.99988	0.00012
1	1	0.6279	0.9279	1.55571	0.99989	0.00011
1	1	0.6280	0.9280	1.55593	0.99989	0.00011
1	1	0.6281	0.9281	1.55615	0.99989	0.00011
1	1	0.6282	0.9282	1.55637	0.99990	0.00010
1	1	0.6283	0.9283	1.55658	0.99990	0.00010
1	1	0.6284	0.9284	1.55678	0.99990	0.00010
1	1	0.6285	0.9285	1.55697	0.99990	0.00010
1	1	0.6286	0.9286	1.55717	0.99991	0.00009
1	1	0.6287	0.9287	1.55735	0.99991	0.00009
1	1	0.6288	0.9288	1.55753	0.99991	0.00009
1	1	0.6289	0.9289	1.55771	0.99991	0.00009
1	1	0.6289	0.9289	1.55788	0.99992	0.00008

Table D.1 *(Continued)*

A Simulation of a Single Artificial Neuron

@100 Cycles		0.6305	0.9305	1.5611	1.0000	0.0000
Input Value	Desired Output	Wbias	Weight	SumI*W	Yout	dError
1	1	0.6290	0.9290	1.55805	0.99992	0.00008
1	1	0.6291	0.9291	1.55821	0.99992	0.00008
1	1	0.6292	0.9292	1.55837	0.99992	0.00008
1	1	0.6293	0.9293	1.55852	0.99992	0.00008
1	1	0.6293	0.9293	1.55867	0.99993	0.00007
1	1	0.6294	0.9294	1.55882	0.99993	0.00007
1	1	0.6295	0.9295	1.55896	0.99993	0.00007
1	1	0.6296	0.9296	1.55910	0.99993	0.00007
1	1	0.6296	0.9296	1.55924	0.99993	0.00007
1	1	0.6297	0.9297	1.55937	0.99993	0.00007
1	1	0.6298	0.9298	1.55950	0.99994	0.00006
1	1	0.6298	0.9298	1.55963	0.99994	0.00006
1	1	0.6299	0.9299	1.55976	0.99994	0.00006
1	1	0.6299	0.9299	1.55988	0.99994	0.00006
1	1	0.6300	0.9300	1.56000	0.99994	0.00006
1	1	0.6301	0.9301	1.56011	0.99994	0.00006
1	1	0.6301	0.9301	1.56023	0.99994	0.00006
1	1	0.6302	0.9302	1.56034	0.99995	0.00005
1	1	0.6302	0.9302	1.56045	0.99995	0.00005
1	1	0.6303	0.9303	1.56056	0.99995	0.00005
1	1	0.6303	0.9303	1.56066	0.99995	0.00005
1	1	0.6304	0.9304	1.56076	0.99995	0.00005
1	1	0.6304	0.9304	1.56086	0.99995	0.00005
1	1	0.6305	0.9305	1.56096	0.99995	0.00005
1	1	0.6305	0.9305	1.56106	0.99995	0.00005

curs in fewer iterations. You could also extend the worksheet to accommodate 200 cycles, for example, or enter data for multiple processing elements. You could then enter formulas to connect the processing elements in a simple network—which could quickly become a complex endeavor.

(We have experimented with a five-node network, using 50 columns and 1,000 rows. When we press F9 on this one, it's time to go out for coffee as the recalculation takes several minutes.)

5 PE Network Example

We talked earlier about ways to represent XOR in a network (see chapter 7). Suppose you wanted to use the five processing element (XOR) network pictured in figure D.2 and build a Lotus 1-2-3 representation of, say, processing element number 4. In this example, the sigmoid transfer function is used. To calculate the error, take the delta error, (Dout - Y_4), and multiply by the first derivative of the transfer function ($Y_4*(1-Y_4)$), as shown in the computations in figure D.2.[1] We have used a learning coefficient of 1 in our example. (Usually the learning coefficient is given a value between .1 and 1; a negative learning coefficient is sometimes called a "forgetting" term.)

Using the data from figure D.2 and the corresponding representation of the Lotus worksheet in table D.2, here are the cell input descriptions needed to build your worksheet for this PE:

Description	Cell	Formula	Column Extension
Desired Output	A4	1 (or 0)	
(update)	A5	A4	Copy from A5 to A6 . . A106
Y1 Input Value	B4	0 (or 1)	
(update)	B5	B4	Copy from B5 to B6 . . B106
Y2 Input Value	C4	1 (or 0)	
(update)	C5	C4	Copy from C5 to C6 . . C106
Weight 1-4	D4	Any value	
(update)	D5	(I4*H4 + D4)	Copy from D5 to D6 . . D106
Weight 2-4	E4	Any value	

continued on p. 330

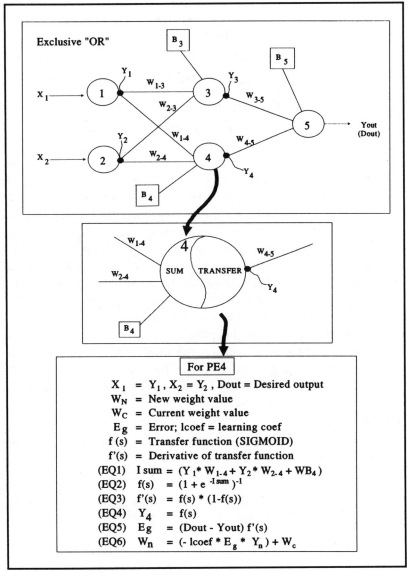

FIGURE D.2   XOR NETWORK SIMULATION

(update)	E5	(I4*H4 + E4)	Copy from E5 to E6 . . E106
Weight Bias-4	F4	Any value	
(update)	F5	(I4*H4 + F4)	Copy from F5 to F6 . . F106
Isum	G4	(B4*D4 + C4*E4 + F4)	Copy from G4 to G5 . . G106
Y4 Output Value	H4	G4*(1 + 2.718 ^-G4) ^-1	Copy from H4 to H5 . . H106
Error	I4	(A4-H4)*(H4*(1-H4))	Copy from I4 to I5 . . I106

Again, remember to use the plus sign (+) before the cell addresses and leading parentheses to indicate numeric values and formulas. You may also wish to copy the final values to the top of your worksheet for easier accessibility to the final calculations. Set the mode for manual recalculation (see /WGRM above).

After your data is entered correctly, save your file. You could now experiment with a combination of inputs, including 0, +1, and −1. Try adding more iterations. What happens to the convergence rate? Can you improve the convergence rate and reduce the error by changing the initial weights? Try your new weights for a variety of cases, keeping in mind that you produce only Y4, the output for PE4, and not the final network output, Yout.

Once you get this far, you have the idea, and you can try extending the worksheet for more than one PE if you wish.

---

1. Philip D. Wasserman, *Neural Computing, Theory and Practice*, New York: Van Nostrand Reinhold, 1989, p. 45–55.

See also:
James L. McClelland and David E. Rumelhart, *Explorations in Parallel Distributed Processing*, Cambridge, MA: MIT Press, 1988, p. 130–141.

Table D.2 Simulation of Neuron 4 from XOR Network

	A	B	C	D	E	F	G	H	I
1	Title: Simulation of Artificial Neuron 4 from XOR Network								
2									
3	Dout	Y1	Y2	W1-4	W2-4	WB-4	Isum	Y4	Error
4	1	0	1	(any)	(any)	(any)	(B4*D4 + C4*E4 + F4)	$G4*(1 + 2.718\ \hat{}\ -G4)\ \hat{}\ -1$	(A4−H4)*(H4*(1−H4))
5	A4	B4	C4	(I4*H4 + D4)	(I4*H4 + E4)	(I4*H4 + F4)	(B5*D5 + C5*E5 + F5)	$G5*(1 + 2.718\ \hat{}\ -G5)\ \hat{}\ -1$	(A5−H5)*(H5*(1−H5))
6	A5	B5	C5	(I5*H5 + D5)	(I5*H5 + E5)	(I5*H5 + F5)	(B6*D6 + C6*E6 + F6)	$G6*(1 + 2.718\ \hat{}\ -G6)\ \hat{}\ -1$	(A6−H6)*(H6*(1−H6))
7	.	.	.	.	.	.	.	.	.
.	.	.	.	.	.	.	.	.	.
.	.	.	.	.	.	.	.	.	.
.	.	.	.	.	.	.	.	.	.
.								.	.
106	.								

Index

Continous Hopfield (CH), 143, 314
Control applications, 72–73
Controllers, 80
Cooper, Leon, 33, 248
Counterpropagation (CPN), 145, 315
Credit risk analysis, 4
Crick, Francis, 33, 57
CYC project, 262–63

Dartmouth Summer Research Project
    on Artificial Intelligence, 28
Data
    compression, 71, 165, 208
        of images, 73
        of training sets, 70
    encoded, 105
    preparation of, for building neural
        networks, 154–55
    preprocessed, 106
    representation of, 113–14, 136
    scaled, 105–6, 107
Database management systems, 98,
    120, 213
Data configuration, 76–77
Data entry, voice-controlled, 6–7
Davis, Bill, 152
Dawes, Bob, 233, 266
DECtalk, 53
Defense Advanced Research Projects
    Agency (DARPA), 23–24, 31
    Neural Network Study, 11, 116, 130,
        142, 179, 267
Delta Rule, 137, 138
Demonstration disk, neural network,
    279–93
    asking questions of, 290–92
    diskette design, 279–80
    installing, 280–81
    introductory screens/options, 281–82
    referencing paths in, 283–90
    rejecting Development Guide path,
        290
    summary, 292–93
Dendrites, neuron, 37, 38
Denker, John, 266
Differential Aptitude Tests (DAT), 249,
    250
Discrete Bidirectional Associative
    Memory (BAM), 313
Discrete Hopfield (DH), 143, 315

Distributed associative memory in
    neural networks, 61–62
DNA sequences, predicting, 7, 81–82,
    240
Doleac, John, 5–6, 226
Draper Prize, 271
Drive-Reinforcement Theory (DRT),
    140, 144, 232, 315
Dvorak, John, 266

Eclectronics, 211
Edge detection, 134
Education in neural networks, 241–43
Edward Smith Papyrus, 26
Eggers, Mitchell D., 231, 259
Einstein, Albert, 14
Eisley, Loren, 36
Electronic Neural Network (ENN), 208
Embedded neural networks, 193, 194
Encephalon project, 209–11
Energy minima, 62
Environment, potential applications of
    neural networks in, 10
Equations used in neural networks,
    146, 147, 311–17
    mathematics for selected paradigms,
        312–17
    symbols for, 311–12
ESPRIT II project, 23, 204
Europe, research on neural networks
    in, 23, 30, 204
Excalibur Technologies, 201
Exclusive-OR problem, 47, 111–12, 328
Expert systems, 71
    handling field service requests with,
        91–92
    heuristics in, 135
    as left brain approach, 92–93, 94
    neural networks as, 88–92
Explanations/justifications in neural
    networks, 75, 234

Face recognition, 17–18, 69–70
Faggin, Frederico, 204
Fast pattern searching applications, 8
Fault tolerance in neural networks, 59,
    64, 120, 230, 259
Federal Aviation Administrator, 4, 98
Feedback network, 51, 112–113, 119,
    125, 142, 215

International Neural Network
conference, 88
International Neural Network Society
(INNS), 31, 117
Inversion, neural network, 172

James, William, 26
Japan
Human Frontiers program, 22, 31
neural network research in, 22–23,
30, 41, 217, 267
studies on right-brain processing,
94–95
Jaynes, E. T., 267
Johns Hopkins University, 236

Kanerva, Pentti, 264–65
Kanji characters, 68, 96, 141–42
Kilby, Jack, 270
Klopf, Harry
Drive-Reinforcement Theory of, 140–
41, 232, 315
Pac-Man symbol and, 62–64
Knowledge, 103–4
recall process, 92, 93, 94
storage of, in neural networks, 55–
56, 61–64
Knowledge base, 88, 89
Knowledge-based diagnostics systems,
239
Kohonen, Teuvo, 30, 31, 123–24, 127,
137
Kohonen learning/networks, 67, 107,
113, 123–124, 127, 137–38, 236
Kosko, Bart, 149
Kuperstein, Michael, 73, 232, 239

Layers of processing elements (nodes),
49, 129
combining, 50
as filters, 52–53
hidden/input/output (see Hidden
layer; Input layer; Output layer)
number of, 110–12
Learning, 40, 41, 48–49, 128–51. See
also Training
architecture of, 142–46
artificial intelligence systems and,
86, 88
autonomous, 223–24
basic mechanism of, 129
defined, 128

forklift robot example of, 65
illustrated in Pac-Man-like symbol,
62–64
laws (see Learning rules)
modes of, 132–36
rates of, 114, 133–35
reinforcement, 224, 225
research on, 146–50, 224–28
self-, 86
supervised, 132
feedback recall, 145(table)
feedforward recall, 144(table)
unsupervised, 132–33
feedback recall, 143(table)
feedforward recall, 144(table)
Learning Channel, 32
Learning functions, 48–49
Learning paradigms. See Paradigm(s)
Learning rules, 131, 136–42, 232–33
ADALINE, 117
back propagation, 138–39
Delta, 137
Drive-Reinforcement Theory, 140–41
Fukushima's Neocognitron model,
141–42, 148
gradient descent rule, 137
Grossberg learning, 139–40
Hebb's, 27, 136, 137
knowledge acquisition for, 88, 89
Kohonen's Learning Law, 137–38
simulated annealing, 142
stochastic, 141
Least means squares algorithm, 68–69,
117, 137
Lenat, Douglas, 260–63
Linear Associative Memory (LAM),
144, 316
Linear functions, 130, 188(table)
limitations on, 47
Lippman, Richard P., 37, 267
Loan(s), evaluating risk in mortgage,
3–4, 70
Loan approval neural network, 156–59
Los Alamos National Laboratory,
predicting DNA sequences at, 7,
81–82, 236, 240
Lupo, Jasper, 23, 100, 265

MacBrain software, 256
Macintosh computers, 256
McClintock, Barbara, 260
McCorduck, Pamela, 34, 128

Statistical mechanics method of
learning, 142
Statistical methods, 79–83
vs. neural networks, 172–73
process control, 6, 80, 110
statistical pattern reconstruction, 68–
69
statistics defined, 79
Stochastic learning, 141
Stoisits, R. F., 88
Stubbs, Derek, 90, 197, 265
Summation function, 46, 107
Supervised learning, 132
feedback recall, 145(table)
feedforward recall, 144(table)
Symbol recognition, automatic, 258
Symposium on Networks in Brain and
Computer Architecture, 229
Synapse, *38*
activity of, 39, 229
Synaptics Corporation, 204
Syntonic Systems, 208

Tanh transfer function, 188(table)
Tapang, Carlos, 208
Tax evasion, reducing, 96–97
Technology integration. *See* Integration
of neural networks to other
technology
Technology transfer, 226–27
Telecommunications, adaptive noise
canceling in, 3
Temporal Associative Memory (TAM),
143, 317
Testbench product, 239
Testing neural networks, 182–89
Texas Instruments, 22, 70, 205, 208,
258, 270, 279
field service requests using expert
systems at, 91–92
Text-to-speech applications, 8, 70, 71,
114
NETtalk, 53–54
Thermal Neutron Analysis (TNA)
bomb detector, 4–5, 98
Third-generation computing, 85–86
Threshold, 44, 46
Threshold function, 47, *48*, 130
neuron synapse activity, 39
Topology, 124, 138
Toshiba Corporation, 96, 238

Tracking state of dynamic systems,
experiment on, 16, *17*
Training, 67, 76, 132. *See also* Learning
off-line, 75, 134
research on, 222–28
techniques, 135–36
time required for, 134, 135, 182
Training sets, 132, 136
reducing size of, 70
Transfer functions, 47, *48*, 107–9, 129–
30, 188(table)
Transformations, 52, 73
Transputer parallel processing chip,
203, 257
Traveling salesman problem, 51–52,
74, 142
Trolio, Andrew, 258
Trowbridge, Dave, 32
Turing, Alan, 26
classical test devised by, 83, *84*

U.S.-Japan Joint Conference on
Cooperative/Competitive Neural
Networks, 31
U.S. Postal Service, 7–8, 241
University of North Texas, 229
Unsupervised learning, 132–33
feedback recall, 143(table)
feedforward recall, 144(table)

Vectors, 45
VHSIC (Very High-Speed Integrated
Circuits), 257
Video-camera images, preprocessing
input from, 106
Visual processing of input data, 106
Viterbi network, 236
VLSI (Very Large Scale Integration),
208, 218, 228, 257
Voice synthesizer. (*See* Speech
generation
Von Neumann, John, 27, 28, 33

Weather prediction, 17–18, 70
Wechsler Adult Intelligence Scale, *249*
Weight(s), *45*, 130
analyzing hidden layers to
understand, 235
changing, in real time, 232
learning and adjustments of, 48–49,
.109